Clarity for Learning

Clarity for Learning

Five Essential Practices That Empower Students and Teachers

John Almarode

Kara Vandas

CORWIN

FOR INFORMATION:

Corwin

A SAGE Company

2455 Teller Road

Thousand Oaks, California 91320

(800) 233-9936

www.corwin.com

SAGE Publications Ltd.

1 Oliver's Yard

55 City Road

London EC1Y 1SP

United Kingdom

SAGE Publications India Pvt. Ltd.

B 1/I 1 Mohan Cooperative Industrial Area

Mathura Road, New Delhi 110 044

India

SAGE Publications Asia-Pacific Pte. Ltd.

3 Church Street

#10-04 Samsung Hub

Singapore 049483

Program Director: Jessica Allan

Associate Editor: Lucas Schleicher

Editorial Assistant: Mia Rodriguez

Production Editor: Kelly DeRosa

Copy Editor: Cate Huisman

Typesetter: C&M Digitals (P) Ltd.

Proofreader: Dennis Webb

Indexer: Wendy Allex

Cover Designer: Scott Van Atta

Printed in the United States of America

ISBN 978-1-5063-8469-6

This book is printed on acid-free paper.

Certified Chain of Custody
Promoting Sustainable Forestry
www.sfiprogram.org
SFI-01268

SUSTAINABLE FORESTRY INITIATIVE

SFI label applies to text stock

19 20 21 22 23 10 9 8 7 6 5 4 3 2

CONTENTS

SHARING CLARITY

ASSESSING WITH CLARITY

FEEDBACK WITH CLARITY

CLARITY IN COLLABORATION

Access the companion website at
resources.corwin.com/ClarityforLearning
for videos, full-color examples of learning intentions
and success criteria, and student examples.

FOREWORD

It helps to be very clear about what you want your students to learn. Surely, this is self-evident; it need not be said. But for many students, the teacher's instructions, intentions for the lesson, expectations of the students with respect to behaviors and involvement, and understanding of the level of performance needed are far from evident. For many students, it is often not clear what teachers want them to do or understand, or what level of performance is required. Why should students be made to guess what the teacher means, wants, and expects?

Teacher clarity relates to being clear about what you want your students to know and be able to do, clearly demonstrating relevant skills and processes that you expect students to employ, and checking that students have a clear understanding of any new material that is needed to gain success in the lesson (Fendick, 1990). Fendick's meta-analysis coded articles about clarity of speech, organization (uses success criteria, covers all topics on post-test, reviews student work), explanation (explains simply and interestingly, at right pace), examples and guided practice (gives examples of how to do the work, answers student questions, gives enough time, gives feedback), and assessment of student learning (asks questions, encourages discussions, checks work). He found 39 studies with an average correlation of these factors to achievement outcomes of $r = .35$, which converts to an effect size of .67. This means that teacher clarity ranks among the top interventions that can best enhance student learning.

John Almarode and Kara Vandas have five main steps to establish clarity in the classroom: (1) crafting learning intentions and success criteria, (2) co-constructing these with learners, (3) creating opportunities for students to respond (e.g., via assignments and assessments), (4) giving and receiving effective feedback, and (5) sharing learning and progress between students and teachers. A lot of attention is thus placed on making clear the purpose of the lesson and the level of cognitive complexity of the lesson, and providing a standard or reference point for the students to know when "good is good enough."

The forerunner of success criteria has been around for some time: It was the UK National Curriculum in 1989 that enshrined learning intentions, but too many of the implementations made these intentions low-level, atomistic, and rather jingoistic claims. So, success criteria were introduced to help move from the lower to higher levels of thinking and comprehending. For many, success criteria remain very product based (i.e., by the end of the lesson(s) you will have . . . .), and they provide no information on how to achieve these products. Then more process-oriented success criteria were introduced by Shirley Clarke (2001), linking the end with a process for achieving the end, and ensuring that the success criteria also provided a benchmark for the quality of learning. This made them more aligned with the US rubrics. Another step was then to co-construct them with the students so the students had a deeper understanding of the criteria, and the criteria did not become merely words the students wrote or phrases they repeated.

The aims of the success criteria were to enable students to know what the aims of the lesson mean, have some first understanding of the steps and processes to attain these aims, know when success has been achieved or some sense of how close they are to the success, enable them to seek and receive feedback to further them toward this success, be more clear about where improvements need to be made, discuss strategies relative to this improvement, and smell the roses when they attain success.

There are many forms of success criteria. In my own teaching I prefer surface (about the content, the ideas) and deeper (relating the ideas, extending the ideas) success criteria for each lesson. I also prefer two tasks or test questions, one for surface and the other for deep—and I make it explicit to students which is which. I want them to know I value both the content and the comprehension, relating and extending the ideas. When first introducing a series of lessons, I may favor a higher percentage of surface success criteria, but I then must balance this proportion of surface and deep success criteria as the lessons progress. The aim throughout is clarity. It should not be the students' task to guess what I value, what level of performance and understanding I desire, and when and where they are successful. When they are in doubt, I note students tend to prefer surface success criteria, as they are easier to learn, and meeting them increases the chance of looking successful (especially when there are no stated deep success criteria). Many students (rightly or wrongly) believe teachers want students to tell them back what the students have been told!

The clarity does not stop, however, with the teacher proclaiming success criteria. It also involves the teacher seeing learning through the eyes of students, listening and evaluating student progress to know when to intervene, knowing when and how best to provide feedback and when to back off and let students wallow in the learning pit, and knowing how to ensure there are appropriate levels of challenge (not too hard, not too boring) such that students are not too anxious or lacking confidence. The authors of *Clarity for Learning* have an excellent section of worked examples that bring clarity to life. In my own teaching, I also have used exemplars of *A*-grade assignments and assessments from previous years, and these are posted on my website—once again to ensure it is not a guessing game for my graduate students to work out what I mean by success!

And clarity does not stop in the classroom; hence the chapter on collaborating beyond the class and school. The advent of professional learning communities, collaborative efficacy, and networks of schools are founded on the clarity of the success criteria. Unless, I would argue, these criteria are related to maximizing the impact of the adults on the students, then they are probably going to have little effect. Too often they are more about curriculum, best practice, assessment, resources, and many compliance issues that may be fun (or not) but are hardly likely to make much difference. Success criteria, whether they have been developed brilliantly or not, can be a focus of critique, collaboration, and improvement among teachers and school leaders, as they provide opportunities to hear how educators see their own notions of success in their teaching.

It is no surprise that a book about clarity is set out with clear directions about what the reader is expected to take away from this book by the end. This makes it a pleasure to read, and, like most excellent success criteria, it allows for more to come, invites a quest for deeper implementation, and encourages a keenness to continuously ask your students this question: "Am I clear about tasks, aims, expectations, and what I mean by success?"

John Hattie, Professor of Education
Director of Melbourne Education Research Institute
University of Melbourne

ACKNOWLEDGMENTS

This book is a true reflection of the hard work that goes on every day in schools around the globe. The journey to clarity presented in this book highlights the enduring commitment educators have for students and making an impact on their learning. We hope that readers discover that the voices that are the most powerful and meaningful are those from the classroom,

Thank you to each of you who contributed—for providing a window into your thinking, for your love and passion for teaching, and for your impact on students!

- A. R. Ware Elementary School, Staunton, VA
  - Dr. Sharon Barker, Billy Brown

- Bauder Elementary School, Poudre School District, Fort Collins, CO
  - Brian Carpenter, Jami Montoya-Ulibarri, Kelsi Idler, Kelli Hoyberg Nielsen, Kelly Hogeland, Sue Weisman, Emily White, Shawna Reger, Ashley Torres, Jennifer Morrison, Rebecca Schkade

- Barren County Public Schools, Glasgow, KY
  - Bo Matthews, Brian Clifford, Scott Harper, Josh Maples, Tara Griffith

- Caldwell School District, Caldwell, ID
  - Jodie Mills, Richard Jamison, Meghan Wonderlich, Isaiah Folau, Jenny Hartvigsen, Cindy Wells, Ben Jackson, Melissa Langan, Heather Mueller, Shay Swan, Tate B. Castleton, Angelica Blanco, Kevin Sitts, Rozanne Gans, Gwen Hogg, Candace Bilbrey

- Green River Regional Educational Cooperative, Bowling Green, KY
  - Kyle Cassidy, Geavonda Stevenson, Terri Stice, Kellie Thompson

- Iroquois Point Elementary School, Ewa Beach, HI
  - Christina Ramie, Ofelia Reed, Thomasina Simmons, Tammie Sawada

- J. Sterling Morton High School District, Cicero, IL
  - Dr. Terrance Mootz, Mary Corbett, Richard Graham

- Lake Wilcox, Richmond Hill, Ontario
  - Mike Cerullo and Claudio Tulipano

- Liberty Public Schools, Liberty, MO
  - Dr. Jeanette Westfall, Carrie Gabriel, Joanie New

- Lone Tree Elementary School, Lone Tree, CO
  - Kay Tucker, Alicia Pepe, Lori Black, Kim Leroi, Tanya Marchman-Twete, Kristian Odegaard

- Louisa County Public Schools, Mineral, VA
  - Doug Straley, Dr. Lisa Chen
- Orange County Public Schools, Orange, VA
  - Dr. Brenda Tanner, Judy Anderson, Renee Honaker
- Spotsylvania County Public Schools, Fredericksburg, VA
  - Dr. Scott Baker, Carol Flenard, Michael Mudd, Keith Wolfe, Jennifer Belako, Mike Brown, Kristine Lentz-Johnson
- York Region District School Board, Aurora, Ontario
  - Rick Rosemin, Trevor Krikst, Lisa Donohue, Yana Ioffe, Diana Dal Bello, Jeff Borsuk, Melanie Chamberland, Melissa Doucas, Loucas Maronitis

FROM JOHN ALMARODE

Kara, thank you for the collaboration on this incredible journey. I am so glad that you agreed to partner with me on this work. Through our many conversations about clarity, I have learned so much about clarity for learning.

To Ms. Cross. The person that inspired me to become a teacher was my sixth-grade science teacher, Ms. Cross. Her classroom was magic. Each day we were clear on what we were learning, how we were going to go about that learning, and what a successful day looked like in Room 30.

To my students. The greatest honor of my professional life is teaching young learners. Period. During my time in the classroom, I have enjoyed this honor over and over again. Just by interacting with each of them, I developed a clearer understanding of their perspective. This taught me about clarity. Just by opening up the classroom to their voices, I developed a clearer view of the experiences that shaped their learning journey.

I am blessed with the opportunity to visit and work with administrators and teachers all across the world. I am forever grateful for this opportunity to collaborate with them, learn from them, and draw inspiration from them. Thank you for welcoming me into your classrooms. This work is better because of you.

Doug Fisher and Nancy Frey have been excellent mentors, colleagues, and friends. Their guidance, thought-provoking questions, conversations, and feedback about clarity have had an amazing and positive influence on this work. I am so grateful for their time and dedication to teaching and learning—they make me a better teacher and learner. Doug and Nancy, thank you.

The contents of this book are not just an academic exercise. I have two young children at home. Tessa and Jackson are my greatest accomplishments. With that being said, the desire for an enriching and engaging learning environment is personal. Tessa just finished kindergarten. Her teacher, Ms. Paulson, provided incredible clarity that allowed my daughter to grow in her learning. Jackson, two years later, will enter kindergarten. My hope is the same for him. Tessa and Jackson, thanks for putting a personal face on why I do what I do!

And last, but certainly not least, I want to thank my wife, Dani. I am still married after yet another book project. Her support is amazing. Your unyielding support in each and every endeavor does not go unnoticed. I am grateful you are my wife, and I am even more grateful that we are partners in life. Thank you.

FROM KARA VANDAS

John, it has been a pleasure to work alongside you and write together. I am honored to be your partner in this work. It has been a lot of hard work, but more than that, a lot of laughter!

To my family, Matt and Myer, I want to thank you for your enduring confidence in me, your patience, and your love. I could not do what I do without the two of you!

To the schools we are partners with, I am honored to be your partner and often feel like I should pinch myself because I can't believe how cool my job is in supporting all of you. You inspire me every day. Thank you for what you do for kids!

To Kristin Anderson, I so appreciate that you have a vision and deep understanding of the work we all do and can see things in others that they sometimes don't see in themselves. Thank you for putting us up to this!

To Larry Ainsworth and Mary Jane O'Connell, who gave John and me the go-ahead for this book but also provided so much thinking, mentoring over the years, and support. We are standing on the shoulders of giants!

To Corwin, which is an organization that promotes the profession of education and impacts student learning around the globe. Thank you for allowing me to be a part of that story, that work, and that impact!

PUBLISHER'S ACKNOWLEDGMENTS

Corwin gratefully acknowledges the contributions of the following reviewers:

Melissa Miller
Middle School Science Teacher
Randall G. Lynch Middle School
Farmington, AR

Marcia LeCompte
Montessori Teacher
East Baton Rouge Parish School System
Baton Rouge, LA

Jane Hunn
Teacher
Tippecanoe Valley Middle School
Akron, IN

Joan Eggert
Eighth-Grade ELA Teacher
Madison Metropolitan School District
Madison, WI

Gayla LeMay
Teacher
Louise Radloff Middle School
Duluth, GA

Faith Chaney-Grant
English Language Arts Teacher
Springfield Public Schools R-12
Springfield, MO

Debra K. Las
Science Teacher
Rochester Public Schools, ISD #535
Rochester, MN

Deanne Brunlinger
NBCT Science Teacher, Department Chair
Elkhorn Area High School
Elkhorn, WI

ABOUT THE AUTHORS

John Almarode, PhD, has worked with schools, classrooms, and teachers all over the world. John began his career in Augusta County, Virginia, teaching mathematics and science to a wide range of students. In addition to spending his time in PreK–12 schools and classrooms, he is an associate professor in the department of Early, Elementary, and Reading Education and the codirector of James Madison University's Center for STEM Education and Outreach. In 2015, John was named the Sarah Miller Luck Endowed Professor of Education. However, what really sustains John—and what marks his greatest accomplishment—is his family. John lives in Waynesboro, Virginia, with his wife, Danielle, a fellow educator; their two children, Tessa and Jackson; and their Labrador retrievers, Angel and Forest. John can be reached at www.johnalmarode.com.

Kara Vandas is an educator with an enduring passion for empowering learners. She began her career in education at an alternative school for youth at-risk. Kara spent several more years in the classroom in public education as a middle and high school educator and then transitioned to coaching and professional learning positions that allowed her to support teachers and leaders. Her current role as an author and consultant takes her around the world to partner with schools and

school districts. She also presents nationally and internationally at conferences, with a focus on learner agency and efficacy.

Kara is the co-author of *Partnering With Students: Building Ownership of Learning* and holds a Master's degree of Education in Curriculum and Instruction from Regis University. She has worked in K-12 education for nearly 20 years with a focus in instruction, curriculum design, using data to drive instruction, science education, learning environments, formative assessment, Visible Learning, and more. She also volunteers as a board member at her child's local school, where she and her family live in Castle Rock, Colorado. She loves the outdoors and spends much of her free time with family and friends.

INTRODUCTION

Clarity in Teaching and Learning

Truly successful decision-making relies on a balance between deliberate and instinctive thinking.

Malcolm Gladwell

The opportunity to double the rate of learning in your classroom, or any classroom for that matter, is enticing to every educator. Recent research strongly suggests that this is not only possible but also attainable with successful decisions in our schools and classrooms that are both deliberate and instinctive. John Hattie (2009, 2012), through his Visible Learning research, has compiled meta-analyses of influences on student learning. Drawing from the worldwide body of existing research, Professor Hattie compiled a list of influences on student learning as well as the relative strength of these influences. When Hattie (2009) organized the significant influences on student achievement into broad categories, he found six groups of contributors:

1. Student characteristics

2. The teacher

3. The home

4. The school

5. Curricular characteristics

6. Teaching practices

As you might expect, the greatest variance in student achievement is correlated with the contributions each learner brings to the classroom, each and every day. However, the second largest contribution is the teacher. In other words, the teacher matters a lot!

Fisher, Frey, and Hattie (2016) assert that learners deserve a great teacher, not by chance, but by design. "By design" refers to the strong belief that the decisions we make in our classrooms should be purposeful and intentional based on what works best in teaching and learning. This is the deliberate part of successful decision making described in the Malcolm Gladwell quote at the opening of this introduction. However, we cannot discount the instinctive element in our decisions based on the tacit knowledge acquired from direct experience in our classrooms or schools. This is the instinctive part of successful decision making.

Learners enter our classrooms from different cultures, with different experiences and prior knowledge. Our job, then, is to meet learners where they are and move them forward, having an impact on their learning. However, the gap between our desire to have an impact on the learning of our students and actually having an impact is determined by our willingness to struggle and persist with these decisions until we identify what works best for each and every learner in our schools and classrooms. As research on teaching and learning continues to unpack the influences that matter most for student learning, a new challenge is evident. There are many things that have a strong impact on student learning. This is good news in that great stuff is happening in our schools and classrooms every day. The less-than-good news is that too many influences to think about can be overwhelming and cloud the focus of a novice teacher or even an experienced or expert teacher. The ideas contained in the following chapters strive to address this challenge and answer the following essential question: What is the one thing that will not only have a significant influence on the learning in my classroom, but also serve as a foundation for which the other significant influences are possible?

The answer: clarity in teaching and learning. Let us look at two classrooms to get at what we mean by clarity in teaching and learning.

CLASSROOM ONE: MR. KLEIN'S HIGH SCHOOL CHEMISTRY CLASS

On Monday morning at 8:25 a.m., high school students file into Mr. Klein's chemistry class after a weekend of social events, sporting events, and just enough time devoted to homework so that they can be prepared for Monday's discussion on balancing equations of chemical reactions. As students take their seats, Mr. Klein begins the class by directing their attention to the interactive whiteboard, which reads,

Learning intention: We are learning to balance chemical equations.

Why? So that we can ensure that all atoms from the reactants are accounted for in the products created in the chemical reaction.

Success Criteria: I will use my understanding of atomic structure and the periodic table to

1. Balance single-replacement reactions.
2. Balance double-replacement reactions.
3. Balance reactions with polyatomic ions.
4. Explain how matter was conserved throughout each chemical reaction.

To supplement the learning intention and associated success criteria, Mr. Klein tells his students,

> Today, we are going to use our understanding of atomic structure and the periodic table of elements to determine how much of each reactant is needed in a chemical reaction, and what the resulting compounds and by-products are. You know you have been successful when you can balance single-replacement reactions, double-replacement reactions, and reactions involving polyatomic ions. You will also be able to explain how matter was conserved in the reaction.

Students grab spots at their laboratory benches and get out their notebooks designated for chemistry. Mr. Klein's class continues with modeling of examples and nonexamples, student discussion and practice, whole-class and partner discussion about how matter is conserved, and, finally, with a self-assessment for each student as to whether or not he or she met each success criterion and which they need to practice more.

CLASSROOM TWO: MS. HEIZER'S FIFTH-GRADE CLASS

On the other side of town, fifth graders arrive in Ms. Heizer's classroom, having had just as active a weekend as Mr. Klein's students. Ms. Heizer's students begin their morning routine by unpacking their book bags, placing their lunches in their designated "cubby," placing their "take-home" folders in the basket on her desk, and quickly finding their seats to start the morning work. Students notice that today's morning work is on figurative language and retrieve their literacy notebooks from their desks. Following the step-by-step instructions, students copy down the different types of figurative language, define each one using their student dictionaries, also in their desks, and then retrieve and complete a handout where they are asked to circle, highlight, or underline examples of figurative language in a nonfiction story.

THE DIFFERENCE

To the outside observer, these two classrooms appear to be productive, well-organized, efficient, and effective classrooms. Outwardly, there appear to be zero behavior challenges as the students, by this account, are compliant with the routines and procedures expected by Mr. Klein and Ms. Heizer. How could these classrooms not yield successful learning? Much to the surprise of many, the students in one of these classrooms show greater than one year's worth of growth in this one year of schooling. Students in the other classroom fall short of this growth. To identify the difference between the two classrooms, ask how the students in the two classrooms would respond to the following three questions:

1. What am I learning?

2. Why am I learning it?

3. How will I know I have learned it?

What would Ms. Heizer's student say?

Mr. Klein purposefully and intentionally provided his students with a learning intention for the day, followed by clear criteria for success. His deliberate decisions about making the day's learning visible provided the clarity for his students to answer the three questions: (1) What am I learning? (2) Why am I learning it? and (3) How will I know I have learned it? Ms. Heizer took great care in explaining to students what they were doing but missed the opportunity to explain what they were learning, and why and how they could be successful in their learning. Therefore, her students may have felt they were successful if they completed the worksheet but missed the learning that was intended about figurative language. So, there is one thing that could make a significant difference in the success of Ms. Heizer's decision making: teacher clarity that provides students with clarity in their learning.

STARTING WITH CLARITY

Clarity in teaching and learning is the one thing that makes a significant impact on the growth in learning for students in any classroom and also serves as a foundation for which the other significant influences are possible. *Learning is most successful when teachers see learning through the eyes of their students and students see themselves as their own teachers: This is Visible Learning (Hattie, 2009, 2012).* Thus, one of the essential features of Visible Learning is clarity. Based on Hattie's Visible Learning research (2009, 2012) and his quantification of learning effects, an effect size of 0.40 equates to a year's growth in learning in a year's time. With an average effect size of 0.75, teacher clarity results in almost twice the average effect size of one year of formal schooling. Fendick (1990) defined clarity as the compilation of organizing instruction, explaining content, providing examples, guided practice, and assessment of learning. Each of these components contributes to student learning. Clarity in each of the following components provides for effect sizes (ES) as shown (Fendick, 1990):

- Organizing instruction   ES = 0.64

- Explaining content   ES = 0.70

- Providing examples and guided practice   ES = 0.46

- Assessment of student learning   ES = 0.64

Hattie (2009) describes clarity as communicating the learning intentions and success criteria for the learning intentions so that students can identify where they are going in their learning, how they are progressing, and where they will go next, thus providing students enough clarity to own their own learning.

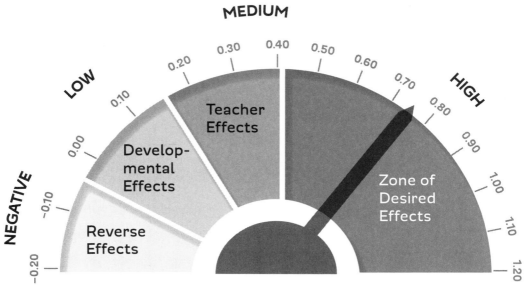

In addition, teacher clarity makes many of the other effect sizes in the Visible Learning research possible. For example, when teachers are clear on what students are learning, they can better select learning experiences that specifically target the necessary learning. Similarly, when teachers know why students are learning what they are learning, they can better design learning experiences that are authentic and relevant to learners. Finally, when teachers know what success looks like, they can show learners what success looks like, design opportunities for students to make their own thinking and learning visible, give and receive feedback, and gather evidence about where to go next in the teaching and learning. All this, because of teacher clarity.

Ensuring teacher clarity is present in the K–12 classroom is paramount in maximizing student growth in all academic areas. However, in addition to teachers seeing learning through the eyes of their students, students must see themselves as their own teachers. Therefore, we must consider clarity from both the teacher's perspective and the learner's perspective. From the perspective of the learner, student clarity is achieved when students know what is to be learned, how they are progressing in their learning, and what they need to learn next. In Hattie's work, this is referred to as *student expectations*, or students are referred to as *assessment-capable learners*; this achievement has an average effect size of 1.33 (Hattie, 2009, 2012; Frey, Hattie, & Fisher, 2018).

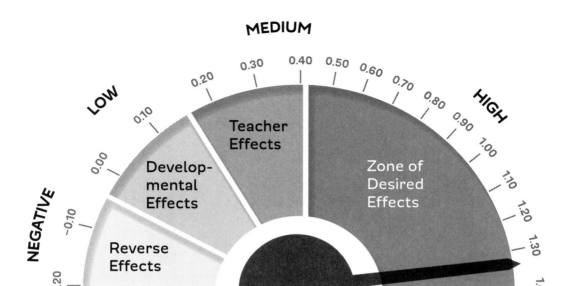

ASSESSMENT-CAPABLE LEARNERS *d* = 1.33

That said, the effect of students achieving clarity can more than triple the rate of learning. From the assimilation of these two research constructs, what follows in this book operationalizes teacher clarity and student expectations into five essential components of clarity for both teachers and students:

1. Crafting learning intentions and success criteria

2. Co-constructing learning intentions and success criteria with learners

3. Creating opportunities for students to respond (i.e., formative assessment)

4. Providing effective feedback on and for learning

5. Sharing learning and progress between students and teachers

This book will present an instructional framework that provides readers with a systematic means to ensure that both teacher and student clarity are not only present, but are catalysts for accelerating learning.

Achieving teacher clarity works best, and doing what works best matters. As teachers, success in our classrooms and schools comes down to the decisions we make each and every day. For each of these decisions to have the greatest impact on student learning, the decisions have to strike the ideal balance between deliberate and instinctive thinking. We make deliberate decisions about what and how to teach content, all while relying on our instincts as we build positive relationships and respond to students' needs in our classrooms and schools. This balance differs from teacher to teacher, student to student, and across each content area and grade level. This book will define the deliberate actions of a teacher to achieve clarity, which in turn will inform the instinctive part of teaching, making it more purposeful. Ultimately, learning will accelerate for both the teacher and the students.

CLARITY IN READING: WHAT TO EXPECT FROM THIS BOOK

There are three main purposes in writing this book: (1) present an instructional process, or framework, for achieving teacher and student clarity in the K–12 classroom; (2) build an understanding of the components necessary to engage students in their own learning in the classroom through learning intentions, success criteria, opportunities to respond, and feedback; and (3) engage readers in reflective practice about their teaching by assessing their impact on student learning. This book will support districts, schools, classrooms, and teachers as they work to increase their impact on student learning through developing a shared language of learning among all stakeholders in the learning process (i.e., administrators, instructional leaders, teachers, and, most important, students).

The five essential components of clarity for both teachers and students form the outline for the instructional process presented in this book, starting with the development of learning intentions success criteria: *gaining clarity*. Assimilating the work of Larry Ainsworth (2016), Shirley Clarke (2014), Michael Absolum (2010), and John Hattie (2012), the initial section on gaining clarity will guide readers through the steps for constructing learning intentions and success criteria that balance surface and deep learning while at the same time finding the right level of challenge.

Sharing clarity, the second component, involves developing a shared understanding of the learning expectations, confirming that both teachers and students understand what success looks like. Part three of the process will provide readers with an opportunity to unpack the relationship between learning intentions, success criteria, and formative assessment: *assessing with clarity*. Ensuring that we see learning through the eyes of students, formative assessment will be framed as students' opportunities to respond. Each opportunity to respond is an opportunity to provide effective feedback to learners. *Feedback with clarity* makes up the fourth part of the process by presenting the characteristics of effective feedback and how to provide guidance that is attuned to student progress and thus improves learning. To make meaning of the process, the final component of the process of this book will demonstrate how students, teachers, and collaborative groups of educators share learning and progress: *clarity in collaboration*.

The contents of this book will provide a resource for teachers and leaders to deepen their understanding in these powerful practices while seeing examples from across North America of how these practices are already being used in schools and classrooms. We will strive to provide useful and practical information, ideas, and strategies intended to make classrooms more inviting, engaging,

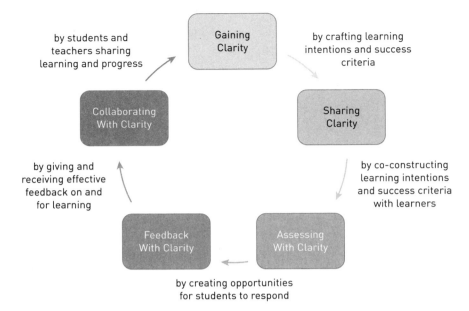

and successful for all learners so that they can answer the three questions: (1) What am I learning? (2) Why am I learning it? (3) How will I know I have learned it?

In the coming pages, not only will this book present a way forward for achieving clarity in your school or classroom, each chapter will model the concepts, ideas, and essential practices for creating and sustaining clarity and connecting clarity to other powerful and evidence-based practices, like formative assessment and feedback. The following in-text features are designed to reinforce each idea and promote, well, clarity of the information in the book:

1. **Learning intention and success criteria** are presented at the start of each chapter for the reader. The learning intention is a clear statement about what you should learn as a result of engaging in the chapter. The success criteria specify what evidence will show whether or not you have met the learning intention. You will notice a slightly different format in each chapter as to how they are presented, as we feel strongly that there is not just one way to write or share them. Rather, it is critical to have them, use them, and know if they are working to clarify learning for students.

2. **Guiding questions** will be provided throughout the book to provide thinking prompts for readers to use as they work through creating clarity in their own classrooms.

3. **Common clarity questions.** As you work to improve the clarity of learning in your school or classroom, you will likely have questions.

Through our work with schools and classrooms around the globe, we have assembled some of the most commonly asked questions. These questions, and responses, have been placed throughout the book with the content that is most helpful in answering the questions.

4. **Common clarity misconceptions.** Although this may go without saying, misconceptions are likely to pop up. Throughout the upcoming chapters, we will identify and discuss common misconceptions about clarity.

5. **Reflection and next steps** will close out every chapter. Closure is important. Each task or question is designed to consolidate information from the chapter into big ideas and takeaways. This, of course, will also enhance assessing for clarity and providing feedback for clarity, and thus increase the likelihood of achieving clarity of assessment and feedback in your school or classroom.

6. **The litmus test:** a test that provides a decisive answer. How you will know you have clarity? Questions posed at the end of the chapter that will help you evaluate whether you have achieved clarity in your classroom for each component. For example, how do you know if you have achieved this particular component of the clarity journey in your school or classroom?

7. **A community of practice:** This brings up the final and most important feature of the book: examples, exemplars, and models of success from a community of practitioners. Educators from around the country have shared vignettes and authentic classroom examples. Each content chapter, or chapter that directly discusses one of the five components of teacher clarity, will be followed by an applications chapter that provides vignettes and examples of clarity from colleagues around North America. These chapters are full of examples that highlight how district, schools, and classrooms have moved from complacency to clarity.

These examples can be applied to your classroom, school, or district as is or be tweaked to better fit your specific context. Furthermore, the ideas apply across all grade levels and content areas.

IMPLEMENTING RESEARCH AND STANDARDS THROUGH CLARITY

The instructional process or framework for achieving clarity aligns with national and state-level standards. In other words, this framework fosters and nurtures your journey as we gain clarity, share clarity, assess with clarity, give feedback with clarity, and collaborate with clarity in the context of accountability. This framework is built from the latest research (e.g., Absolum, 2010; Ainsworth, 2016; Clarke, 2014; and Hattie, 2012) on what works best in teaching and learning, incorporating examples from classrooms that support this journey.

A SELF-ASSESSMENT OF CLARITY

Let's preview what you will understand (learning intention) and be able to do (success criteria) by the end of this book. Take a moment to engage in a preassessment of the learning that you will experience while reading this book. Where are you now? Then, once you have read and worked on each component of the book, we encourage you to return to this assessment, marking in a different color or with a different date how your learning has progressed and changed.

Component of Clarity	Success Criteria	Self-Assessment*		
		NY	S	A
Defining Clarity (The Clarity Problem)	• Describe what is meant by clarity.			
	• Explain the relationship between clarity, learning intentions, and success criteria.			
	• Develop a way to determine whether you have a clarity problem in your school or classroom.			
	• Apply the language of clarity to your own school or classroom.			
Gaining Clarity	• Describe what a learning intention and success criteria are and are not.			
	• Explain criteria for writing effective learning intentions and success criteria.			
	• Answer common questions and address common misconceptions about learning intentions and success criteria.			
Sharing Clarity	• Define what co-constructing is and why it is essential.			
	• Explain what teachers must think through prior to co-constructing criteria with students.			
	• Describe several methods for co-constructing success criteria collaboratively.			

Component of Clarity	Success Criteria	Self-Assessment*		
		NY	S	A
	• Express the rationale for using worked examples and exemplars to further clarify criteria and offer multiple pathways to success for students.			
	• Answer common questions and address common misconceptions about the process of co-constructing success criteria.			
	• Share clarity with students in your own school or classroom.			
Assessing With Clarity	• Analyze the relationship between learning intentions, success criteria, and opportunities for students to respond.			
	• Create opportunities to respond that align with specific success criteria.			
Feedback With Clarity	• Use opportunities to respond to gain feedback from your students about your teaching.			
	• Apply the research on effective feedback to both the learners in your classroom and yourself.			
	• Adjust your feedback based on the specific learning intentions and success criteria.			
Clarity in Collaboration	• Use feedback from your students to adjust your instruction for better clarity.			
	• Collaborate with students, teachers, and leaders to develop clarity at all levels.			

*Self-Assessment Marks: NY (Not Yet), S (Sometimes), A (Always)

CLARITY AS DELIBERATE DECISIONS

Unfortunately, multiple scenarios cloud our decision making and distract us from being deliberate about clarity. For example, the end of the school year is notoriously associated with standardized testing that creates a high-stakes climate around student learning, teacher evaluation, and school accreditation. As a result, we focus on teaching for the test at the cost of overlooking the what, why, and how of our students learning. "Because it is on the test" is a common justification for each day's learning. Regardless of which high-stakes scenarios dominate your thinking, each moment in your classroom or school provides an opportunity to focus on and strive for clarity. This journey to achieving clarity comes from deliberate decisions about what matters most in teaching and learning. These decision points, and the decisions we make at these junctions, will have a significant and lasting impact on student learning. Focusing on the five essential components of clarity will not only boost student learning, but also serve as a foundation upon which everything is possible in your school or classroom. From research to reality, providing a process puts this into practice and is the purpose of this book. So, let's get started.

THE CLARITY
PROBLEM

WHAT IS THE CLARITY PROBLEM?

Consider the following scenario. Below is a set of directions leading to a specific destination.

1. Go to the end and turn right.

2. After driving 800 meters, turn right at the traffic light.

3. Now, drive approximately 1,600 meters and turn left at the traffic light.

4. Finally, at the second traffic light from there, make a left.

5. Go halfway and the destination is on your right.

Where did you end up either in your mind or, regrettably, in your car? If you said the local frozen yogurt bar in the hometown of one of the authors, you were correct. If not, I am sorry you were not successful. As you read this set of directions, how did you feel? Were you confused? Did you feel a bit frustrated with this task? Whether in your imagination or your car, you likely found several challenges that prevented you from successfully arriving at the local frozen yogurt bar. For example, you had no idea of the starting point, which was the author's garage. Second, if you were not familiar with the metric system, the units would be hard to follow. What if English was not your primary language? Because you did not know the specifics of the destination, you had only one path to the end. Finally, once you got to an endpoint, the only guidance you had at that time was, "The destination is on your right." You would be unable to answer the questions: What am I doing? Why am I doing this? and How will I know when I get there? Furthermore, you would not have known what to take with you on your journey, because you had no idea what you were going to do when you got there.

The same problem with clarity you just experienced in failing to have frozen yogurt is also a problem in the classroom all too often. Is our students' learning journey like the one above, or are they part of the journey, knowing the destination, milestones, and language of learning to be successful?

EVIDENCE OF THE CLARITY PROBLEM

Leaders That Have the Disposition: Carol Flenard, Assistant Superintendent of Instruction

Spotsylvania County Public Schools (SCPS) is the 12th-largest school division in the state of Virginia. SCPS consists of 29 schools and has an enrollment of approximately 24,000 students. It is a rural school system that rests between Washington, D.C. and Richmond and has experienced significant changes in student demographics over the past 10 years. Like many school divisions in Virginia, SCPS experienced state and federal sanctions for underachieving schools due to an increase in rigor on state assessments and accountability revisions. At one point, 10 of the 29 schools were in a warning status. When a school system in Virginia finds itself in this unfortunate position, the Virginia Department of Education (VDOE) provides support through the Office of School Improvement (OSI).

As the assistant superintendent of instruction, I am honored to lead an incredible instructional leadership team. As a team, we determined that we would apply the guidance provided by the state to all of our schools, collectively. A mass support system for the 10 warned schools was developed that included individuals from the instructional leadership team, instructional coaches, and administrators from each of the schools. We began by providing systemwide professional learning on unpacking standards and writing cumbersome objectives on the board for students. We did see significant improvement, as 9 out of the 10 warned schools reached the accountability requirements in one year. The increase in the schools' achievement of state and federal requirements was due to a focus on the alignment of the written, taught, and tested curriculum rather than the posting of an objective. After improving to meet the minimum requirements, the schools saw little to no further growth. In other words, 25 to 30 percent of students continued to fail the state standardized tests, and achievement gaps were significant. As an instructional leadership team, we desired more for all our students. Achievement is not about meeting state or federal requirements, but about true student learning.

With our shift from state compliance to student learning as a school division, we began our work through a professional learning plan that was developed on high-yield instructional practices that included a bottom-up, top-down approach to support buy-in and momentum at the school level. Learning opportunities were provided to division and building-level leadership, teacher leaders, and instructional coaches at various venues.

In order to gauge where SCPS was as a division in terms of these instructional practices, school administrators created walkthrough protocols unique to their buildings. They identified which practices they wanted to include and used the data from their walkthroughs to generate goals for staff and the school. Walkthroughs with the instructional leadership team and administrators helped to determine the level of implementation of high-effect-size instructional practices in our schools.

As this professional learning occurred, I was afforded opportunities to visit other school divisions. As a typical practice, before visiting a school, I review achievement data that is accessible via the VDOE website. Upon reviewing this data, I noticed that the schools I was about to visit in a neighboring division were performing higher than some of our own (SCPS) schools and with larger, more diverse populations. I was eager to observe classroom instruction. What I noticed immediately was that there was not necessarily amazing instruction taking place. In fact, in some classrooms I felt like I had stepped back in time. However, when I engaged students and asked them what they were learning, why were they learning the material, and how they knew if they were accurately completing their tasks, an overwhelming number of students could answer those three questions. The students knew the expectations and owned their learning. I found myself reflecting about how some classrooms with whole-group, teacher-led delivery of instruction performed similarly to the classroom with dynamic instruction with the teacher as a moderator. The gains in learning and student achievement were relevant to the clarity provided to the students and not the delivery of the material. Even though I gained insight regarding clarity during my visits to another school division, I believe further inquiry is needed regarding the multiple factors influencing student learning and achievement.

Given this visit to a neighboring division and our own SCPS walkthrough experiences and data, I discussed a lack of consistency in the level of teacher clarity in classrooms throughout the division with the instructional leadership team. We then discussed these findings as a team, which resulted in the conclusion that a common division walkthrough that focused on the following three questions of teacher clarity was necessary for Year 2 of the work:

- What are you learning?

- Why are you learning it?

- How will you know when you've learned it? (see Almarode, Fisher, Frey, & Hattie, 2018; Fisher, Frey, & Hattie, 2016; Hattie, Fisher, Frey, Gojak, Moore, & Mellman, 2017)

Now, as administrators and the instructional leadership team complete walkthroughs, we ask students these three questions. The data from these questions on the common division walkthrough are used in three targeted ways. The first is to determine school strengths and opportunities in terms of the three questions focused on teacher clarity. This data is used to inform next steps in professional learning for school leadership and staff. The second is to drive conversations between school-level administration and the instructional leadership team members who support each school. Discussion is focused on comparisons of what each is seeing in the classroom in terms of clarity, a determination of common expectations on student responses, and staff learning needs based on the data. Finally, the instructional leadership team is able to discuss their observations of clarity, teacher communication of the three questions, and common expectations of student responses. The alignment of common walkthrough data, common expectations of student responses to the three questions, and use of data to inform next steps in professional learning provides SCPS with the ability to support the practice of teacher clarity systemically.

Our work with instructional practices and clarity is not complete. As noted, we have begun the work of gathering data at the division and school levels on these important concepts to better understand the use of the data, provide future professional learning opportunities, and drive our school and division improvement efforts. Preliminary data indicates that our next steps are related to how our students know if they've achieved the learning intention for the day and to providing students with ample and varied opportunities to respond.

Teachers That Have the Disposition to Ask: Beverley Acres Elementary School

The York District School Board lies just outside of the greater Toronto area. As part of the district's modern learning initiative, an initiative to prepare learners for the twenty-first century and beyond, a cadre of teachers from Beverley Acres Elementary School submitted a proposal to investigate their students' perception of the learning in each of their classrooms. Loucas Maronitis and his four colleagues who initiated this project expected that their learners would be able to identify what they were learning, the specific content or skills they needed, and where they needed to go next in their learning journey. Below is a brief summary of the specific focus within four of their classrooms.

- Classes 1 and 2 (Melanie and Melissa): We want students to know why it was important to learn and understand history. Students should be able to communicate how the feedback received for one task or subject is related to another task or subject.

- Class 3 (Loucas): I want students to be able to communicate why they are researching, reading, and sharing information through a variety of authentic activities, moving away from task-based to process-based work.

- Class 4 (Jeff): I want students to be able to focus on specific developments and processes in order to better themselves in very specific ways. Their focus should put learning ahead of the task and allow students to continue to work on their development beyond the task itself.

One of their main evidence sources was student voice, which was acquired through a survey the teachers developed that sought their students' perspectives on teaching and learning at Beverley Acres Elementary School. They felt that if they wished to understand what was happening in their classrooms, why not ask the students?

When the four teachers amassed the student survey responses, they found the following:

1. Many students were unable to state that writing in their reading journals helps them with their writing in other subject areas. That means a significant number of students were not sure why they were doing what they were doing in their learning.

2. Students were able to identify how they were learning to research, read, write, and share ideas through various structures (not necessarily tasks), but they struggled to understand and communicate the why behind their researching, reading, sharing information, and thoughts through a variety of activities.

3. Many students could not communicate the purpose of working through this process or learning to use these skills.

4. Another area of the survey that stood out was that students felt they did not have a voice in their education, which is why the teachers needed them to have a voice through the survey and recognize that providing their voice fueled learning for the teacher and for themselves.

5. The other area that stood out was that students felt as though they were not getting enough feedback, and the feedback that they received did not help them decide where to go next in their learning.

> *I did not necessarily want students to recognize that what I provided was "feedback", but to take the advice, suggestions, and questions that I put to them, internalize this feedback, and use it to aid in their quest to enhance their learning development.*

While surprised about some of the results, the teachers believed that their teaching needed to change.

Although student responses indicated many positives about the teaching and learning in these four classrooms, the previously presented evidence highlights what the teachers found to be a clarity problem in their classrooms.

We will visit several districts and schools like Spotsylvania County and Beverley Acres Elementary School throughout the next several chapters to participate in their journey in addressing this clarity problem. To be clear, these educators reached conclusions not unique to their schools and classrooms. This is the **clarity problem**, and it is common in many schools and classrooms across the world.

CATEGORIES OF CLARITY PROBLEMS

The clarity problem manifests in schools and classrooms in five different ways:

1. Fragmented teaching and learning

2. Activity-driven instruction

3. Misaligned strategies

4. Lack of progress-monitoring of learning

5. Unhelpful assessment data

Through our work with districts, schools, classrooms, teachers, and students, we, the authors, have engaged with educators in countless professional development workshops, planning meetings, faculty meetings, coaching conversations, and classroom walkthroughs. The data generated from these interactions points to common aspects of the clarity problem and of what the clarity problem looks like in each context.

Fragmented Teaching and Learning

What is it? Learning experiences are not connected in a way that promote learners to make connections and deepen learning; rather they appear to be a series of disconnected lessons.

How does it manifest? Students learn discrete concepts and skills but fail to see the big picture and make deep connections, and misconceptions are prevalent due to the disconnectedness and lack of depth of understanding. That said, students often fail to fully transfer new learning into their own skills and concepts as part of their learner toolbox.

Examples of Fragmented Teaching and Learning

In the middle school science classroom, students are learning about the structure and function of a living cell. For this specific manifestation, a lack of clarity will lead to the teaching and learning of each structure and its function as discrete vocabulary terms or concepts. A teacher might present the nucleus, chloroplasts, mitochondria, cell membrane, and cell wall as simply terms in science that students must be able to define and then identify on a model of a cell. Without clarity, learning evolves into series of fragmented or discrete topics, and students do not develop an understanding that the functioning of a cell as a whole system is a product of the specialized functioning of each of its parts.

Another example of fragmented teaching comes from pacing guides that become checklists of content covered rather than the intentional and purposeful progression of big ideas, essential knowledge, and necessary skills. If the teaching and learning in your classroom is packaged in fragmented, individual packets of information or lessons linked to a strict pacing guide, you may have a clarity problem. If teachers feel the pressure to keep up with a pacing guide, regardless of whether or not students have shown competency in the skills and concepts, you might have a clarity problem. If the pacing guide allows little time for preassessing, slowing down to go deep in learning, or reteaching if students haven't got it, you may have a clarity problem.

Activity-Driven Instruction

What is it? The activity takes precedence over learning.

How does it manifest? When the teaching and learning in our classrooms involves a "cool" activity that is not necessarily connected to clear learning intentions or the success criteria, we likely have a clarity problem. It often happens for the best of reasons or intentions: We wish to engage students. For example, activity-driven learning occurs when a teacher does his or her favorite unit on frogs, dinosaurs, or Agatha Christie simply because students enjoy the unit and the teacher is passionate about the content. Activity-driven learning is often the barrier to clarity in science classrooms but many other content areas as well. Focusing on demonstrations, exciting laboratory investigations, and cool science tricks, teachers and learners alike lose focus on the learning. Learning the necessary skills and concepts is put on the back burner behind what is enjoyable to learners or matches a teacher's passion. Because engagement in classrooms around the world is a common issue, teachers spend a great deal of time searching for exciting, entertaining, and, quite possibly, engaging activities. This often takes place at the beginning of learning, prior to establishing learning intentions and success criteria, and can lead to students focused on the specifics of the task and not what they are learning from the task and why they are being asked to complete the task.

An Example of Activity-Driven Learning

In a first-grade social studies class, learners are identifying national monuments and their meaning in the history of the United States. To get her students excited about and engaged with the monuments exploration, the teacher asked learners to work in groups and build models of the monuments. During the process, learners spent so much time on the selection of materials, the construction of the model, coloring, cutting, pasting, and the dynamics of working in a group that the outcome of this learning was lost. When asked, students weren't able to explain how certain national monuments represented the history of the United States; rather, they described what they created and how they went about creating it. Let us be clear here as well: The project-based experience is not discouraged, but the focus of the lesson—on the activity and not the learning intention and success criteria—distracted students from the clarity of purpose. If the teaching and learning in your classroom begins with Google, Pinterest, or finding a cool activity, you may have a clarity problem. If the goal of the activity is to engage students for a lesson or two before the real learning begins, you might have a clarity problem. If students fixate on the task or experience and are unable to explain what they learned and what they need to learn next, you definitely have a clarity problem.

Misaligned Strategies

What is it? The strategy being used in the classroom does not match the learning needs of the students (as evidenced by their work samples and assessment evidence) or the rigor required in the standards.

How does it manifest? If you have a headache, you are not going to put a Band-Aid on your forehead. Likewise, if your car has a flat tire, you are not going to schedule an appointment at the auto body and paint shop. Teaching and learning works the same way. If teachers have not gained clarity and then shared that clarity with learners, there is a better-than-desired chance that the learning experience will not line up with the intended learning outcomes. The level of thinking expected and demonstrated during the learning should be in alignment with the learning intentions, success criteria, and student work and assessment evidence. Thus, the strategies, tasks, and assignments selected provide a specific purpose in moving learning forward.

An Example of Misaligned Teaching and Learning

In this example, third-grade students were given the following assignment:

Learning Intention	Success Criterion	Strategy	
I will understand how the structures of a plant contribute to the functions that allow plants to survive.	I can compare and contrast the different ways that plants reproduce and survive.	To address this particular success criterion, the classroom teacher provided each learner with a t-chart graphic organizer:	
		Angiosperms	**Gymnosperms**
		Each student was given an envelope with slips of paper on which were written individual terms, statements, and examples. The task was to sort the slips of paper into the two columns. That is, students were to determine whether the term, statement, or example described or represented an angiosperm or a gymnosperm.	

Stepping back, we can see that the task requires students to *sort or identify,* while the expectation is that they *compare and contrast.* In this case, the strategy provided a beginning step to compare and contrast but did not actually require students to describe ways that angiosperms and gymnosperms were alike or different or to justify their reasoning for the comparison or contrast. If the specific strategy, task, or assignment does not evoke the same level of thinking, or progress fully to the same level of thinking, as the learning intention and success criteria, you may have a clarity problem. If student learning remains at the surface level, while the standards call for deeper learning, you might have a clarity problem.

Lack of Progress Monitoring of Learning

What is it? Teacher and learners are unsure or unaware of the progress made toward the intended learning.

How does it manifest? As learners engage in the learning process, the successful progression of learning involves monitoring students through formative assessment and effective feedback. However, if we do not offer students opportunities to recall, reorganize, and make meaning of their learning, or if we do not give them opportunities to make their thinking visible, we cannot adjust instruction to support their learning, and they are not able to think about their own learning and make their own adjustments as self-directed learners.

Examples of a Lack of Progress Monitoring in Teaching and Learning

Consider a high school government class, where students are working on their understanding of popular sovereignty as represented in the Constitution and its significance in America today (learning intention). The success criteria are that learners "can (1) describe popular sovereignty, (2) identify specific statements in the Constitution that define popular sovereignty, and (3) give examples of how this concept is significant in 2017." The teacher, to keep learners engaged, has provided fill-in or skeleton notes that students will fill in as they move through a presentation projected on a screen at the front of the room. Although the process of filling in notes may keep students focused on the notes, the act of filling in notes provides no data on how students are progressing in their understanding of popular sovereignty or their progress toward meeting the success criteria. Furthermore, learners do not have a real indication of their own learning simply because their thinking is not visible. If students are not provided multiple opportunities to make their thinking visible, or if a teacher does not know where the students are in their learning, you may have a clarity problem. If students are busy filling in worksheets, blanks, and boxes; but haven't articulated their learning in some way by explaining what they are learning, how they are progressing, and where to next; you might have a clarity problem.

Unhelpful Assessment Data or Tools

What is it? Assessment data does not inform next steps in teaching and learning.

How does it manifest? What happens if you are gathering data through formative assessment, only to find that the data does not tell you what you thought it would tell you? This scenario happens regularly in classrooms, as assessments may be premade from the previous year, curriculum materials, state assessment items, or a test generator. Such assessments may not fully align to the teaching and learning that has taken place thus far in the classroom, the students' needs, or the learning intentions and success criteria.

This also happens when teachers are given or find rubrics to base the learning on that are vague and give little information about how students can progress in their learning. Some rubrics are well written, align to success criteria, and are useful in moving learning forward, while others fall far short. This issue often stems from the use of subjective or unclear terms such as *adequate* or *sometimes*. It also stems from a rubric failing to explain what it means to meet the success criteria. This happens when rubrics have multiple levels but no expectation of which level proves that the necessary learning has taken place. Tools like this are unclear for teachers, students, and parents alike, and just because we found it on Teachers Pay Teachers, in our curriculum resources, or made it on RubiStar does not mean we have a tool that moves learning forward.

An Example of Unhelpful Assessment Data for Teaching and Learning

This example comes from a sixth-grade mathematics classroom, where learners are working on using number patterns to create tables, establish numeric rules, develop equations, and then create graphs of these patterns. The teacher, aware that evidence is needed to monitor the learning progression of students, has created an online assessment with questions or problems that resemble the standardized, end-of-course assessment for this particular grade level. Once students have submitted their responses, the teacher downloads the student responses and their scores on this online assessment and begins to analyze the learners' data. During the data analysis, the teacher calculates the mean, median, and frequency distributions for each question or problem. Developing charts to be used in the next grade-level planning meeting, the teacher begins to make inferences about student learning needs.

What this teacher will soon discover is that he knows very little about the learners' progressions in using number patterns beyond which questions they selected correct answers for and which questions they selected incorrect answers for. As a mathematics teacher, he also knows that there is an element of guessing to the assessment as well. The teacher has data, but the data is not helpful in identifying next steps in student learning. What exactly caused the student to select the wrong answer? Was it his or her computation? Did he or she respond in haste or by guessing? Are there true gaps in his or her understanding? Furthermore, the teacher is now limited in his ability to provide effective feedback beyond whether an answer was correct or incorrect. If the opportunities for students to make their thinking visible do not provide insight into their current level of thinking so that you can identify next steps in teaching and learning, you may have a clarity problem. If a rubric is used to quantify learning but fails to provide students with next steps in learning or specific feedback, you might have a clarity problem.

Each of the five manifestations of a clarity problem can show up as individual opportunities for improving clarity, and to be sure, we have each encountered them in our own classrooms. There may also be combinations of manifestations. In either situation, focusing on crafting learning intentions and success criteria, co-constructing learning intentions and success criteria with learners, creating opportunities for students to respond (i.e., using formative assessment), providing effective feedback on and for learning, and sharing learning and progress between teachers and students will enhance both teaching and learning in any school or classroom. Take a moment, and reflect on your own classroom or school. Which of the categories or what combination of categories of clarity problems do you see? What feedback would you provide classroom teachers to assist them with their clarity problem?

CONCLUSION

Learning is most successful when "teachers see learning through the eyes of their students and students see themselves as their own teachers: Visible Learning" (Hattie, 2009, p. 238). This is the essence of clarity. Clarity comes as a result of crafting learning intentions and success criteria aligned to standards, co-constructing learning intentions and success criteria with learners, creating opportunities for students to respond (i.e., using formative assessment), giving and receiving effective feedback on and for learning, and sharing learning and progress between teachers and learners. In other words, finding clarity is hard work, but when clarity is achieved, it provides clear direction and purpose for the learning. Furthermore, teachers have the focus to guide their intentional and purposeful selection of strategies to engage learners in progression toward the learning intentions and success criteria. Students are empowered with the knowledge of what they are learning, how they are progressing, and where to next for them individually. This progression must be an active, collaborative partnership between the teacher and his or her learners.

The solution is to ensure that:

1. We craft learning intentions and success criteria.

2. We co-construct learning intentions and success criteria with learners.

3. We create opportunities for students to respond (i.e., we use formative assessment).

4. We give and receive effective feedback on and for learning.

5. Students and teachers share learning and progress.

LITMUS TEST

Rate yourself using the following question prompts:

Fragmented Teaching and Learning: Does learning in your school or classroom feel like a series of discrete topics?

Never	Sometimes	Always

Activity-Driven Instruction: Do you and your colleagues pick an activity first, fitting it into the content? Or do you first determine what learners must know, understand, and be able to do?

Never	Sometimes	Always

Misaligned Strategies: Do the strategies, activities, and tasks in your school or classroom ask students to engage in or progress to the cognitive level or complexity required by the standard(s)?

Never	Sometimes	Always

Lack of Progress Monitoring of Learning: Do you have a clear picture of where your students are in their learning progression? Do students have a clear picture? If we walked into your classroom and randomly selected a student, could you or the student tell me where he or she is in the learning progression?

Never	Sometimes	Always

Unhelpful Assessment Data: Do you have large amounts of data that do not indicate what the students are learning, how they are learning it, and where they are going next in their learning?

Never	Sometimes	Always

If you selected "some" or "always" as your answer to any of the above questions, you likely have a clarity problem. With that said, the next section, Reflection and Next Steps, will help address this clarity problem.

REFLECTION AND NEXT STEPS

1. The two scenarios at the beginning of this chapter portrayed how data was collected around teacher clarity in two school systems, in Virginia and Toronto. Develop a comparable plan for assessing the level of clarity in your school or classroom. What evidence will you collect? From whom will you collect this evidence?

2. After you collect your evidence, what conclusions can you draw from the data?

Conclusions

3. Which components of clarity need additional support in your school or classroom? What evidence supports your claim?

Components	Evidence
Crafting learning intentions and success criteria	
Co-constructing learning intentions and success criteria with learners	
Creating opportunities for students to respond	
Providing effective feedback on and for learning	
Sharing learning and progress among students, teachers, and leaders	

GAINING CLARITY: CRAFTING LEARNING INTENTIONS AND SUCCESS CRITERIA

READER'S SUCCESS CRITERIA

I know I have learned it when I am able to

Short-Term Success Criteria:

1. Describe what a learning intention is and what success criteria are and are not.

2. Explain criteria for writing effective learning intentions and success criteria.

3. Answer common questions and address common misconceptions about learning intentions and success criteria.

Long-Term Success Criteria:

4. Use common language when referring to Learning Intentions and Success Criteria with colleagues and students.

5. Collaborate with colleagues to develop clarity.

Notice the different wording with the learning intention and success criteria for this chapter. How is the wording different from the previous and subsequent chapters? What approach to learning intentions and success criteria fits you best? What works best for your students?

A PERSONAL ACCOUNT OF CLARITY FROM THE WORLD OF EDUCATION

When I (Kara Vandas) was finishing my master's degree in education, I took a course on data analysis from a certain professor that will remain unnamed. She asked us to complete many tasks in data analysis, including one on using survey data from students, teachers, and administrators to determine needs within a school. The professor's explanation of the task was three sentences long, and I initially thought that it would be *that* simple. How hard could it be to interview a few people? I developed a short survey and engaged in interviewing students, teachers, and administrators as asked by the professor. I wrote up the results and turned the assignment in, thinking I had done just what was intended for this task. You see, as a learner, I was accustomed to getting A's and thought I had hit the mark, especially based on the limited explanation of the task. However, a few days later, my work was returned to me with a C at the top. No additional feedback was provided to explain the meaning behind the grade. "What? How could this happen?" I thought to myself. I determined I needed to talk with the professor to understand further this gap between my understanding, expectations, and grade on the assignment. After class, I asked her about the assignment and let her know that I must have misunderstood the learning expectations. Her response was, "That was evident."

I was not sure what to say after she insulted me. I wanted to give her a long explanation of how the learning expectations were unclear. However, I realized in talking with her that she took no responsibility for this component, and that somehow, getting the C was entirely my fault for not fully understanding what she expected. What was missing? *Clarity.*

The first step in our clarity journey starts before the buses arrive, the bell rings, and we as teachers utter the first word to our learners. In this chapter, we will explore the work of the teacher that must be done before students take their seats in the classroom. To frame the journey to clarity for both teachers and learners, we have marked our starting point on the following learning map.

> ❝
>
> *Clarity around understanding the standards and what must be learned and taught begins with the teacher. . . . It is absolutely imperative that the teacher find clarity in the standards in order to translate clear learning expectations for students. If the teacher is unclear about what students must know and be able to do, it is impossible for students to follow or own their learning.*
>
> (O'Connell & Vandas, 2015, p.54)

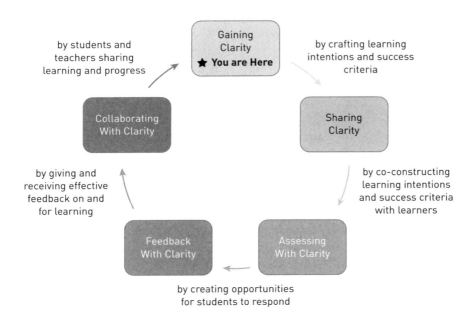

To begin the clarity journey, we begin with what is to be learned.

LEARNING INTENTIONS

A learning intention is just that; *it is the intended learning.* Learning intentions specify what students are supposed to learn. Learning intentions in the classroom should be clear and focused on the outcome of the learning. They are not an agenda of tasks to complete or a list of curriculum resources used during the lesson or day. For example, compare these two statements:

- I can explain how graphing ordered pairs helps me to predict and compare data.

- I will graph ordered pairs and answer questions about the data.

Learning Intentions are what we intend students to learn. (Hattie, 2012, p. 48)

The first statement clearly relays what the learners are expected to learn or understand in this particular mathematics class. The second statement focuses on a task that the students will complete.

Think of a time when you were asked to complete a task but were unclear on what was being asked of you. Think of the confusion you felt and the frustration that came from trying to complete the task without understanding the expected outcome. At every level in the field of education—as teachers, principals, and district-level administrators—we are sometimes asked to do things and are not given an understanding of the intention behind the request. Whether the request is to use a new educational program or to implement a districtwide policy, we struggle to find the motivation to implement these requests with fidelity. When we do this, we do what is requested out of compliance and not commitment or for the purpose of learning. Too often students are in the same dilemma, as they are engaged in hours of activities and instruction each day with one subject coming after another subject. How often is there confusion as to what is being learned or how lessons are connected? Do you ever hear, "What are we doing?" or "Why are we doing this?" in the classroom? These questions are a clear sign that something is amiss with the learning intention. Students not only want clarity about what they are to learn, but they require this clarification for any goal-oriented behavior to be attempted or accomplished.

Clarity of the expectations helps learners collaborate or align their personal interests and level of willingness to engage with the goal of meeting the learning intentions. Hattie and Donoghue (2016) have shown that when students are aware of what they are learning and what it means to be successful *before* undertaking the task, this leads to more goal-directed behaviors. Gaining clarity through clear learning intention(s) is the first step to providing students with the necessary information to embark on a pathway to success.

Consider the following tasks:

1. Finding the density of three mystery substances in a science lab

2. Reading *A Wrinkle in Time* by Madeleine L'Engle

3. Sorting three-dimensional solids based on various characteristics (e.g., faces, edges, vertices, etc.)

4. Identifying the horizon line in various pieces of art

5. Creating a concept map or graphic organizer representing the three branches of the US government

Each of these tasks represents what students will do in these specific classrooms. For example, in a fifth-grade classroom, the learners will engage in the act of reading *A Wrinkle in Time*. Similarly, learners in a civics or government class will use their textbook or other sources to fill in a graphic organizer. There is nothing wrong with any of these five tasks; all can be linked to evidence-based practices. However, each of these five examples focuses only on the task and not the expected learning associated with each task. Yes, learners are expected to complete a laboratory that asks them to calculate the density of a mystery substance, but what are they learning from this task? Why does this specific lesson call for this particular task? What will this task support students in knowing or understanding about density?

If we don't provide clarity about what learners are expected to learn from a specific task, activity, or strategy, learners will most likely view these events as exercises that simply require compliance. In other words, they will try to "get it done."

Let us revisit the five tasks. Only this time, they are transformed to reflect the intended learning associated with each one.

Task	Learning Intention
Finding the density of three mystery substances	I am learning about the relationship between the mass of a substance and the volume that mass occupies.
Reading *A Wrinkle in Time* by Madeleine L'Engle	I am learning about the roles that characters, thoughts, words, and actions play in making inferences about the plot in fiction.
Sorting three-dimensional solids based on various characteristics (e.g., faces, edges, vertices, etc.)	I am learning the essential characteristics of three-dimensional solids.
Identifying the horizon line in various pieces of art	I am learning about the relationship between a horizon line and perspective in various pieces of art.
Creating a concept map or graphic organizer representing the three branches of the US government	I am learning about the balance of powers among the three branches of government in the United States of America.

In the previous five examples, a transition occurred from the task to a statement about intended learning. This is a major step forward toward clarity. However, just because a teacher writes down a learning intention in the lesson plan, on the board, or in a syllabus; and briefly talks about it, has students restate it, and even summarizes the learning for the day; doesn't mean any of the students understand what they are learning, why they are learning it, and how to be successful.

"What is the intended learning?" This one question should drive all planning and assessment in our schools and classrooms. Label these learning statements "content standards," "benchmarks," "grade-level indicators," "grade-level expectations," "essential learnings," "learning outcomes," "lesson objectives," "learning intentions," or whatever you like; they all represent *learning intentions*, or *statements of intended learning*. If we don't begin with clear statements of the intended learning, we won't end with sound assessments" (Stiggins, Arter, Chappuis, & Chappuis, 2006, p. 54).

Learning Intentions are also known as

- Learning goals
- Learning outcomes
- Objectives
- Aims
- Learning targets

Having clear learning intentions in the classroom is more than throwing a standard on the whiteboard or telling students the day's or the unit's outcome.

EFFECTIVE LEARNING INTENTIONS

Several criteria exist for getting the most out of planning and providing students with learning intentions. Larry Ainsworth (2016), through his research and work with schools across the globe, compiled the following list of criteria for effective learning intentions.

- Written
    - As the learning *destination*—"*Where* are we going?"
    - As a summary or general restatement of the standard(s)
    - As a global statement without specifics (i.e., "learn to write an opinion piece" or "learn to use ratios and proportions to solve a problem")
    - In age-appropriate, kid-friendly language but retaining the rigor and intent of the standard

- Includes
  - No specific details from the standard (specifics will be addressed in the success criteria.)
  - Key terms and vocabulary
  - No references to specific *context* (textual, curricular, situational, procedural, etc.)
  - An explanation of *why* this is important—for students *and* teachers

Let's return to the five tasks and their learning intentions in the table in the previous section. Do you see these essential characteristics in these examples?

We have not yet included the *why*. Providing students with why the learning is relevant is a critical component to their understanding and motivation. It is our job to determine why and share it with students, whether in written form, in conversation, or both. The *why* does not have to be that the learning intended is critical to the survival of all life on Earth. Many teachers report struggling with why some math concepts, science concepts, et cetera, are pertinent to students. For example, a teacher might wonder why it is important for students to know how much they would weigh if they traveled to different planets or the moon. Clearly most students won't be taking a space journey soon. However, the *why* can center on what is needed for next steps in learning, how the knowledge will be used in future learning, making connections in learning, and yes, how it may be used in the real world. In the case of calculating one's weight on different planets and celestial bodies, the reason centers on understanding that the force of gravity varies depending on multiple factors like the size of a celestial body or its distance from other celestial bodies. Understanding how gravity varies ensures students have a deep understanding of the properties of gravity; and thus, a better understanding of how the solar system and space function; which, coincidently, is critical for our survival on Earth.

Take a few moments and compare the learning intentions in the following table with the above criteria for effective learning intentions. Fill in the right column with specific characteristics exemplified by each example.

Task	Learning Intention		Criteria for Effective Learning Intentions
Finding the density of three mystery substances	**What:** I am learning about the relationship between the mass of a substance and the volume that mass occupies.	**Why:** So I can describe the intrinsic properties of matter.	
Reading *A Wrinkle in Time* by Madeleine L'Engle	**What:** I am learning about the role that characters' thoughts, words, and actions play in making inferences about the plot in fiction.	**Why:** So I can use inferences when I read any text that will help me to make connections and better understand what I am reading.	

(Continued)

(Continued)

Task	Learning Intention		Criteria for Effective Learning Intentions
Sorting three-dimensional solids based on various characteristics (e.g., faces, edges, vertices, etc.)	**What:** I am learning the essential characteristics of three-dimensional solids.	**Why:** So I can determine quantitative relationships within solids (e.g., volume, surface area, and angles)	
Identifying the horizon line in various pieces of art	**What:** I am learning about the relationship between a horizon line and perspective in various pieces of art.	**Why:** So I can learn to use perspective in my own art in order to better represent the world around me and also to ensure my art makes an impact on the viewer.	
Creating a concept map or graphic organizer representing the three branches of the US government.	**What:** I am learning about the balance of powers among the three branches of government in the United States of America.	**Why:** So I can describe the responsibility of each branch of government and how each branch serves to keep the others in check.	

COMMON QUESTIONS AND MISCONCEPTIONS ABOUT LEARNING INTENTIONS

As we strive to gain clarity through the development and articulation of learning intentions, questions arise about the process and characteristics of learning intentions. For example,

- How do we know what the learning intention is for specific content?

- What about rigor?

- Does every standard need one, two, three, or more learning intentions?

- What if I have a spiraled curriculum? Will I have a lot of different learning intentions at the end of the year?

- Do I have a different learning intention each day, or one for the entire week, month, or unit of study?

Each of the above questions, or some variation of it, represents a common concern or misconception about learning intentions. To ensure that we are successful in gaining clarity for our sake and the learners' sake, let us look at each of these questions.

1. How do we know what the learning intention is?

Answer: Learning intentions come from the academic content standards for a grade level, course, or topic, but they can also come from other sources when standards are not available. For example, a high school mathematics course will generate learning intentions from the Common Core State Standards or a similar set of mathematics standards, whereas in a high school dual-enrollment course, the expectations come from the curriculum of the college or university.

2. What about rigor?

Answer: Rigor is the combination of difficulty and complexity (Almarode, Fisher, Frey, & Hattie, 2018; Hattie, Fisher, Frey, Gojak, Moore, & Mellman, 2017). Difficulty refers to the amount of effort, while complexity refers to the type of thinking. For example, the learning intention, "I am learning about the role that characters' thoughts, words, and actions play in making inferences about the plot in work of fiction" should align with the level of rigor required by the standard, whether it comes from the Common Core or from an individual state or provincial standard. The difficulty should align with the type of fictional work (i.e., short story versus chapter book), while the complexity should align with the cognitive demand of the learning (i.e., describe the role, compare and contrast different works, evaluate different works, or create works). Again, rigor will come from the standards. However, the learning intention is not the only means by which students will have the rigor communicated to them. In fact, the success criteria, worked examples, and exemplars and nonexamples clarify the learning intention even more. We will address some of these ideas in subsequent chapters.

3. Does every standard need a learning intention?

Answer: Yes and no. Successfully meeting any standard requires learning. Therefore, every standard has a learning intention. That is why the answer to this question is yes. However, some standards can be integrated with other standards. For example, a standard on scientific processes (e.g., observing, collecting data, analyzing data, making inferences, etc.) can be embedded in a unit on weather. Therefore, the learning intention may focus on weather, with specific tasks and activities incorporating specific scientific processes. In order to clarify learning and show students how learning is connected within a unit of study, inquiry cycle, topic, or "chunk" of instruction, we recommend grouping related standards and selecting those standards from the group that represent the "big picture" of learning. Such standards show how students put all their learning together, and in turn, show us what they know and that they are ready for the next level of learning. This interconnectedness is why the answer to this question is also no. To continue to clarify this question, we recommend reading questions 4 and 5 as well.

4. What if I have a spiraled curriculum?

Answer: There are different views on how to approach a spiraled curriculum. For example, Frey, Hattie, and Fisher (2018) recommend that the learning intention focus on the specific day. In other words, what is the learning intention for today? However, there are long-term learning intentions within each of the content areas (Ainsworth, 2016). For example, in a spiraled reading curriculum, one can look at the reading standards for the grade level for the year, identify the priority or essential standards, and develop a long-term learning intention or intentions that can be referenced all year long. For example, "We are learning to make connections when we read" or "We are learning to develop the skills of technical reading." This can be shared with learners so that they know where they are headed over the next several weeks, giving them a frame in which to place the daily learning intention. For a chunk of instruction or daily lesson within the spiral, the learning intentions may be, "We are learning to identify a text-to-self connection with the setting of a story" or "We are learning to use pictures within text to make predictions about what the text is about."

At the end of the day, the question is not, however, how many learning intentions can we create? Rather, the question is, how can we gain clarity and share the clarity of learning expectations with students? That said, we encourage teachers to develop more global learning intentions first and then use them until they need greater clarity for students to understand what they are learning. Then, break the learning down into chunked or daily learning intentions. This point will become more clear as success criteria are developed that can provide students will additional clarity. Keep reading!

5. How do unit or long-term learning intentions relate to using daily learning intentions?

Answer: In the answer before this one, we shared a framework for thinking about learning intentions that includes long-term learning intentions, as well as daily learning intentions. We recommend reviewing that to get a sense of how long-term and daily learning intentions can work together. However, the real answer is about connection. One of the key factors in deepening learning is being able to make connections within the learning. By having long-term and daily learning intentions that work together, students are encouraged to make connections in their learning: The long-term learning intentions provide the answer to the big-picture question, "Where are we going?" and the daily learning intentions provide a small chunk of the learning it will take to get there. Therefore, the daily learning intentions provide the building blocks for getting to the long-term learning intention.

GENERATING LEARNING INTENTIONS FROM CONTENT STANDARDS

The commonly asked questions around learning intentions lead us into the next part of our discussion on gaining clarity, an in-depth discussion about generating learning intentions. Learning intentions come from state and provincial standards, the Common Core State Standards, the Next Generation Science Standards

(NGSS), or any set of standards associated with a particular content area. To gain clarity in learning, teachers must use these standards, along with the associated curriculum documents (i.e., frameworks and/or pacing guides). While learning intentions come from the standards, there is more than one way to derive learning intentions from standards, so we have provided a set of guiding questions for the work of generating learning intentions.

GUIDING QUESTIONS FOR DEVELOPING LEARNING INTENTIONS

1. In reading through the standards, does a big-picture learning outcome emerge? If so, what it is?

2. Does the big-picture learning outcome encompass what all of the standards in that section, chunk, or grouping are aiming for in terms of student learning?

3. Would a set of more specific components or success criteria provide the needed clarity as to how to successfully reach the big-picture learning outcome?

If you are able to answer each of the questions with a yes, you have what is needed to develop a learning intention that represents the global, unit, or individual learning expectation. What follows is an example, based on Common Core Reading for Literature Grade 1 standards.

Common Core Reading for Literature Grade 1 Standards Key Ideas and Details	
1. Ask and answer questions about key details in a text.	
2. Retell stories, including key details, and demonstrate understanding of their central message or lesson.	
3. Describe characters, settings, and major events in a story, using key details.	
Guiding Question	**Answer**
1. In reading through the standards, does a big-picture learning outcome emerge? If so, what it is?	Yes, the big-picture outcome that emerges is **that students are able to accurately retell a story.**
2. Does the big-picture learning outcome encompass what all of the standards in that section, chunk, or grouping are aiming for in terms of student learning?	Yes, **if students accurately retell a story, they will do all the things included in Standards 1–3.**
3. Would a set of more specific components or success criteria provide the needed clarity as to how to successfully reach the big-picture learning outcome?	Yes, the **success criteria could define what it means to accurately retell a story**, using language from each of the standards. **Examples might include the following:** • **Asks questions about the pictures in the story** • **Describes main character** • **Tells main events in order**
Resulting Learning Intention	**We are learning to retell a story.**

SUCCESS CRITERIA

Learning intentions are just one part of gaining clarity in learning. "There are two parts to supporting a learner to become clear about what is to be learned: naming or identifying the learning (learning intentions) and describing the learning (models or exemplars and success criteria). These are two parts to a whole, and you must not lose sight of that whole" (Absolum, 2010, pp. 81–82). Once we are clear on the learning intention, what will convince us, and our learners, that they are progressing toward or have met the intention?

Success criteria describe the evidence students must produce to show they have achieved the learning intention. Consider the earlier example used to define learning intentions, "I will understand that graphing ordered pairs helps me to predict and compare data." There are often several success criteria for a single learning intention. Success criteria specify evidence that demonstrates a learner has an understanding or is progressing toward understanding of a learning intention. By achieving all of the success criteria, learners have proven they have met the learning intention fully. For example, what would demonstrate that students understand that *graphing ordered pairs helps to predict and compare data?* Success criteria for this particular learning intention might be:

- I can identify which component of the ordered pair represents x and which component represents y.

- I can explain how the ordered pair corresponds with specific quadrants in the x-y plane.

- I can describe trends in a collection of ordered pairs.

This evidence, spelled out in the success criteria, will support learners as they take ownership of their own learning as well as teachers as they monitor student learning. In the gaining clarity journey, success criteria are the major milestones or landmarks, ensuring that all those involved in the learning experience know how they are progressing toward the intended learning outcome. In order for students to engage in the learning, they need to understand what success looks like. What will it take to reach the goal? How will students monitor their progress toward the goal? How will they know if they wish to invest in the learning?

EFFECTIVE SUCCESS CRITERIA

Just as with learning intentions, there exist criteria for getting the most out of success criteria, making them something that learners not only use, but that allow each learner to thrive, give and receive feedback, and engage deeply in learning.

SUCCESS CRITERIA

- Success criteria provide the "way of knowing that the desired learning (learning intention) has been achieved" (Hattie, 2009, p. 47).

- "Success criteria help students to gain a better understanding of what successful learning might look like in ways that they can recognize from what they know now. . . . They spell out in greater detail the learning intention" (Absolum, 2010, p. 83).

- "Success criteria are standards or rules which students use to make judgements about the quality of performance. Students use success criteria to determine what progress they are making toward achieving learning goals. Criteria show what success 'looks like,' and when used to assess, give both the teacher and the student feedback about learning. Whereas learning goals answer the question, "Where am I going?" success criteria help students to answer the question, "*How* am I going?" ("Learning Goals," 2010).

- I introduced the term Learning Intention to my students and explained that this was going to be the *flashlight* in my teaching and their learning. We talked about our learning being like a journey through a tunnel. This was where I introduced success criteria, and we likened them to *signposts* along the way through the tunnel. Often a picture of the flashlight was placed beside the words Learning Intention and signposts beside the success criteria. (Absolum, 2010, p. 83)

Success criteria are also known as

- Key competencies

- Evidence of learning

- Components to include on a scoring guide or rubric in the proficient or "meets" column

Effective success criteria

- Specify what students are to *do* to demonstrate learning

- Provide a "map" to the learning destination—"*How* are we going?"

- Identify the *details* needed to achieve the learning intention

- Use specific terms from the standard(s) and maintain the rigor of the standard(s)

- Include objective wording only, no subjective language (i.e., *some, few, many*, etc.)

- May include *other* details not included in the standard, but necessary to achieve the learning intention(s)

Consider the five tasks and learning intentions presented earlier in this chapter. Now examine the success criteria associated with each learning intention.

Task	Learning Intention	Success Criteria
Finding the density of three mystery substances	I am learning about the relationship between the mass of a substance and the volume that mass occupies.	• I can determine the mass and volume of a given substance. • I can graph the volume of different mass values of the substances. • I can explain the relationship between mass and volume from the graph. • I can calculate the density of a substance from the graph.
Reading *A Wrinkle in Time* by Madeleine L'Engle	I am learning about the role that characters' thoughts, words, and actions play in making inferences about the plot in fiction.	• I can describe the characters, setting, and plot in a given piece of fiction. • I can support my descriptions with evidence from the text. • I can make inferences about characters and plot using evidence from the text.
Sorting three-dimensional solids based on various characteristics (e.g., faces, edges, vertices, etc.)	I am learning the essential characteristics of three-dimensional solids.	• I can describe the characteristics of three-dimensional solids. • I can compare and contrast different solids using the characteristics. • I can use the essential characteristics to sort three-dimensional solids. • I can justify my sorting using the essential characteristics.
Identifying the horizon line in various pieces of art	I am learning about the relationship between a horizon line and perspective in various pieces of art.	• I can compare and contrast horizon lines in different pieces of art. • I can explain how the horizon line is related to perspective and how it contributes to the visual impact of an artwork. • I can create my own piece of artwork that uses a horizon line to show perspective.
Creating a concept map or graphic organizer representing the three branches of the US government	I am learning about the balance of powers among the three branches of government in the United States of America.	• I can name the three branches of government. • I can describe the primary function of each branch of government. • I can compare and contrast each of the functions. • I can describe the limitations of each branch of government. • I can apply these limitations to the balance of power.

COMMON QUESTIONS AND MISCONCEPTIONS ABOUT SUCCESS CRITERIA

1. If success criteria represent the achievement of the learning intentions, then how do I know where to begin instruction? Are success criteria different from a learning progression?

Answer: In short, success criteria and learning progressions are connected. If the success criteria represent what students will do to achieve the learning intentions, then the learning progression represents the pathway or incremental steps that begin with prerequisite skills and concepts and progress as we travel forward through the learning process to achieve each success criterion.

Take a second look at the success criteria associated with the learning intention, "I will understand that graphing ordered pairs helps me to predict and compare data." Listing the success criteria as a list, they would appear this way:

1. I can identify which component of the ordered pair represents x and which component represents y.

2. I can explain how the ordered pair corresponds with specific quadrants in the x-y plane.

3. I can describe trends in a collection of ordered pairs.

The learning progression pairs with the success criteria and represents the incremental steps that begin with surface or foundational skills and concepts and build up. We often hear instructional coaches and teachers say, "Those may be the learning intention and success criteria, but my students are nowhere near being able to do that." Besides adding the word *yet* to the end of that statement, this is where the learning progression plays a pivotal role in gaining clarity. We begin by determining the learning intentions and success criteria and then chart the course of learning by establishing the most logical progression of learning. Doing so allows both students and teachers to see a pathway to meeting the learning expectations. If students perceive they are or actually are far from meeting the learning intention, providing them with incremental steps can be a game changer. Success breeds success, and students who see their own progress begin to crave more, and so it goes until students are on an "upward spiral" of success (Dweck, 2006). As teachers, our job is to get students on a winning streak and keep them there (Stiggins, 2015). We must gain clarity to accomplish this important task. The progression may also include skills and concepts beyond the success criteria if and when they prove they have achieved all of the success criteria.

Learning progressions are our professional estimation of how learning will progress from one skill or concept to another. As teachers, we quickly learn how students engage with, interpret, and make meaning of concepts within our grade-level or content areas. In addition, educational researchers have devoted significant efforts to understanding how learners progress in their learning within different content areas (e.g., Almarode, Fisher, Frey, & Hattie, 2018; Popham, 2008). As mentioned earlier, a strategy for developing learning progressions is to use the success criteria, breaking them down into small steps or prerequisite knowledge and skills that students will need to prove they have met the learning intention(s) as well as those that are beyond the rigor of the standard.

2. Do students need to be aware of all of the success criteria at the beginning of a unit of study? In other words, do I show students all of the success criteria for a given unit of study or chunk of learning?

Answer: Students benefit from knowing where the learning is heading. For learners to know that there are several success criteria that they will reach provides clarity and a focus for learning. Success criteria help students see the progress they are making as they check off each success criterion on the way to meeting the learning intention. If the number of success criteria is overwhelming to learners, we encourage teachers to begin with a more generalized set of success criteria and build understanding as learning progresses, even adding additional criteria as learning progresses. Consider the following example:

GRADE 7 ARGUMENTATIVE WRITING

Learning Intention	Success Criteria
We are learning to write an argument supported by relevant evidence.	• I can state my claim. • I can state the opposing claim. • I can support my claim with relevant evidence. • I can organize my evidence in a logical way. • I can show relationships between claim, opposing claim, and evidence. • I can provide a conclusion that aligns to the evidence.

The teacher may provide the criteria to the seventh-grade class at the beginning of the learning, but he or she can, over time, further define each criterion. For instance, the teacher may have a mini-lesson on what makes a strong claim. Students may be offered multiple examples of claims, both strong and weak, and be asked to determine which are strong claims and why. The class may then collaboratively define or develop criteria for what makes an effective claim. In this example, the learning experience further defines the general set of success criteria and informs students in greater detail what an effective claim looks like, deepening their learning and providing clarity for their own writing. In truth, success criteria become clearer and more defined over time for students if they are used well. Students can then use the criteria to monitor their progress and understand how all the learning is connected.

3. Do all students have the same success criteria?

Answer: Because the success criteria are derived from the grade-level or content standards, the expectation is the same for all students. What may differ is the starting point in the learning progression and the scaffolding or support necessary to progress toward the learning intention. This is differentiation. The pathway through the success criteria may vary greatly student-to-student, but the grade-level or content expectations remain consistent. "In order to have a maximum impact, success criteria need to be known by teachers first. All pupils need to have the same learning objective, the same context, and the same criteria. Differentiate the activity rather than the success criteria." (Clarke, 2008, pp. 92–93)

4. What if my learning intentions and success criteria sound like the same thing?

Answer: If the learning intentions and success criteria are the same or sound the same, chances are that there is too much detail in the learning intentions, and/or the success criteria are too general/broad. Recall that a learning intention is just that; *it is the intended learning*. Learning intentions specify what students are supposed to learn in general terms. They are not an agenda of tasks to complete, or a list of curriculum resources used during the lesson or day, and they do not specify how students will achieve the learning. Success criteria describe the evidence students must produce to show they have achieved the learning intention; thus, the specificity as to how to reach the learning intention should be established with the success criteria.

5. Are success criteria used only with products we want students to produce, or can they be used for processes too?

Answer: Success criteria can be used for products, processes, and conceptual understanding. The goal is to ensure that the success criteria provide the ingredients to meeting the learning intentions. Look at the example below to see how each form of success criteria may be used.

LEARNING INTENTION

WE ARE LEARNING TO DEVELOP ART
USING A VARIETY OF TECHNIQUES.

Success Criteria

Process

- I can produce a concept sketch.
- I can identify three different techniques and describe how they will be used within the final piece.

Product

- I can produce my own art that contains three different techniques.
- I can integrate the techniques to produce a cohesive composition.

Conceptual Understanding

- I can explain how different techniques influence the impact of a piece of art.

6. What is the relationship between language objectives, used to support language learners, and success criteria?

Answer: There is a clear connection between providing students language objectives and the practice that takes place in the classroom of asking students to use the language they are learning. In order to fully learn a language, students must practice reading, writing, speaking, and listening in that language; it is critical to their success. There are two simple options as to how to connect language objectives and success criteria. The first way is to post the language objectives alongside the learning intentions and success criteria. This is recommended if the practice of using language objectives is deeply embedded in the culture and practices within a school. The second way is to ensure that the success criteria incorporate language skills, asking students to speak, listen, et cetera as the language objectives provide part of the ingredients to meeting the learning intention. In the example that follows, you will see that when students are asked to share their conceptual understanding, they are asked to do so by explaining. As long as teachers are thoughtful about having students use and practice language when learning, then either format can be effective. Review the example below to see how the two formats relate.

LANGUAGE OBJECTIVES COMPARISON

Kindergarten Math Example: Two Formats

Format 1: Includes Content, Language and Social Objectives	**Format 2:** Includes Language and Social Objectives as Success Criteria
Learning Intentions: **Content Learning Objective:** We are learning to count to 100 and beyond. **Language Learning Objective:** We are learning to talk to others about numbers and counting. **Social Learning Objective:** We are learning to work together to practice counting.	**Learning Intention:** We are learning to count to 100 and beyond.
Success Criteria: • I can count objects and call them by number names • I can count in sequence • I can make groups of objects and count them • I can compare groups of objects (less, more, and equal) • I can write numbers • I can count on	**Success Criteria:** • I can count objects and call them by number names • I can count in sequence • I can make groups of objects and count them • I can compare groups of objects (less, more, and equal) • I can write numbers • I can count on

Kindergarten Math Example: Two Formats	
• I can skip count by 2, 5, and 10	• I can skip count by 2, 5, and 10
• I can tell about patterns in numbers	• I can tell about patterns in numbers
	• I can work with others to practice counting
	• I can talk to others about numbers and counting

Explanation: In this example, you can see the structure on the left includes a content, language and social objective for learning, where on the right, the same expectations appear. However, the Learning Intention remains a general statement of learning and the Success Criteria includes the language and social expectations.

In addition, we recommend that whether a teacher used the expectations formatted on the right or the left of this chart that they take time to add success criteria over time, as kindergarten students are ready for the next steps in learning to count to 100 and beyond.

GENERATING SUCCESS CRITERIA

As mentioned before, success criteria come from standards and provide the ingredients or evidence for meeting the learning intentions. How do we derive success criteria? You may choose to use the following guiding questions:

GUIDING QUESTIONS FOR DEVELOPING SUCCESS CRITERIA

In achieving the standard(s) and meeting the learning intention(s),

1. What evidence would show you that students have achieved conceptual understanding?
2. What process might they need to follow to show their understanding?
3. What product would show that they know?
4. What language will they need to use to share their evidence of learning?

It is important to note that not all standards will have conceptual, process, and product success criteria. Some may have only conceptual and process criteria, for example. Therefore, the guiding questions are to be used to think through and determine the success criteria that best represent the learning required in achieving a standard or standards.

Consider the Grade 3 learning intentions generated from the NGSS. How would you break down the learning intention "I am learning about the relationship between forces and the motion of an object" into the ingredients for success using the guiding questions?

Standard	Students who demonstrate understanding can: 3-PS2-1. Plan and conduct an investigation to provide evidence of the effects of balanced and unbalanced forces on the motion of an object.
Learning Intention	We are learning about the relationship between forces and the motion of an object.

Success Criteria	Guiding Questions for Developing Success Criteria:
	
	1. What evidence would show you that students have achieved conceptual understanding?
	  • Define balanced and unbalanced forces.
	  • Explain how balanced and unbalanced forces affect movement of an object.
	
	2. What process might they need to follow to show their understanding?
	  • Conduct an experiment to prove how balanced and unbalanced forces affect motion.
	
	3. What product would show that they know?
	  • Write a summary of the evidence from the investigation.
	
	4. What language will they need to use to show they know?
	  • Students will need to explain and write (see #1 and #3).

PLANNING AS A NEXT STEP

By completing the process of gaining clarity, you have extracted what learners need to know, understand, and be able to do to meet the standards; and therefore, you are now poised to further plan for instruction, feedback, and assessment. The following questions may already be percolating in your mind, and we encourage you to make those connections. In addition, we will continue to unpack these concepts throughout the remainder of the book.

1. What prior knowledge is necessary for learners to successfully engage in this content? What learning experiences must they have to successfully build their prior learning and background knowledge? What scaffolding is necessary for all learners to successfully engage in higher-order thinking?

2. What learning experiences will encourage and engage learners and align to the success criteria? How will we make thinking visible to capture student

thinking? What opportunities to respond work best for these levels of thinking? How will we ensure that the opportunities to respond are really eliciting the level of thinking desired in learners?

3. How will the learning experiences promote multiple ways of interacting with the content? Cooperative learning? Small group? Whole group? What materials or manipulatives will be available to learners? What thinking strategies will be used to scaffold thinking?

4. What might students who have proven the success criteria engage in to go beyond the standard(s)? How can they apply or transfer their learning?

THE LITMUS TEST

Are the learning intentions and success criteria in my classroom working to clarify learning for students?

The litmus test, therefore, is whether or not students can explain what they are learning, why they are learning it, how they are progressing, and what they need to learn next. If they are able to explain these things, then clarity has been achieved. However, if not, there is more work to be done to provide clarity to students that is meaningful to them. This may include switching up the format of how you provide learning intentions and success criteria to them. We recommend asking the students, as they are the ones we are doing all of this work for and can inform us about what constitutes student-friendly language, formats, et cetera. In addition, the following chapter will address how best to share clarity with students and may add insight to the classroom practices you are already using or wish to try in the future.

We have intentionally written learning intentions and success criteria in a variety of formats throughout the book. Review the beginning of each chapter as well as samples throughout the book to notice the differences, as there is no right or wrong format; rather it comes down to clarity.

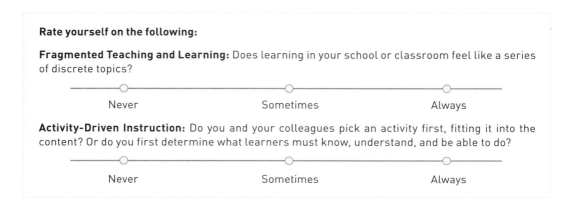

Rate yourself on the following:

Fragmented Teaching and Learning: Does learning in your school or classroom feel like a series of discrete topics?

Never   Sometimes   Always

Activity-Driven Instruction: Do you and your colleagues pick an activity first, fitting it into the content? Or do you first determine what learners must know, understand, and be able to do?

Never   Sometimes   Always

SUMMARIZING GAINING CLARITY

3 Questions	Powerful Practices	Students Can
What am I learning?	Learning intention Success criteria	• Articulate what they are learning
Why am I learning it?	Sharing the *why*	• Relate what they are learning to the purpose of learning
How will I know I have learned it?	Success criteria Examples and exemplars Feedback and formative assessment Learning progression	• Monitor their own progress • Articulate which success criteria have been achieved • Explain what they have not yet mastered and need to work toward next • Understand how to transfer their learning to a new challenge or problem

REFLECTION, NEXT STEPS, AND EVIDENCE

As you reflect on gaining clarity, use the following matrix to guide progress. The reflection questions can support you in considering how your school and classroom are gaining clarity. The next steps provide guidance on how to implement specific tasks into your discussions around gaining clarity. Finally, the last column, or evidence, highlights what evidence will give you the best picture about gaining clarity in your school and classroom.

Reflection Questions	Next Steps	Evidence
Is the goal of learning clear? • Teachers • Students • Parents	Using the standards, course expectations, and next level of learning needs, ensure the learning intentions • State the goal of learning • Use student-friendly language • Provide the "why"	Students are the best indicator as to whether or not the learning intention is clear. Ask them by • Polling the class • Hosting a focus group to ask if it is clear and what could make the learning intention more clear • Using an exit ticket that requires them to explain the intention and what they have learned so far
Are success criteria provided that show how to meet the learning intention/goal? • Teachers • Students • Parents	Provide success criteria to students. Ensure that success criteria show how to meet the learning intention.	Ask students to explain how they can meet the learning intention. Ask students to progress monitor their own learning using the success criteria.
Does the learning progression provide a probable pathway from current state to desired state of learning?	Use a preassessment to determine students' current state of understanding. Craft a most likely sequence of incremental learning steps to get students from their current state to achieve the success criteria and beyond.	Ask students if they can explain the steps to meeting a single success criterion.

GAINING CLARITY IN ACTION: VOICES FROM THE FIELD

Gaining clarity involves utilizing our standards of learning, whether they are local or national standards, and purposefully identifying the learning intentions for those standards. Effective learning intentions provide a clear target for both teachers and learners. These targets, then, allow us to articulate the evidence we are looking for as learners progress toward the learning intentions. These are the success criteria and the learning progressions for teaching and learning. As you might have guessed, how teachers gain clarity varies across districts, schools, and classrooms.

To assist in our clarity journey, we have incorporated voices from the field. What follows are multiple examples from schools and classrooms throughout North America. In addition to examples of learning intentions and success criteria, district leaders, principals, and classroom teachers shared their perspectives on gaining clarity.

VOICES FROM THE FIELD

From an Instructional Coach and Principal: Gaining Clarity

Names: Richard Jamison (coach), Meghan Wonderlich (principal), Caldwell School District, Caldwell, ID

Leadership: Preparation and Planning

The leadership team met over the summer to identify an area of focus for the school that would align with the district's vision of being a Visual Learning school district. After some discussion of the focus from the previous year, it was decided this year's focus would be on developing a deeper understanding of how well-developed learning intentions and success criteria aid in providing teacher clarity and influence students' feelings of success in their classrooms. During this meeting, we identified how we would introduce these concepts to the staff at the beginning of the year and began to solidify our own understanding of how learning intentions and success criteria help with teacher clarity.

We used our first staff meeting of the year to present what learning intentions and success criteria are and how they can be used in the classroom. During the presentation, Meghan and I made sure that teachers left with a basic understanding of how learning intentions come directly from the content standards and should be the goal of learning, the major takeaway from the day's lesson. We also wanted teachers to know that showing they had met success criteria was how students would demonstrate their understanding of the learning intention. In addition to the staff meeting, we provided professional development opportunities for teachers that were offered during their prep times or after school. The PDs were differentiated for teachers, providing them the opportunity to choose the level that made the most sense for them and that matched their current understanding of learning intentions and success criteria. The three levels offered were Novice—"I'm just starting to learn this," Apprentice—"I'm starting to get it, but I still need some coaching," and Practitioner—"I can do this mostly myself. I would like to know what my next steps are." All three levels provided teachers with plenty of examples and a space to share ideas and ask questions. We also planned to conduct interviews of students in order to allow teachers to reflect on how their students are remembering the learning intention and success criteria. The students' responses were recorded on video and shared with their teachers. The teachers then reflected on these videos and rated the students' responses.

Instructional Coaching

As the instructional coach, I made sure to make myself available to teachers in order to support them with this process. In addition to providing the PD during prep time and supporting staff meetings, the majority of my coaching opportunities were "on the fly" coaching. Teachers would call me into their rooms and ask, "How do these learning intentions look?" or "Can you take a look at my success criteria?" In these situations, I would read the learning intentions and success criteria, and then ask some questions about them—questions like these: "What is your learning goal?" or "What do you want your students knowing as they walk out the door?" For success criteria, I tried to assume the perspective of the students by asking teachers about how they thought their students would understand what they were being asked to do. I would also ask questions trying to determine whether the success criteria were aligned with the learning intentions and trying to see how they were all related to each other.

Besides the prep time PD, I met with all department lead teachers and worked closely with them in order to better support each team's development. These meeting were one on one and allowed for specific questions to be asked and a chance to plan next steps for their team. These meetings provided feedback to me as the coach and allowed me to better support teams of teachers by knowing where the team was on the continuum of understanding and implementation.

Another focus I had was to encourage and support teachers in their ideas and vision of how students might use their learning intentions and success criteria. Whether it was having students sign the poster underneath the learning intention, or using colored dots to allow students to reflect on their own understanding of the day's intentions, I encouraged teachers to try things out and to see what happened. I was their sounding board for ideas, made suggestions where I saw fit, and then encouraged teachers to try their ideas. In the end, I wanted to make sure the teachers had a clear picture of what they were doing and how it could impact students, because that is what this process is about; what we do as teachers has great impact on students. They better we understand what we are doing in the classroom and clearer this process is for students, the greater impact we will have on students' success in school.

Example of Learning Intention and Success Criteria: Math	Example of Learning Intention and Success Criteria: English Language Arts

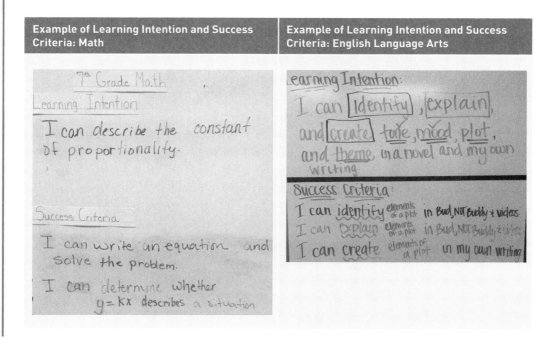

From a Middle School Instructional Coach and Special Needs Math Teacher: Gaining Clarity

Names: Carrie Gabriel, Joanie New, Liberty Public Schools, Liberty, MO

Breaking the Learning Intention Down Into a Step-by-Step Learning Progression

Coach's Perspective

While our coaching team was learning about Visible Learning, we viewed a video of a kindergarten student who was able to describe exactly where she was in progressing toward her writing goal, where she had been, and what she needed to do to move toward proficiency with respect to the goal. I briefly shared the impact this video had on me, and special education teacher Joanie New viewed it as well and was also motivated to try something similar with her struggling students. We broke down a math standard and identified the success criteria, which ultimately became the steps in a progression toward proficiency for the standard. She posted them in her classroom and used them to track student growth toward the goal.

(Continued)

(Continued)

A Sample of the Learning Progression for Rates and Ratios

RATIO/RATES VISIBLE LEARNING

**Steps in Learning Progression
(Prerequisite Skills)**

I CAN IDENTIFY A FRACTION

Fraction	Not a fraction	
½, ¾, 2 ⅝, ⅓, 5 ¾	.97865 1.3333	6 8

**Steps in Learning Progression
(Prerequisite Skills)**

I CAN IDENTIFY EQUIVALENT FRACTIONS IN PICTURES

**Steps in Learning Progression
(Prerequisite Skills)**

I CAN DETERMINE IF TWO OR MORE FRACTIONS ARE EQUIVALENT

$$\frac{1}{2} \quad \frac{2}{4} \quad \frac{8}{16}$$

Unit Success Criteria

I CAN IDENTIFY EQUIVALENT RATIOS.

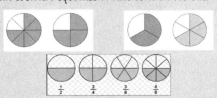

Unit Success Criteria

I CAN SET UP A PROPORTION AND SOLVE

Sam raked 3 bags of leaves in 16 minutes. If he continues to work at the same rate, about how long will it take him to rake 5 bags?

Proportion with Units	Work - Solution
$\frac{3 \text{ bags}}{16 \text{ min}} = \frac{5 \text{ bags}}{x \text{ min}}$	$3x = 5 \cdot 16$ $3x = 80$ $x = 26.7$ 26.7 min

Unit Success Criteria

I CAN SET UP AND SOLVE A PROPORTION

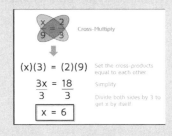

$$\frac{5}{12} = \frac{15}{x}$$

$5x = 180$

$5x = 180$

$\div 5 \quad \div 5$

$x = 36$

(x)(3) = (2)(9) Set the cross-products equal to each other

$\frac{3x}{3} = \frac{18}{3}$ Simplify

Divide both sides by 3 to get x by itself

$x = 6$

Although we believe all students would benefit from having their learning targets made visible, we felt this was especially important for students who tend to struggle with mastering content, especially doing so at the same pace as their peers.

The progressions were used to track learning and to help motivate students to move toward being proficient in the standard. We've found that when students were not provided with the same structure, they tended to struggle with comprehension of the standard. Joanie is very intentional about identifying the goals, naming the vocabulary associated with each goal, and having students have a visual cue to help them track progress.

As a coach, I've had the opportunity to see the impact within and outside of Joanie's classroom. The work she is doing has been shared and talked about with other teachers, and they now have started to do similar work: sharing targets with students so they can see the progression toward a goal. These teachers like the visual for students and have started incorporating it into other units and sharing it with other teachers in the building as well as with collaborative teams outside of the building. It is exciting to see teachers take ownership, see the impact, and share with others. My hope is that it will spread like wildfire!

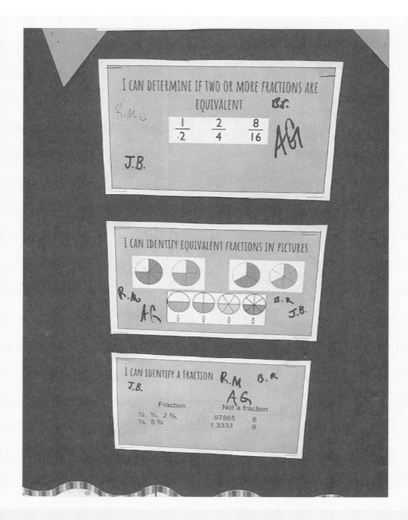

The above photo shows how students sign their initials when they have achieved each step in the learning progression.

(Continued)

(Continued)

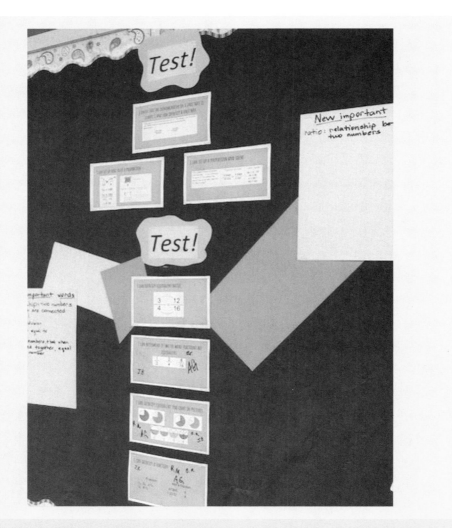

The above photo shows how students move through the progression and to the success criteria as they attain skills and concepts.

Teacher's Perspective

For my student who has been diagnosed with an emotional disability, it has made all of the difference between being motivated or not for math, and now math is his favorite subject. That didn't happen until we started Visual Learning. For him to see what he has to accomplish ahead of time has motivated him to work, and he feels more successful because he sees check marks toward his progress. He knows how much work he has to do each class period and he does it. He used to be so disruptive that the rest of the class couldn't work. I love it because it helps me be organized, and I use it to stay accountable to the curriculum and then use it to remind the students of our work. Using initials on the board helps hold them accountable for the work they have already done. If they say they can't do something, I show them the progressions on the board and remind them that they CAN already do it. I am not going to give the final test until I know they are ready. It really helps them emotionally. Personally, it helps me be organized in the chaos of a differentiated classroom.

Two Examples of Gaining Clarity Collectively

The two examples that follow both address the need for teacher teams to review standards and develop learning intentions and success criteria from them. Each school uses a different method, but both get to the same end. These examples appear here to provide multiple methods of addressing the need to work from the standards to gain collective clarity. Consider the following questions:

- Are the learning intentions presented as the learning *destination*—"*Where are we going?*"

- Are the learning intentions presented as a summary or general restatement of the learning?

- Are the learning intentions a global statement without specifics (i.e., "learn to write an opinion piece" or "learn to use a ratios and proportions to solve a problem")?

- Are the learning intentions in age-appropriate, kid-friendly language that retains the rigor and intent of the standard?

- Do the learning intentions avoid specific details from the standard? (Specifics will be addressed in the success criteria.)

- Do the learning intentions include key terms and vocabulary (e.g., academic vocabulary)?

- Do the learning intentions provide insight into *why* this learning is important—for students *and* teachers?

For the success criteria, how do the previous examples align with our discussion about effective success criteria? Consider the following questions (adapted from Ainsworth, 2016):

- Do the success criteria specify what students are to *do* to demonstrate learning?

- Do the success criteria provide a "map" to the learning destination—"*How are we going?*"

- Do the success criteria identify the *details* of what is needed to achieve the learning intention?

- Do the success criteria use specific terms from the standard(s) and maintain the rigor of the standard(s)?

- Do the success criteria include objective wording only, no subjective language (e.g., *some, few, many,* etc.)?

- Do the success criteria include *other* details not included in the standard, but necessary to achieve the learning intention(s)?

From the standards: Have the schools developed learning intentions and success criteria that fully address the rigor and purpose of the standards?

To get to clear learning intentions and success criteria, staff at Van Buren Elementary and A. R. Ware Elementary School devoted significant time to unpacking the standards of learning during their common planning meetings and teacher workdays. This systematic process results in effectively gaining clarity for both teachers and learners.

From a Principal and Grade 5 Team: Gaining Clarity by Plotting Standards

Team Members: Isaiah Folau, Jenny Hartvigsen, Cindy Wells, Ben Jackson. Principal: Melissa Langan, Van Buren Elementary, Caldwell, ID

A Grade-Level Team's Perspective: Gaining Clarity

As a grade-level team, we worked together in an Impact Team setting to define our learning intentions, learning progressions, and success criteria for our fractions unit. To begin, we reviewed all of the fifth-grade standards that we would address during our eight-week math unit. We categorized the overarching standards that we considered the "big ideas" of the unit.

From there, we deconstructed those overarching standards into smaller learning progressions that would support the big ideas of the unit, and then plotted them on a timeline in order from the beginning of the unit to the end. Finally, our team brainstormed the crucial skills students would need to be proficient. We then co-constructed our success criteria with students in friendly language. We organized our unit this way because it gave our team an instruction direction and clarity. It provided us a roadmap for our unit as well as an opportunity to coordinate our daily objectives with our unit goal.

Standards for Unit of Instruction Plotted on Webb's Depth of Knowledge				
Webb's Depth of Knowledge				
STND	Recall	Skills & Concepts	Strategic Thinking & Reasoning	Extended Thinking
5.NF.1		Add and subtract fractions with unlike denominators, including mixed numbers, by replacing given fractions with equivalent fractions in such a way as to produce an equivalent sum or difference of fractions with like denominators.		
5.NF.2			Solve word problems involving addition and subtraction of fractions referring to the same whole, including cases with unlike denominators, e.g., by using visual fraction models or equations to represent the problem. Use benchmark fractions and number sense of fractions to estimate mentally and assess the reasonableness of answers.	

STND	Recall	Skills & Concepts	Strategic Thinking & Reasoning	Extended Thinking
5.NF.3		Interpret a fraction as division of the numerator by the denominator. Solve word problems involving division of whole numbers leading to answers in the form of fractions or mixed numbers, e.g., by using visual fraction models or equations to represent the problem.		
5.NF.4		Apply and extend previous understandings of multiplication to multiply a fraction or a whole number by a fraction.		
5.NF.5		Interpret multiplication as scaling or resizing.		
5.NF.6			Solve real-world problems involving multiplication of fractions and mixed numbers, e.g., by using visual fraction models or equations to represent the problem. ←——————————→	
5.NF.7			Apply and extend previous understandings of division to divide unit fractions by whole numbers and whole numbers by unit fractions. ←——————————→	
5.OA.2	I can represent a calculation expressed verbally with a numerical expression. I can analyze expressions without solving them.			

(Continued)

(Continued)

Learning Intentions & Success Criteria Derived From Plotting Standards

Learning Intentions

- I can apply each operation to fractions (add, subtract, multiply, divide).
- I can communicate my understanding of fractions using high-level math vocabulary.

Success Criteria

- I can create equivalent fractions.
- I can add and subtract fractions with unlike denominators.
    - Ratio tables
    - Bar models
        - Number line
    - Identity property of multiplication (multiplying by x to make 1 or a whole)
- I can match fractions to their number problems.
- I can multiply fractions (mixed number, whole number, fraction).
    - Area model
- I can divide fractions (fraction by a whole and whole by a fraction).
- We can explain our thought process clearly using high-level math vocabulary.
- We will be able to interpret and analyze contextual problems and create a matching equation.

Student Friendly Success Criteria

- I can create equivalent fractions.
- I can add and subtract fractions.
- I can multiply and divide fractions.
- I can use different models for a variety of problems.
    - Ratio tables
    - Bar models
    - Area model
    - Identity property
- We will be able to interpret and analyze contextual problems and create a matching equation.

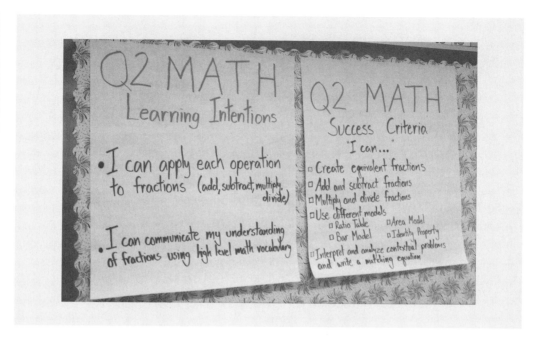

Determining the Learning Progression

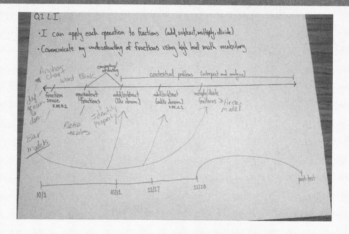

Using this document, the team worked on a timeline for teaching and for how they would work through the learning progression within the standards.

(Continued)

(Continued)

To accomplish our unit goals, when students review our daily objectives we intentionally link them back to our learning intentions and progressions. Students self-assess their learning on a daily basis using our success criteria. In addition, as an impact team we plan lessons together each week and evaluate where each of our classes is on the unit learning continuum. This enables us to evaluate where we are in our progress toward our learning progressions, to analyze student misconceptions and success with our progressions, and to take action with enhancements, interventions, and next steps.

By using this process, our end goal has become clear to us, and this in turn has brought clarity to our students. Students have marked ownership of their learning and now have a visual representation of where they have been, where they are, and where they are going next. Their depth of knowledge has increased, and their appropriate use of academic language has significantly increased.

From Two Coprincipals: Gaining Clarity by Unpacking Standards

Names: Sharon Barker and Billy Brown, A. R. Ware Elementary School, Staunton, VA

The Perspective of Two Highly Collaborative Instructional Leaders

In our classrooms at Ware, learning intentions and success criteria are foundational. They set the agenda for the day and instructional unit. Teachers at Ware post learning intentions and success criteria daily so that our students can refer back to them throughout their learning. Our goal is for our students to be active participants in their own learning, so telling students up front what they will be learning (and reinforcing this throughout the lesson) is an avenue for students to make connections to new learning and to begin to self-monitor their own learning understanding.

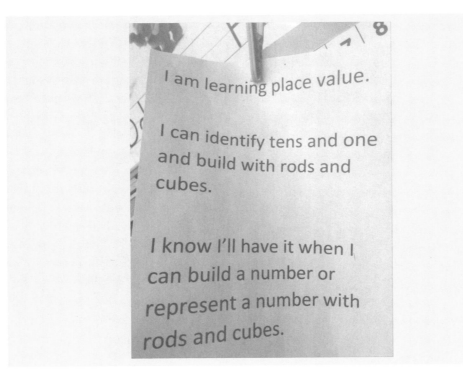

I am learning place value.

I can identify tens and one and build with rods and cubes.

I know I'll have it when I can build a number or represent a number with rods and cubes.

Our teachers are more focused on what students are learning than on what students are doing (the activity). Focusing on learning intentions and success criteria has caused our teachers to be more purposeful in their planning, delivery, and reflections. The language teachers use when speaking with students has also changed: Our teachers are talking with students about what they are learning rather than what they are doing. Our students are using learning intentions and success criteria as a monitoring tool during instruction. When Billy and I are in classrooms, we ask students the three important questions: 1. What are you learning? 2. Why are you learning it? 3. How are you going to know you are successful? Our students at Ware will direct us to where the teacher has posted the learning intentions and success criteria and talk about where they are in terms of the success criteria. It's powerful when students are able to talk not only about their learning but about where they are on the learning continuum and what they need to do to further their own learning.

Our teachers use learning intentions and success criteria as the cornerstone of their planning and instruction. Learning intentions and success criteria are posted throughout the room and referred to throughout instruction. When we first started on this journey, teachers were taking a lot of verbiage from the state standards when writing their learning intentions and success criteria. As we have learned and grown more comfortable with this process, teachers are writing learning intentions and success criteria in more student-friendly language. As a result, students are apt to use learning intentions and success criteria, because they are viewed as a strategy for understanding.

In Virginia, we use state Standards of Learning (SOL) and supporting documents such as the Curriculum Framework, which are specific in terms of student learning outcomes. Our teachers at Ware rely heavily on the Curriculum Framework, which the state provides for each grade level/subject, when planning. Learning intentions and success criteria are derived from state-provided standards and documents to ensure alignment.

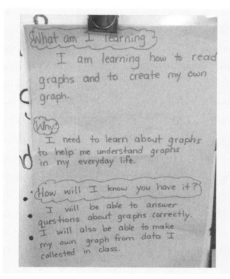

It takes time for teachers to really sit down with their colleagues and discuss the curriculum. There is also a mindshift that has to happen for teachers in the planning process. Teacher used to plan by focusing on the types of activities or tasks they wanted students to accomplish. Now, teachers plan first by focusing on the end results, student learning and understanding. Then, teachers work on developing the activities and tasks that will help accomplish that goal for the students in their classroom. So, our teachers at Ware plan with the end in mind and for the learners in their classroom, because the tasks and activities they select are based on the needs of their students. This requires teachers to engage in deep conversation (and ask questions of each other) so that together they can have a common understanding of learning outcomes. Then, once teachers have those common learning outcomes, they are able to go back and plan for instruction that will move the students in their class forward on the learning continuum. Teachers are also able to think about and plan for the type of feedback their students will need to help advance learning/understanding. This whole planning process requires teachers to know their students and where each student is in her or his learning/understanding. Getting to know students, as individuals and as learners, takes time.

Developing, supporting, and promoting teacher efficacy is so important. We are fortunate at Ware to have a math coach and a literacy coach who are able to work with teachers individually and in grade-level groups to discuss the curriculum and deepen teacher understanding. A deeper understanding of the curriculum helps teachers craft purposeful learning intentions and success criteria. Teachers

(Continued)

(Continued)

and students are then able to use the success criteria as scaffolding, or check-ins, in monitoring understanding.

I also think providing teacher with examples of well-crafted learning intentions and success criteria is important. As a faculty at Ware, we have also taken the time to review examples of learning intentions and success criteria that we considered to be well crafted as well as those that we felt could be improved upon. Carving out time for colleagues from different grade levels to have meaningful conversations with each other helps build collective capacity.

From a Team of Teachers: Gaining Clarity

Names: Principal Yana Ioffe; Team Members Jeff Borsuk, Melanie Chamberland, Melissa Doucas, Loucas Maronitis, Beverley Acres Public School, York Region District School Board, Ontario, Canada

The Perspective of a Collaborative Inquiry Team

Jeff: For me, providing students with learning goals is also giving them context. They need to know what they are learning in order to know what I'm looking for and how this impacts their development. Because of this, in the name of teacher clarity, I also provide students with the reason that they are learning whatever it is we are working on together. Both of these as well as the success criteria get posted up in the classroom as a visual reminder and shared with parents online so that the conversations and learning can continue at home. The co-creation of success criteria plays a vital role, because students need to chunk their goal. Instead of working toward an overall expectation, they, along with me, build the framework to their success. By doing this, students are both involved in the process of their learning and assessment, and are articulating the path, as they see it, to meet the learning goal. With guidance, the students should have a clear picture of their journey to successfully meet the goal before even getting started on a given task.

The assessment part is quite important. Students need to have a clear understanding of how they are being assessed. We triangulate assessment in Ontario. So when students aren't working on something with a rubric that breaks down expectations, they still know what they need to do. The feedback they receive, in fact, nearly always points to the learning intentions and success criteria.

Melanie: For myself and my students, learning goals (intentions) let students know where we are going. At the start of each unit, I set out learning intentions for the whole unit. I used to give more specific learning goals, but now I find that for my intermediate students (Grade 7), having more general learning goals helps them have ownership over some of the specifics of their learning and how they share that learning with me and with others. Thus, instead of saying something like "We are learning to write persuasive essays," I would now say, "We are learning to use persuasive techniques to convince others to think, say, or do something we want them to." In our persuasive unit this year, some students created movie posters, some wrote letters, some wrote newspaper articles, but they all showed they could use persuasive techniques! Also, once I have presented our learning intentions, and before discussing success criteria with students, I have started to ask students *why* they think we are exploring a certain topic or technique. It's very interesting to hear their thinking, and helps them to see that there might be more than one reason to learn something. We can then co-create success criteria with input from both the teacher and students. When starting a unit, I know that some things are going to be nonnegotiable in terms of success criteria, but students always come up with reasonable criteria that can be used to assess their learning journey. As Jeff mentioned above, it means that students are involved in the process of their learning and their assessment, and helps them see where they are, where they need to go, and how they might choose to get there.

Melissa: Learning goals are referred to at the beginning of each unit of study as well as throughout the unit. Sometimes, we will do an activity or lesson with a discrepant event, so that students will be able to work with me to figure out what it is we will be studying or learning.

Overall learning goals for the unit of study are posted on the board in the classroom for that curriculum area.

Learning goals also appear on assignment pages and in my Google Classroom. We refer to what we are learning and why when making connections between lessons and across subjects. For instance, "Yesterday we were using the Pythagorean theorem to calculate the length of the hypotenuse of a triangle. Today, now that we know the dimension of the unknown side, we are going to use what we learned yesterday to calculate the area and perimeter of the triangle."

Students have gotten used to creating success criteria for assignments and learning activities. If we are aiming to create a specific type of product, they are quick to describe what a successful or effective product of that type would contain/look like. For instance, my students are creating public service announcements (PSAs) in health class. After watching several examples and discussing their relevance and effectiveness, students created the following criteria for a successful PSA: is informative, is meant for a specific audience, has a focused subject, has a clear goal/message, uses appropriate persuasive techniques for the subject and audience, and is not created to make a profit/to sell anything. The exercise of having the students come up with these criteria on their own was helpful to me, because it helped me to check their understanding and see if they were listening actively and thinking critically about what we are doing in class. It's powerful for them to create these criteria, so that they know exactly what to do when they are planning and creating their own PSAs.

I'm still not at the stage of having daily learning goals and success criteria written down for each lesson. I have seen it in learning sessions and in some classrooms, and am interested in adopting this practice in my class, but I'm not there yet.

Jeff: The teaching and learning in my classes have been impacted in a significant way because of the direct message provided to the students. No longer do the students believe they are working through a task in order to master the task itself. Because students are being told about the development/process/learning goal and why they need it, they can focus their efforts on building toward it, instead of trying to perfect the task. To be fair, it isn't simply the learning goals and success criteria alone that allow for students to view their learning in this way, but rather the explicit instruction around their goals.

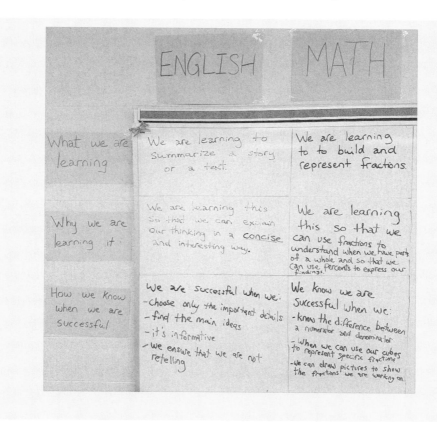

(Continued)

(Continued)

Melanie: I think what's most important to mention is that the way that I look at learning goals and success criteria has changed relative to the work we did in last year's modern learning collaborative. As I mentioned above, instead of having a few specific look-fors, we are working through broader goals and criteria. While this might sound counterintuitive, it has helped my students to meet the learning goals and success criteria more consistently, because it's not about assessing the task. Our learning goals and success criteria are about critical thinking skills (think, "What were the effects of colonialism in North America in the 1700s and the ongoing effects of colonialism today?" instead of "How did the Europeans interact with indigenous peoples in the 1700s?") and learning to apply specific skills that can then be used across multiple domains.

Melissa: Talking with students and parents about what we are learning, why we are learning it, and how they can demonstrate their learning has changed the type of discussions I am having with students and the types of discussions I hear students having with one another. While there is still a list of criteria attached to many of my rubrics, there are fewer specific items and more general questions: "Did you learn this? Did you communicate this effectively?" Students are then more likely to bring up things they did in assignments for one class in discussions on assignments for a different class. (It's less about using a ruler to label names of cities, and more about making sure we are clear and accurate when we present information.)

Jeff: In mathematics we often speak of the "big ideas." The learning intentions focus on building toward finding success within one singular big idea. It allows students to focus directly where I, their teacher, want them placing their focus. Also, should a student lose focus and forget why she is working through a task, she can simply look up at the board and read about the what, why, and how of the learning intentions.

Melanie: The learning goals presented at the beginning of a unit of study, and the success criteria that are then constructed with students, help me as a teacher determine where to focus not only my instruction (through mini lessons, readings, multimedia, etc.) but also my feedback. Because I teach all my classes in French (the students' second language), it is helpful for the students to know what points of language will (or will not) be assessed for any given unit or task. Using the learning goals and success criteria also allow students to easily peer- or self-assess in order to improve their work, as they know what I (and thus they) will be looking for.

Melissa: As Melanie mentioned, presenting the learning goals and co-constructing success criteria with the students helps me to focus my feedback to students and keeps students focused on what's important. It also helps students work together when they are collaborating on a task or in peer-editing circles. They are more specific in their feedback, and it is anchored in the list of criteria that was co-constructed with the class earlier.

As well, if a student is off the mark in terms of what he submits, I have to reflect and assess whether the student is experiencing difficulties with that particular area, or whether my teaching (the instruction, format, content, criteria set out) is unclear. If it is a wider group, I need to look at what it is I asked them for, and where communication was unclear. How students use success criteria helps me to design and plan further instruction.

Jeff: The standards (curriculum expectations) are the guide on what needs to be taught. They dictate the learning intentions. The learning in class should support the curriculum expectations. The success criteria are a breakdown of how to meet the goals depicted in the learning intentions. They can be considered look-fors or a guide. By co-constructing success criteria with students, we enable them to share their voice in the process of their learning.

Melanie: As I mentioned above, the standards (curriculum expectations) give me the big ideas I need to cover with my students in a given school year. I know that I will need to guide my students through learning about strong and stable structures, the fall of New France, the War of 1812, et cetera. From there, I can develop the broad learning intentions that will guide my students through the content. Thus, the standards and the learning intentions are the "what." The success criteria, co-constructed with the students, are the "how." The standards let me know what topics my students and I will attempt to uncover, but not *how* we need to go about doing so. This gives me as a teacher, and my students as learners, stewardship over our mutual journey in a given year. It is why, even though the curriculum remains largely unchanged, each year my teaching looks very different as I work to try to meet the needs of the students in my classroom.

Melissa: The standards tell me what content or skill I need to address within the school year. I use the expectations, along with students' interests and experiences as well as their strengths/areas of need, to plan an outline of units and lessons for the year. Each unit of study will cover a few big ideas, and I try to use student-friendly language to set up learning goals of those units and subtasks. I usually keep some of the same tasks from year to year, with slight modifications based on how students progressed and how they felt about them. If I noticed that a task seemed to be too simple for one class, then I adjusted for the next year, and so on.

Once students know the "what" of a particular unit of study, they have become quite adept at finding examples and describing "how" they can show their learning. Co-creating success criteria for assignments allows them to work together to frame a common understanding of what exactly they will do in order to be successful. When I co-create the success criteria with students, I have far fewer students or groups asking what we are supposed to be doing and fewer students who are underperforming. They set high expectations for themselves and understand how to meet them.

This year, I am teaching some subjects for the first time. I find that I have read the curriculum and grouped standards/expectations together into sections/chunks that make sense to me and that seem to have overlap. (For instance, Grade 8 Math, Geometry strand—Pythagorean relationship/Grade 8 Math, Measurement strand—area and perimeter of a triangle). I am collaborating with my colleagues to design units and lessons that work best to teach the students in a way that will be engaging and will hopefully help them to make deeper and long-lasting connections.

I find that in a Grade 8 class, I am able to be honest about my newness to this curriculum area and open to students' help and suggestions with planning. For our number sense unit on fractions, I asked for student input in creating the learning goals and planning the timeline for the unit. Students were able to see the curriculum expectations as laid out by the ministry, and we tried to unpack that language and make meaning of it. Where there is some overlap in the curriculum between grades, and certain students had said "We know this!" at the outset of the unit, it was helpful to look at the specific differences between the Grade 7 and 8 expectations and focus my teaching in that area.

Jeff: The biggest challenges in creating learning intentions are

- Making them in student-friendly language
- Ensuring that they work in concert with previous and future intentions to build foundational big ideas
- Being too vague or too specific

I create these myself without any support, without any guidance. Perhaps, those who are new to teaching or new to teaching a specific subject would benefit from a list of learning intentions and success criteria. This would allow educators to tweak provided goals in order to fit the needs of their program.

Melanie: For me, one of the biggest challenges in creating learning goals and success criteria has to do with the formal reporting framework of the Ontario Provincial Report Card. So much

(Continued)

(Continued)

of the learning my students do is cross-curricular, joining history with geography, drama, music, and art, for instance. But, I only teach history and geography to my students. While I do work collaboratively with the drama, music, and art teachers to let them know what we are doing in class, the way that one giant project must be communicated in a few lines on a formal report card doesn't really express the depth of student learning. Beyond that, some of the challenges I face are

- Creating learning goals and success criteria that reflect high expectations for all students, while providing multiple entry points for *all* learners in the classroom. I want all my students to learn something new. The goals and success criteria have to be broad enough that high-level students can push themselves to go beyond the common ideas (which they often already know before any teaching on my part!), and lower-level students can meet the expectations and expand their knowledge and understanding.

- Adequately capturing the learning goals and success criteria in student- and parent-friendly language, especially when working in a second-language program.

- Making sure that the goals focus not only on knowledge of facts and application of those facts, but also on enduring processes and skills that the students can carry across subject areas and from year to year.

I think that support in the form of professional learning opportunities and communities is invaluable, because being unconsciously unskilled (you don't know what you don't know) at something doesn't allow room for growth for you or your learners. Professional learning opportunities can cause some discomfort as you become consciously unskilled (you realize there are things you don't know) but can help you then move to being skilled in new areas. Continuing to share ideas with other educators and a wide variety of students helps hone the skills needed to create better learning goals and success criteria, because you hear a variety of ideas and experiences to inform your thinking.

Melissa: A few challenges I have with learning goals and success criteria are these:

- Creating learning goals and success criteria that reflect high expectations for all students, irrespective of achievement levels. As Melanie mentioned, we want all students to be learning. Sometimes it's tough to create success criteria that are broad enough to allow students to push themselves to reach higher levels (deeper thinking, more critical questioning, richer cross-curricular connections).

- Creating success criteria that focus on learning processes instead of products, and growth over achievement.

- Creating rich and engaging tasks with several learning goals, and ensuring that the success criteria do not become a grocery list of elements to include rather than important ideas/skills/processes to use.

We have had several professional learning opportunities on this topic, and I found those sessions to be very helpful when I first started using learning goals and success criteria with my classes. Nowadays, I appreciate working with my colleagues more informally—having them provide feedback on my wording to and with students and parents. I learn a lot by making mistakes and having my students tell me when the language is unclear. Sometimes it will be too late for that task, but not for that process, skill, or strategy. Continued work with colleagues, other teachers, and students is beneficial in assessing what's going well and what's not, and in refining my practice.

CONCLUSION

The voices from the field provide a glimpse of what gaining clarity looks like in the classroom. The previous examples and the associated commentary highlight the different approaches taken by schools and classrooms. However, each of the examples provide clarity in learning by allowing both teachers and students to answer the questions, (1) What am I learning? (2) Why am I learning it? and (3) How will I know that I have learned it?

REFLECTION

How will you think differently about clarity, based on what you have read?

What ideas have you generated that you will try in your own classroom or school?

SHARING CLARITY: CO-CONSTRUCTING SUCCESS CRITERIA WITH LEARNERS

READER'S LEARNING INTENTION

I am learning the power and purpose of co-constructing success criteria as a strategy for clarifying learning intentions.

READER'S SUCCESS CRITERIA

By the end of this chapter the reader will be able to

Surface	Deep	Transfer
• Define what co-constructing is and why it clarifies learning expectations	• Explain what teachers must think through prior to co-constructing criteria with students	• Answer common questions and address common misconceptions about the process of co-constructing success criteria
	• Describe several methods for co-constructing success criteria collaboratively	• Share clarity by co-constructing success criteria with students in the reader's own school or classroom
	• Explain the rationale for using worked examples and exemplars to further clarify criteria	

Source: McDowell (2017, p. 48)

The worst learning scenario is to be unaware of expectations or how your work will be judged and to have no guidelines about how to achieve the objective in the first place.

Shirley Clarke

(Clarke, 2008, p. 81)

In the quotation, Shirley Clarke explains the experience of many students who struggle, wonder, and put effort toward learning but are unsure of what success or achievement really looks like. In such scenarios, students often struggle to set goals and to understand why the topic or skills they are learning are important, how different learning activities and experiences fit together, and how to monitor their own progress. Not only is this not fair to students, it also inhibits learning and impedes motivation. Learning should not be a mystery, as our brains are wired for learning, but we seek focus, clarity, and patterns to help us make meaning. However, for too long, students have struggled to find clarity in our expectations for learning.

A TRUE STORY: LEARNING IS A MYSTERY

Going into my sophomore year of high school, I was so terrified of a legendary history teacher, whose name I will protect. I had heard story after story about him from my older sisters and knew I was in for a challenging experience. I knew he was very rigorous and expected a lot from students, and I was worried his class would ruin my GPA. I was not that confident of a learner, as I had a tough start to school, so I was just starting to believe I could get good grades in high school after a successful freshman year.

Then came the first assignment. It was an essay. I was anxious, as to this point, I hadn't written many technical essays. I worked hard to impress my teacher and turned my essay in with anticipation that, at least for now, my grade was safe. A week later, we received our graded essays back.

As mine was handed to me, I saw big red letters across the top and pulled it close to me so others couldn't see. At first as I glanced down, it didn't register, but the word across my paper read, "Bologna!" accompanied by a "D." I was horrified and wondered how many others received similar feedback.

I crept out of class that day, stuffing my paper as far into my binder as possible, and avoided eye contact with friends I usually talked to in the hallway. I was heartbroken and upset, and looking back, the thing that upset me the most was that I had no idea how to make it better. I didn't know what he wanted from my writing. What I did know is that I had failed terribly and would most likely continue to do so. I could kiss the good grades, my GPA, and scholarships goodbye.

Looking back now as an educator, I think that with just a few simple changes, my teacher could have given me a pathway to success. I wish he had shared with me what he was looking for and given our class some examples of well-written essays he had received in the past (on different topics, of course). I might then have seen a way forward. As it stood, I felt sure I would fail.

—Kara Vandas, coauthor

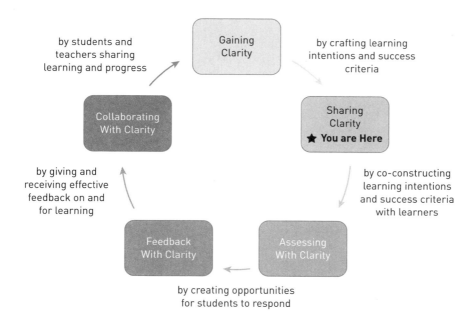

WHY CO-CONSTRUCTING MATTERS

We have an opportunity to change the clarity issue for students, and in doing so, greatly accelerate learning, impact student motivation, and build more confident learners. The power of the Visible Learning research is that it equips educators with the knowledge of what works best. At the top of the list of influences for students, we find the concept of *assessment-capable learners,* which had a d = 1.33 effect size (Hattie, 2012), more than tripling the typical rate of learning. What does that mean? It means students can make three years growth in one year's time. It means that kids that are significantly behind can make up three years of learning in one year. What exactly are assessment-capable learners? They are students who are able to articulate what is to be learned and what success looks like, describe and discuss their progress toward meeting the criteria, and determine their next steps in learning. Assessment-capable learners are able to select the right tools, at the right time in their learning journey. In addition, such students are able to set, monitor, and attain personal learning goals, while exploring and selecting learning strategies that work for them. Assessment-capable learners seek feedback, recognize their mistakes as learning opportunities, and support their peers in the learning journey (Frey, Hattie, & Fisher, 2018). One way to monitor whether students are developing into assessment-capable learners is in their responses to these three questions:

- Where am I going? (They know and are able to explain the learning intention[s].)

- How am I doing? (They know and can articulate the success criteria and their progress toward meeting each criterion.)

- Where to next? (They use the success criteria to assess their progress and determine their next steps for learning.)

Thus, one impetus for students truly knowing the success criteria, and for teachers taking the time to co-construct the criteria with them, is to enable them to develop the skills of an assessment-capable learner. However, co-constructing success criteria with students is more than handing them a list of tasks they must complete; rather, it is *building a shared understanding of learning expectations and a pathway to make progress.* It is a roadmap that lays the foundation for deep learning.

Research published in 2016 by Hattie and Donoghue provides further impetus for students knowing success criteria and co-constructing the criteria collaboratively. The research looked deeply at the learning process and examined how over 400 learning strategies affected student learning outcomes. The findings on the use of success criteria were astonishing, as they determined that students knowing the success criteria provided an average effect size of d = 1.13, while the average effect size of learning strategies was approximately d = 0.53. What does this mean? It means that providing students clarity around what success looks like can accelerate learning to more than double the normal rate. In addition, the meta-analysis found that results were highest for developing success criteria across the learning phases, which points toward the process of co-constructing success with students over time to develop a shared understanding.

But co-constructing success criteria with students is far greater and more important than accelerating learning for students, which is an incredibly powerful outcome and one we all want. You see, beginning a new topic or unit of study with clarity provides students a "coat hanger on which surface-level knowledge can be organized" (Hattie & Donoghue, 2016). It increases their willingness to engage in the task, helps them see its importance and purpose, increases their level of confidence, decreases anxiety, connects new learning to their prior knowledge, and increases the probability that they will reinvest in subsequent learning opportunities. In short, providing students a clear target to aim at increases their efficacy as learners. If we want to build lifelong, problem-solving, risk-taking learning ninjas, capable of taking on future tasks beyond our imagination, this is how we go about it. We build their efficacy as learners from the beginning by co-constructing with them what success looks like. If you are not seeing the fireworks of how exciting and thrilling this information is, you may want to consider a new profession. Educators, this is powerful, future-changing practice for our students and ourselves! And we have only discussed the idea of co-construction to aid surface-level learning, but its impact increases as we move students from surface-level ideas to deep learning and on to the transfer of learning to new and more complex tasks and situations. "Using success criteria has enabled pupils to have a sense of what their work should include, and, if success criteria are broken down and include examples along the way, quality will be increased" (Clarke, 2008, p. 117).

> **Self efficacy is the belief we have the skills to face challenges and reach our goals.**

CO-CONSTRUCTING SUCCESS CRITERIA: WHY?

1. Provides students a "coat hanger on which surface-level knowledge can be organized" (Hattie & Donoghue, 2016)
2. Increases their willingness to engage in the task and see the importance and purpose
3. Increases their level of confidence, decreases anxiety, connects to their prior knowledge
4. Increases the probability that they will reinvest in subsequent learning opportunities
5. Increases students' self-efficacy as learners

For students to move from surface-level learning to deep learning, they must use strategies that require planning and evaluation of learning in order to monitor their own progress and the learning strategies they have employed. They must ask themselves if they are making the necessary connections and seeing how learning is fitting together, how they are linking new thinking to old thinking. Without knowing and having co-constructed the success criteria, students have much less to base their metacognition on, meaning they will struggle to think about their own thinking, engage in effective self-evaluation and questioning, and seek accurate help and feedback from others. Therefore, if our hope is to have deep learning taking place in our classrooms, co-constructing success criteria is not only a good idea, it is the basis for which students will move from surface to deep learning.

Finally, as students move from deep learning to transferring that learning to new problems and situations, they must be able to evaluate the similarities and differences between the new task and one they have successfully accomplished. This requires a clear understanding of what success looked like last time and how it may be manipulated and modified to fit a new problem.

The bottom line is that if we as educators wish not only to accelerate learning for our students, but also to build their efficacy while we deepen learning, we must learn how to engage with them in co-constructing success criteria. It is both a powerful tool and an engine for learning.

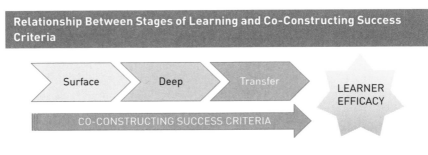

Relationship Between Stages of Learning and Co-Constructing Success Criteria

Surface › Deep › Transfer   LEARNER EFFICACY

CO-CONSTRUCTING SUCCESS CRITERIA

WHAT DOES CO-CONSTRUCTING SUCCESS CRITERIA ENTAIL?

The process can be accomplished using a variety of methods and with students of all ages, but a few basic components are critical when planning to co-create criteria with students.

Planning Ahead

1. Teachers must first have clarity of learning expectations in order to guide the conversation and ensure the learning intention(s) is (are) fully addressed by attaining the success criteria.

2. Teachers select ways to model and use examples and/or exemplars (above standard student work) to deepen understanding of what successful student work looks like.

3. Teachers determine how to best share, model, and construct the success criteria collaboratively with students.

The use of modeling, worked examples, and exemplars is critical to students gaining a shared understanding of success. The reason is that students rarely, if ever, read a standard or learning intention and say, "Oh, I know exactly what to do to achieve that and what my teacher will expect." The same can often be said for providing students a rubric. While rubrics often provide an explanation of how students' work will be scored, they leave a lot of room for interpretation and are often vague in the language used to differentiate each level. In addition, with multiple levels, they can be overwhelming to read and understand for students and often fall short of sharing clarity with students. For example, students may be given a rubric prior to creating a piece of writing. Yet, we see that their work has the basic elements required but the quality is lacking. Why is this? It is a lack of clarity as to what success looks like, and therefore, it becomes a list of things to do that students vaguely understand. Learners require a context for their work, a challenge or exemplar(s) that shows what is just beyond their current appraisal of what they are able to accomplish, and examples to evaluate and discuss.

> *Co-constructing is simply the practice of working with students to develop a shared understanding about what success looks like.*

To be clear, using a rubric is not a discouraged practice; however, it is far more powerful to engage in learning by establishing the criteria for success collaboratively—using modeling, worked examples, and exemplars—than to begin with how student work will be evaluated. In addition, the rubric or scoring guide should be tightly aligned to the success criteria and be used during and at the end of the learning for the purposes of feedback and evaluation, rather than to engage students in learning.

In the following section, we will address modeling structures that can be used for co-constructing and providing examples, as each structure can be used in a variety of ways by teachers and in different subject areas. Just following the examples will be a set of steps that teachers can use to co-construct success criteria with students.

Modeling

Modeling can take many forms, but essentially it involves demonstrating expectations for students so they can see and hear what the expectations look like. Thus, examples of modeling include creating opportunities for learners to follow, imitate, or work from what they have witnessed. As teachers, we often do this component without thinking it is part of the clarity equation, but it is, and it serves as one component of the co-constructing process.

In the service of exploring the power of modeling, take notice of the popularity of food TV today. It is one thing to pick up a cook book or recipe card and attempt to replicate a dish from a list of ingredients and written instructions (which are much like success criteria that are given to students along with directions from the teacher). However, it is infinitely better and instills confidence when we can watch, rewind, and watch again how a trained chef put the ingredients together, listening to the commentary added along the way and watching the chef demonstrate skill after skill until the recipe turns into a mouth-watering entrée or treat. Seeing it modeled is so different from following steps on a recipe card!

> *As a culture shaper, modeling operates on both an explicit and an implicit level. Explicitly, we may demonstrate techniques, processes, and strategies in a way that makes our own thinking visible for students to learn from and appropriate. Implicitly, our actions are constantly on display for our students. They see our passions, our interests, our caring, and our authenticity as thinkers, learners, community members, and leaders. Ritchhart (2015, p. 115)*

This demonstrates the might of modeling, and while there are many ways to model, the clarity equation doesn't stop there. Some of us may never have attempted the complexities of French cooking without Julia Child or the layers of flavor in southwestern cuisine without Bobby Flay to model the way. We amateur chefs crave models to know what success looks like, just as our learners crave models. Models make learning make sense and give learners an impetus to engage more deeply in learning. In fact, recent studies about modeling and the brain have found that observing another do or learn something causes the same neural networks to fire in the brain as doing it yourself (Ritchhart, 2015). In addition, researchers have found that when we identify with the person modeling the learning, more neurons fire than when we don't identify with the person. That said, teachers who have developed relationships with students have an enormous opportunity to shape students' thinking and learning through modeling.

How do we think through what and how we wish to model? First, we want to determine what type of modeling we intend for our students. In other words, what is our purpose? When co-constructing success criteria, our goal is to model so that students have a clear understanding of what success looks like, have an increased willingness to take on the new learning challenge (Hattie & Donoghue, 2016), and have some idea of how to go about the learning.

In *Creating Cultures of Thinking,* author Ron Ritchhart shares four types of modeling that he calls *apprenticeships,* as the goal is to make the implicit explicit in the service of deepening learning over time while developing more equipped learners. We will highlight the four types Ritchhart established and connect the types of modeling to opportunities to co-construct success criteria.

- **Dispositional Apprenticeship:** Being a role model of learning and thinking

  - **What:** Modeling how to think about learning, mistakes, failures, being stuck, and finding ways to get unstuck in one's learning.

  - **Why:** Surfacing the thinking of learners provides students with a model to deal with their own setbacks and struggles when learning.

  - **How:** Model the dispositions of a learner from the beginning of learning and throughout the learning process, so that students begin to stitch the characteristics of a learner together through authentic experiences.

  - **Application to Co-Constructing Success Criteria:** When modeling what success looks like, make explicit the thinking and feelings of the learner so students will know and be prepared for the types of thoughts and feelings they will likely experience during the learning. When the dispositions or characteristics we wish to see in learners are highlighted by the teachers, students begin to pick up on that way of thinking and on using those characteristics as a language of learning (Claxton, 2018).

- **Cognitive Apprenticeship:** Making our thinking visible

  - **What:** Deliberately bringing the thinking to the surface, or making it visible. For example, saying aloud what a good reader does to find text evidence while reading.

  - **Why:** Making thinking visible allows students to observe, think about, and practice different ways of thinking.

  - **How:** Explicitly model through think-alouds, connecting key ideas, wondering, predicting, considering different strategies, and other thinking routines or practices.

  - **Application to Co-Constructing Success Criteria:** Ensure that modeling your thinking is directly related to attaining the success criteria, rather than a task or activity. Thus, focus the modeling on the learning expected from students and how they might approach the learning rather than the doing.

- **Gradual Release of Responsibility:** Modeling for independence

  - **What:** Moving students toward independence in the use of thinking and learning strategies.

  - **Why:** Using the gradual release model provides students a scaffolded way to engage in a new way of thinking or doing when it comes to learning.

  - **How:** Teachers must identify the cognitive processes needed for successful learning to take place and model those processes from I Do (teacher explicitly models the cognitive process), to We Do (teacher and students work through cognitive process), to You Do It Together (small groups of students collaboratively work through the cognitive process), to You Do It Alone (students independently complete the process).

  - **Application to Co-Constructing Success Criteria:** A teacher can first determine what thinking processes are necessary for students to achieve the success criteria. For example, if a success criterion for reading is that students be able to select three relevant pieces of text evidence to support an argument, then the teacher might identify what thinking students must do while reading, and then provide a gradual release of that thinking process for students: First, the teacher would model the strategy with a portion of the text, asking the students to watch how the teacher identified a piece of relevant text evidence. This would then lead into the teacher and students working through the strategy together with a portion of the text. Next, students could practice that same strategy with a partner or in a small group with the next section of text. Finally, students could be asked to independently identify a piece of text evidence. Some might call this a mini lesson on determining relevant text evidence, but it is very much a part of the co-construction process for deeply understanding success criteria as well, because students can then take that thinking process and apply it to texts in the future.

- **Interactive Apprenticeship:** Learning from examples, practice, and reflection

    o **What:** Modeling how to do or accomplish something using examples, practice experiences, and reflection about the experiences, other than cognitive processes. Examples might include modeling how to draw in perspective, how to greet someone in another language, or how different economic systems function in different countries around the world.

    o **Why:** By analyzing models and examples, students are able to discern elements of quality and different approaches to achieving quality.

    o **How,** and **Application to Co-Constructing Success Criteria:** Because there are multiple ways to set up interactive modeling with success criteria, we are going to highlight them with more detail. They include but are not limited to using worked examples, using a series of worked examples from less proficient to proficient, and using exemplars.

Worked Examples

"A worked example is a step-by-step demonstration of how to perform a task or how to solve a problem" (Clark, Nguyen, & Sweller, 2006, p. 190). *Worked examples* are designed to support initial acquisition of cognitive skills through introducing a formulated problem, solution steps, and the final solution (Renkl & Atkinson, 2010). They can take two forms, as they can be a fully worked example or a series of examples that get progressively better over time.

Fully Worked Examples

Fifth-Grade Worked Math Examples: Multiplication, Heather Mueller

Series of Examples

Kindergarten Writing Progression of Worked Examples, Lori Black

Let's start with the first snapshot from the classroom, which is a set of fully worked examples. We may provide students with a worked example of a math problem to show them how they may do the same and then offer them a different problem to solve, asking them to use the worked example as a guide. This is how Heather Mueller uses the worked examples in the first figure above. She has modeled four strategies for solving two-digit multiplication problems for her students, and she has paired each strategy with a learning goal and success criteria. Once she has modeled each, she uses them as tools in her classroom: She not only asks students to use the strategies to check their work on other problems, but she also asks students to determine which strategy they need to work on and places their photos (which can be seen as small rectangles at the bottom of each worked example in the figure) below the worked example that best fits what they need to work on next. She then forms groups and creates learning experiences for each group.

The second example is of a series of worked, kindergarten writing examples that get progressively more proficient, culminating in one example that meets and one that exceeds the success criteria. Lori Black uses the examples to host discussions with students about their next steps in writing and model what the progression of writing looks like. Read more of her example in Chapter 5, page 86.

Exemplars

Using exemplars, or top-quality examples that meet or exceed all success criteria, with students provides a way of showing them what quality looks like and what "criteria in action" look like. It sets a challenge for students and shows them what is possible with hard work over time. It is similar to watching film of a professional athlete and using that film to dissect how to shoot a better free throw or throw a better pitch.

An example of the power of using exemplars appeared at the Denver Art Museum in 2012 and 2013 in Colorado in an exhibit called "Becoming Van Gogh," which was based on the book of the same title by Simon Kelly. Van Gogh was an artist known as a master of color, but what is so interesting is that he didn't begin that way. In fact, the exhibit began with a display of his early work, which was dark and dreary and lacked color. As the exhibit progressed, it highlighted Van Gogh's growth as an artist by placing his works next to those of accomplished artists—including Edgar Degas, Camille Pissarro, and Paul Gauguin—that Van Gogh apprenticed under during his career. Each master he studied under influenced him profoundly, propelling him forward with new techniques and a deeper understanding of color. The end of the art exhibit showed the glory of his learning and showcased the famous paintings with explosive color and captivating images that we know him by today. Without such learning experiences, Van Gogh may never have realized his potential to become a master of color. His growth happened because he patterned his work after that of masters, and in doing so, learned the skills to become a master himself.

The same process holds true for students in our classrooms. It is to look at the best possible examples available to learn from and to pattern after in order to create something beyond oneself (Clarke, 2014). Some may worry this is pushing too hard or setting the expectation too high. However, students report finding it clarifying, especially when more than one exemplar is used to show different styles or ways to meet or exceed the learning expectations. Think of showing kindergarten students a video of a highly proficient reader at the end of kindergarten. It doesn't intimidate them; it inspires the learners to think that they too will read that way one day.

There exist several ways to use exemplars in order to best engage students in discussion about what quality looks like. In fact, when looking for quality in student work, exemplars are the best way to communicate what it looks like and how it might take different forms. For example, by looking at a variety of exemplars on creative writing, students might notice how one uses vivid imagery, while another has a particular strength in using figurative language. In the following list, we have detailed different ways to use exemplars to establish not only the success criteria but also what quality or exceptional work looks like. No rubric can ever accomplish what using a variety of exemplars can when students can see, experience, and discuss what quality work looks like.

Example Methods for Using Exemplars and Worked Examples to Co-Construct Success Criteria

- Use a variety of exemplars that show students different ways to achieve the success criteria and foster creativity. Ask students to notice the differences in the exemplars and highlight the success criteria in each by noticing how each one meets or exceeds the criteria.

- Compare one or more exemplars to a few samples that are not quite as proficient, and ask students to notice and discuss what makes the exemplars truly exemplary.

- Show multiple versions of one student's work that has progressed over time until the student's work became exemplary. Ask students to notice how the student improved over time, highlighting the success criteria that the student achieved in each piece of work.

- In a math or science class, teachers can begin by modeling and using worked examples of how to solve a problem. Next, they can ask students to verbalize and chart how to finish a partially complete problem, find the error, or write an explanation for a correctly solved problem. By asking students to articulate the process and problem-solving strategies being used, they are co-constructing what success looks like and more equipped to problem-solve in future tasks.

Once a teacher has clarity about the standards; has developed learning intentions and success criteria; and has determined what models, examples, and exemplars will show students what the success criteria look like; it is time to share those criteria with students. In the service of working through this process from start to finish, we have outlined the steps in the following section.

STEPS TO CO-CONSTRUCTING SUCCESS CRITERIA

1. Determine **when** to co-construct success criteria with students.

2. Gather the tools students will use: worked examples, exemplars, models.
   - Examples of attainment of the learning intention(s)/standard
   - Examples of exceeding the learning intention (exemplars)
   - Non-examples or works in progress
   - Processes, steps, or multiple approaches to attain the same criteria

3. Determine the method that will be used to share the criteria with students.
   - Studying and differentiating among exemplars in small groups to generate success criteria
   - Modeling by teachers or students—demonstration with a think-aloud
   - Worked examples modeled and then posted for reference
   - Comparing exemplars to other, less-exceptional examples or nonexamples to determine which is better and why

4. Generate initial success criteria with students.
   - Allow students to share criteria after modeling, worked examples, and exemplars have been shared.
   - Add any missing success criteria (teacher noticing if anything is missing and needs to be added, based on the standards and expectations).

5. Categorize and organize criteria to create

    - A t-chart

    - A checklist

    - A rubric (meets and exceeds learning expectations portions of rubric)

    - Another way of representing the criteria

6. Model/practice using the criteria to provide feedback, and set personal goals as to which criteria are to be worked toward next.

7. Revise success criteria and goals over time as learning deepens.

As you may have noticed, Steps 6 and 7 engage students in goals setting and goal getting. This is intentional, and once students are empowered with the knowledge of what success looks like, they then have the ability to more accurately self-assess their own progress and achievement.

GOAL SETTING AND PROGRESS

This can be done through the use of a pre-assessment or any formative evidence of student learning paired with the co-construction process. The natural next step is to ask the students to use what they now know to determine which success criteria they have already accomplished and which represent their next steps in learning. We encourage teachers to host this conversation and self-reflection regularly in the classroom to enable students to notice and see the progress they are making toward accomplishing all the success criteria. Why? Because progress breeds progress, success breeds the desire for more success, and soon students find themselves on an upward spiral of learning (Hattie & Donoghue, 2016). This matters because it builds students' self-efficacy as learners. They have evidence of their learning, they know what they have and have not mastered yet, and they are finding success on a regular basis ("Self-Efficacy," 2010). If we want to build motivation and better learners, this process is paramount to success.

COMMON QUESTIONS AND MISCONCEPTIONS ABOUT CO-CONSTRUCTING

1. Do I always need to co-construct success criteria with students?

Answer: What we would encourage is to use modeling, exemplars, and worked examples often to provide clarity as to what the success criteria mean. The students will get more skilled at this process and so will you. However, we never want to co-construct just for the sake of doing so; if it isn't useful, don't do it. That said, we recommend starting in an area where the students and teacher lack clarity, and it would be very useful to develop it with students.

2. I don't have time to co-construct success criteria. Do I have to co-construct every time I have a new learning intention?

Answer: Two things: (1) The complexity of a task or standard(s) should be reflected in the amount of time you spend in clarifying quality and expectations; therefore, if you are planning to spend several weeks on a standard or topic, it makes sense to spend some significant time co-constructing success criteria. In addition, as each portion of the learning is modeled, explained, experienced, et cetera, students' understanding of the success criteria will continue to deepen. That said, taking time at the beginning to paint a clear picture of "Where are we going?" and what quality looks like is worth the time. Think for example of teaching students to write an argument or opinion piece; it will take several weeks potentially to draft, revise, and finalize the writing. However, if you are just spending a short time on the topic or standard, then the time spent co-constructing success criteria should be shortened to reflect a less rigorous learning experience.

(2) Teachers most always take the time to reteach, review, and provide interventions; however, how much of that time could be saved with a shared understanding of what success looks like? Taking the time early in learning to co-construct the success criteria may save significant time on the back end because students have a deep understanding of what success looks like. Also, it doesn't all need to be accomplished on one day. Co-constructing success criteria often continues throughout a unit or chunk of learning, as mini lessons and further use of examples, modeling, and exemplars will continue to clarify the learning expectations as students' learning deepens.

3. Is there a right or wrong way to co-construct?

Answer: Any experiences that clarify the learning expectations for students will have an impact on them, their willingness to engage in learning and risk taking, and their ability to plan for and take responsibility for their own learning. In many ways, sharing clarity with students through co-construction, using a variety of methods, will keep the experience interesting and student engagement high, as the brain enjoys novelty. If it becomes the same old, same old, students may begin to tire of the process but will likely still appreciate the clarity.

THE LITMUS TEST

Bottom line, you have done a terrific job of sharing clarity with students if they can articulate what the success criteria are and explain what quality work looks like. Some students will need the criteria, exemplars, and examples you have provided to give an explanation, but that is a good sign, as they are using the resources they have been given as learners to talk about learning. You may also want to review the chart below that focuses on developing assessment-capable learners to further explore the outcomes we are looking for in what students can do.

Three Questions of Assessment-Capable Learners	Powerful Practices	Students can
Where am I going?	Learning intention Success criteria	• Articulate what they are learning and what success looks like
How am I going/doing?	Success criteria Examples and exemplars Feedback and formative assessment	• Monitor their own progress • Articulate which success criteria have been achieved
Where to next?	Success criteria Examples and exemplars Feedback and formative assessment	• Explain what they have not yet mastered • Explain how to transfer their learning to a new challenge or problem

REFLECTION, NEXT STEPS, AND EVIDENCE

Reflection	Next Steps	Evidence
Look back at the ways that the learning intentions and success criteria are shared in each of the chapters to this point. How do they differ? Which format would make the most sense for your students? Why?	Ensure the co-constructed success criteria • Are agreed upon and student friendly • Are paired with worked examples, exemplars, and models of success • Are organized and easy for students to use and refer to in order to progress-monitor learning and determine next steps	Ask students to articulate the learning intentions and success criteria in their own words. Ask students if they know how they are progressing in their learning and which success criteria they have accomplished thus far. Ask students what is next for their learning.

SHARING CLARITY IN ACTION: VOICES FROM THE FIELD

Sharing clarity provides a crucial link for students between knowing and doing. In this chapter, you will find many different methods for co-constructing success criteria with students. The goal is to provide you with a variety of examples to spark your own ideas and methods for sharing clarity with students. Take time to review examples from a variety of subjects and grade levels to see how varied and creative the process can be, and then take time to plan your own co-construction of success criteria with students.

VOICES FROM THE FIELD

From a Kindergarten Teacher: Sharing Clarity

Name: Lori Black, Lone Tree Elementary School, Lone Tree, CO

Subject: Writing

After reading your book (*Partnering with Students: Building Ownership of Learning*, 2015) and hearing you speak to our staff during our professional development day last year, I became inspired to use exemplars to guide students to be independent as well as accountable for their writing. But I realized they can't achieve success unless they know what to expect and have something to guide their progress. In kindergarten, we must teach them conventions first before adding in other components such as wise word choice, voice, et cetera.

This year my students are, once again, motivated to write because they have specific tools to use to help them along the way. After explicitly teaching each writing convention (punctuation, finger spaces, capital letter at the beginning, lowercase letters in all their words, and details in their drawings), I taught them how to check their work against our writing goals. I place magnets on our big dry erase board, with one of our writing conventions shown on each magnet. Students take their writing to the board and look at each magnet to make sure their writing has those specific elements. Once they check and then return to their seats to revise, they can look at exemplars (which are actually another student's writing) on a trifold board to evaluate where they are in their writing. Some students even feel safe conferring with other students to help them evaluate their work.

I also conference with each student about the student's passions and encourage students to create stories based on their interests. It's only November, and two-thirds of my class can now write at least two full sentences, and they will write more if they enjoy the topic, and if it's their choice. They actually beg me to let them write, even during their free choice time!

Student assessing his work against success criteria	Students referring to a series of progressively improving examples and exemplars to determine next steps in writing

In the photos, you can see students checking their writing with our writing conventions shown on magnets, and later scoring themselves after self-evaluating using our exemplars. In between, there has been revision and discussion. This has become such a habit in our room that students seem to need the magnetic goals and boards. As the year progresses, I will add more goals to include wise word choice, vivid voice, sentence fluency, et cetera. Eventually, they won't have to use the kindergarten exemplar board, but will instead compare their work to a notebook of first-grade exemplars.

They consistently do this with *all* of their writing. Even when they are writing their cute notes to their friends, they pull out our success criteria (exemplar) board to check their work!

Thanks for inspiring me to inspire them!

From a Teacher: Gaining Clarity

Name: Alicia Pepe, Grade 6, Lone Tree Elementary School, Lone Tree, CO

Subjects: Writing, Reading, and Math

I am a sixth-grade teacher at Lone Tree Elementary in Colorado. During the fall of 2016, our staff was fortunate to have the opportunity to host Kara as our guest speaker to introduce the concept of criteria lists. After the professional development (PD) day in downtown Denver learning about the benefits of students knowing what they are being held accountable for and where they are at in their learning progression, I was excited about the possibility of starting a more simplified version of the collaborative rubric. In the past, I had worked with the students to brainstorm rubrics for the projects or assignments we were working on. However, I found that students often didn't understand the language that I put in the rubric, or they just didn't use the rubric until their final grade was highlighted on it. There is definitely a time and place for rubric usage, but I was in search of a better way for students to track their progress on required criteria for projects and lessons. And then we learned about success criteria!

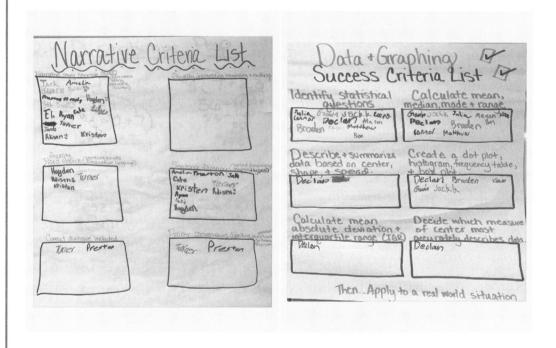

The week following our PD session, I chose to create a criteria list with my students for a narrative piece of writing we were starting. Since students had been writing narrative pieces since they were younger, they had some schema of what it takes to create a quality piece of writing for this genre. After they got together in groups and discussed what their idea of a quality narrative would be, I handed out an exemplar, had them read it, and told them to add to their lists anything they thought they had missed. Once they had some pretty complete lists of skill requirements, we came together as a class, grouped their ideas into six main categories, and added other required standards they had missed to create one comprehensive list of criteria the students needed to meet in order to have a grade-level piece of writing. I have to say, they did a pretty great job identifying all the skills I would

(Continued)

(Continued)

have included on a rubric! With this checklist to guide them, the round of narratives the students produced were of a higher quality than any I had received before. I was shocked that such a great improvement could happen so quickly!

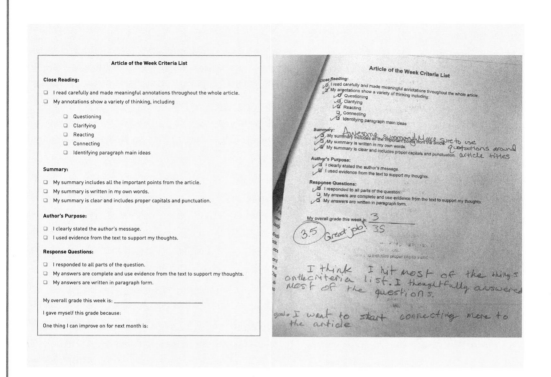

Once we were able to create and use the narrative criteria list, we expanded into creating one for our data and graphing math chapter, our passion projects, our mini quality products, and our other genres of writing. Criteria lists have completely changed the way my students assess their progress through assignments and projects, and I think what I love most about them is that the KIDS ACTUALLY USE THEM! The kids are showing *ownership* of their learning as they flip from one chart to the other to look at where they are in the progression and to add their name to the boxes they have mastered. They are *motivated* to sign their names in the boxes and to show mastery of their skills. The students are able to identify areas for improvement and able to articulate what they would like me to edit on their papers or help them with according to the goals that they have set for growth on the criteria lists. As one student said, "They definitely helped me with knowing what I needed to do and what I already knew." As a teacher, the criteria lists allow me to see what concepts I need to provide mini lessons for and how to group kids for targeted teaching opportunities. I have been amazed at the improvement in students' writing and overall work production by just adding the creation of a criteria list to my lessons.

I am so happy to have learned about criteria lists and to have been able to implement the use of them in my classroom to improve my students' ownership of and accountability for their learning!

From a Second Grade/Kindergarten Teacher: Sharing Clarity

Name: Kim Leroi, Lone Tree Elementary School, Lone Tree, CO

Subject: Writing (Grade 2), Generating Quality Questions (Kindergarten)

About a year ago our staff was introduced to the benefits of using success criteria in the classroom. It seemed logical enough—just have the students come up with the needed criteria to be successful in the assignment. I chose to start with writing. I knew I needed to teach my second graders paragraph writing. Yet, how can I talk about the success criteria when they needed to be instructed on what makes up a good paragraph? I could not speak with them about *topic sentences, transitions,* and *concluding sentences,* since they had no experience with those terms. How can you determine what is important in a task when you haven't experienced it yourself? I also knew that the success criteria needed to come from the students. I decided to teach my class paragraph writing step by step. Each day over a two-week period, I presented lessons on

- Outline formats
- Topic sentences (statement, number statement, and question)
- Transitions and when they are used
- Concluding sentences
- Supporting details

Over the course of the two weeks, I worked with individuals and small groups so everyone could have a solid paragraph. As the students completed their paragraphs, they shared them with the class during Author's Chair. Once I thought my students had a firm understanding of what makes a paragraph, I knew it was time to create the success criteria.

I began the process by giving pairs of students five sentence strips. I told them to come up with as many ideas as they could on what made some paragraphs better than others, and to write these on the sentence strips. Once each pair finished their strips, we discussed them and taped them to the chart paper. Duplicate ideas were not discarded. Instead I taped them on top of each other. Every student's ideas were shared and used for our success criteria.

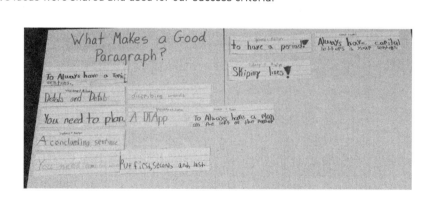

This chart hung in our classroom for the remainder of the year. Students would refer to the chart while they were writing, and with that, they began to take more ownership of the process. I would often hear students ask their peers to read their work for feedback. Having the success criteria visible allowed me to spend more time conferencing with students on improving paragraph structure, since they understood the basics of paragraph writing. The results were impressive. Students were writing the best paragraphs I had seen in many years. They knew what their end goal was and understood the steps to get there.

(Continued)

(Continued)

Success criteria charts then spread to giving presentations and to our summative assessment of our Connecting With Our Community unit. Once we had the understanding of how success criteria could be used, students were empowered to give their thoughts on what was needed to make any task successful. And the best part was that the criteria came from them, not me!

I now teach kindergarten and plan to create success criteria on what makes a good question. Students will analyze different types of questions and will understand the difference between closed- and open-ended questions. What I have found out so far is, once again, the more background information students have, the deeper the question. I asked my kindergarteners to come up with questions after we visited a local botanic garden where they took part in a leaf investigation and learned about the changing of the seasons and why leaves change different colors. Upon returning to class, I asked them to come up with questions on what they saw. Here are some of the questions they came up with:

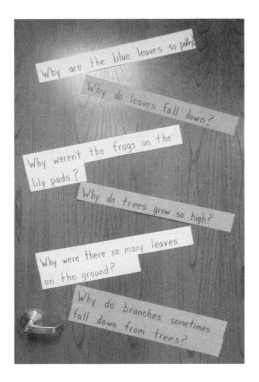

I was thoroughly impressed.

A week later, I asked students to think of questions for another kindergarten class that we were going to meet through a Google Hangout. Their questions were not as developed, nor were they engaged in the process. I found myself leading the whole discussion in order to get a handful of questions from them. It just solidified that students need to understand fully the task at hand before I can ask them to collaborate with me to create success criteria.

I believe that no matter the grade level, using success criteria has proven to be successful. It raises the quality of student work and empowers students to be more independent.

From a Fifth-Grade Teacher: Sharing Clarity

Name: Isaiah Folau, Washington Elementary School, Caldwell, ID

Subject: Math, Constructing a Quality Explanation

A quality explanation in math is composed of two things: a proper explanation of the process, and the correct usage of math vocabulary. At the beginning of each unit, and again as a review at the start of each lesson, vocabulary is introduced and then becomes a habitual part of the vernacular as a way to describe, discuss, and explain. This process piece, repeated with demonstration and trial, becomes innate. The ultimate result, then, is for students to refine their thinking so succinctly and candidly that they are able to describe what they did, and are able to do the same in analysis of another's work.

Learning Intentions and Success Criteria for Math, Grade 5

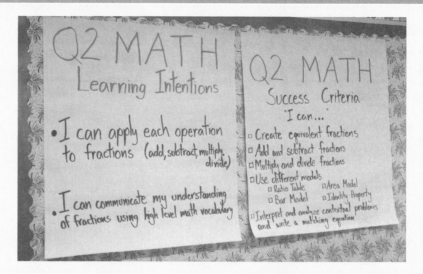

Examples Used to Co-Construct the Success Criteria for a Quality Math Explanation

Expression

$2\frac{1}{5} \times 4$

Explanation 1:

Two composed 4 iterations makes 8 units and they are partitioned like $\frac{1}{5}$ units so that makes it decomposed into wholes of 8. And then when you iterate wholes and $\frac{1}{5}$ you make $\frac{4}{5}$ which after you product them it is $8\frac{4}{5}$.

Explanation 2:

I decomposed the equation and made 2 iterated 4 times and that's 8, and $\frac{1}{5}$ iterated 4 times is $\frac{4}{5}$ and when you compose them back together, you get $8\frac{4}{5}$.

Explanation 3:

2 wholes is the same as $\frac{10}{5}$ plus the extra unit makes $\frac{11}{5}$ and then that iterated 4 times makes $\frac{44}{5}$ which needs to be converted to a mixed number. So 5 goes into 44 eight times with four left over so the answer is $8\frac{4}{5}$.

(Continued)

(Continued)

> ### Learning Intentions and Success Criteria for Math, Grade 5
>
> Notice: The math problem being addressed is shown under the heading, "Expression." Three sample math explanations appear below it, provided by Mr. Folau. After being given the three explanations, students were asked to determine which was the strongest of the explanations and why. Students spent time reviewing and discussing the explanations, they selected the strongest explanation and shared that the criteria for a well-written math explanation includes two parts: 1) correct explanation of the math process and 2) correct use of math vocabulary.

Students can build up to this but need a scaffolded framework of what that looks like. We often begin with Cloze-type sentences, focused on a single part of the process, and aim only for students to use the vocabulary correctly. This then proceeds to a Cloze-type paragraph with the same focus. The next step is for students to be able to write their own paragraphs, and so, to model, I wrote three samples—a best, a good, and a poor response—and we then spent time analyzing them to see whether they described the process and used the vocabulary properly. As we did this frequently, over different problems, longitudinally, students became able to explain their own process on a given problem properly using the key vocabulary.

From a Fifth-Grade Teacher: Sharing Clarity

Name: Tanya Marchman-Twete, Lone Tree Elementary School, Lone Tree, CO

Writing Success Criteria for Reflective Blogs With Whole Group

Reflection is a necessary component to the growth mindset. In order to add specified time for students to reflect on their work and their work behaviors, we adopted a reflective blog time each week. However, we noticed after the first blog that students were literally writing lists of what they had done and really weren't exploring the metacognitive skills we wanted them to tap into. The solution was co-creating success criteria for a good reflective blog.

I think using exemplars is key. When students research what they themselves like to see, read, or participate in, they start to dive deeper, thinking critically about the work they are going to produce. When we start a new lesson plan, the first thing we do is look to see what already exists. By exploring what we like and don't like, we start to formulate the plan of our own lesson.

Therefore, we began by asking students what they already knew about blogs and exploring kid blogs that were on the internet. As teachers, we identified three blogs to have them read and asked the kids to answer the following questions on their own in their journals:

- What is a blog?
- How would you rank these in order of worst to best? Explain how you ranked them.
- What's your favorite and why?

We then came together as a class and discussed what makes a good blog. I took notes on their answers on the board (see example that follows). The following day, we explored the concept of reflections. We talked about what it means to reflect on one's behavior (a concept fifth graders know well). We then pushed their thinking into how they reflect on their work, such as giving and receiving feedback and taking that information to fix their work. The kids participated in a Bloom's taxonomy sort to familiarize themselves with the terminology as it pertains to reflections. We ended that day by brainstorming, as a group, what metacognition looks like when reflecting on one's work. It's important to note that even though we personalize goals in our school, group conversations are key to creating success criteria that will be used by all so that students develop a common language.

Finally, we created a Venn diagram for both blogs and reflection and weeded through our initial brainstorms. We ended up with five key elements or success criteria (see example) that each of their blogs should contain. These are intentionally broad, because the blogs are all individualized and personalized. Each time students blog, they check their work against the criteria, and when I read their blogs, I do as well. The common success criteria have led to deeper reflections that give me a window into their thinking and evolving minds.

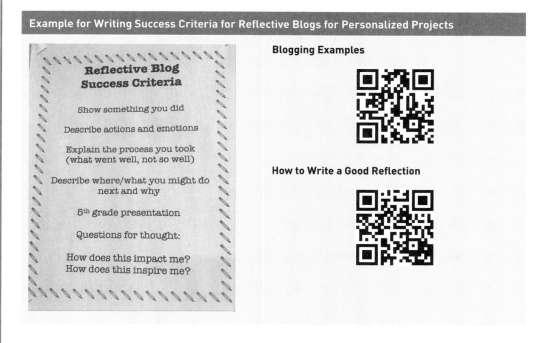

After they have used the success criteria for a while, I do check-ins with students to see how the tool is working for them and if we need to change anything. Students have expressed mixed emotions about these success criteria. One student said that she liked having the tool, because it helped her make sure she had everything she needed in her blog, but she would like to have it electronically so she could have it up on her screen while she was writing. Another student said he didn't like using it at first, because it confined his writing, but he liked to have it for his revisions to "check all the boxes." I find it important to check in with students so that we can personalize the common tool to best fit their needs. In addition, it shows them that they have the power to create tools that work for them and to change the tools if they aren't working.

From a High School Math Teacher: Sharing Clarity

Name: Mary Corbett, J. Sterling Morton High School, Cicero, IL

Birthday Polynomials

The MLO (mastery learning outcome) for the day was, "I can create my own polynomial and analyze its graph by identifying its key features: domain, range, end behavior, intercepts, maxs/mins, and intervals of increasing/decreasing."

The outcome was accomplished by having students create the famous "birthday polynomial." In this activity, students use the digits of their birthday as the coefficients of a polynomial in standard form. They then access the Desmos free online graphing calculator on their laptops or phones to graph their polynomial and play around with the signs of the coefficients until they like how it looks. Students then sketch their polynomial on paper and list and label the key features according to a checklist of success criteria.

(Continued)

(Continued)

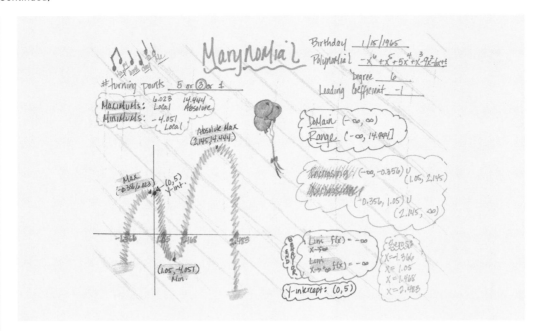

To begin, we practiced writing birthdays into the standard form of a polynomial:

$$6/10/2004 \rightarrow 6x^6 + x^5 + 2x^3 - 4$$

$$12/14/2000 \rightarrow x^7 - 2x^6 - x^5 + x^4 + 2x^3$$

$$3/5/2002 \rightarrow 3x^5 + 5x^4 - 2x^3 + 2$$

The success criteria along with one completed example and one nonexample were then presented. It was later suggested that I have the students grade the example and non-example using the success criteria checklist. I like that idea and will definitely try that next time.

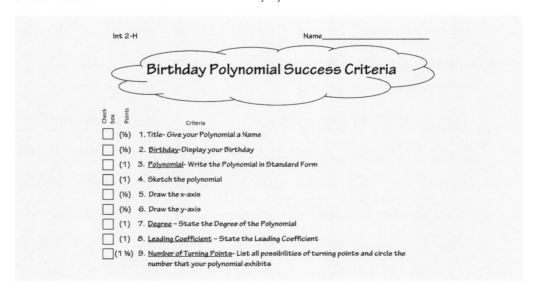

☐ (1) 10. <u>Domain</u> ⎤
                    ⎬ Use interval notation
☐ (1) 11. <u>Range</u> ⎦

☐ (2) 12. <u>End Behavior</u> – Use limit notation: $\lim\limits_{x \to -\infty} f(x) =$ ____ $\lim\limits_{x \to \infty} f(x) =$ ____

☐ (1 ½) 13. <u>Increasing</u> ⎤
                        ⎬ Use interval notation
☐ (1 ½) 14. <u>Decreasing</u> ⎦

☐ (1 ½) 15. <u>Zeros</u> – Place values on x – axis and state with the other key features

☐ (1) 16. <u>Y-intercept</u> – Place value on y – axis and state with the other key features

☐ (1 ½) 17. <u>Maximums</u> ⎤ Place coordinates on graph & label as absolute or local (relative
                      ⎬ also state only the y-values of each with your other key features
☐ (1 ½) 18. <u>Minimums</u> ⎦

☐ (3) 19. <u>Presentation</u> – Neat, organized, and colorful

The students took a lot of interest in their unique polynomials, and because each polynomial was individualized, students were unable to copy answers from each other, forcing them to ask questions or seek help if they were confused. Some students had a point of inflection in their graph and struggled deciding whether that point was a maximum or minimum. This put them deep into the learning pit, where they discovered the inflection point was neither a max nor a min. You could see the excitement on students' faces and sense the appreciation they had for the struggle, as they realized what they accomplished working their way out of the pit on their own.

Having the success criteria on a checklist along with an example and nonexample clarified the expectations of the learning outcome. Creating their own unique polynomials provided the students a sense of ownership of their learning, resulting in pride in their accomplishment.

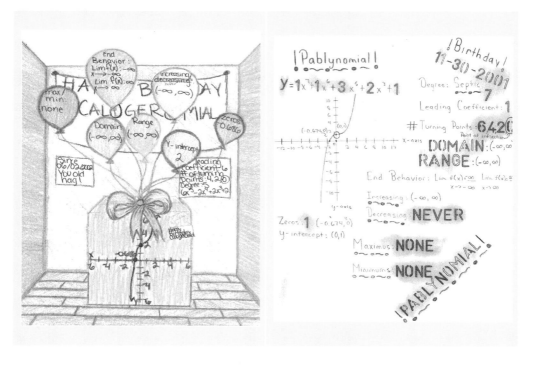

(Continued)

(Continued)

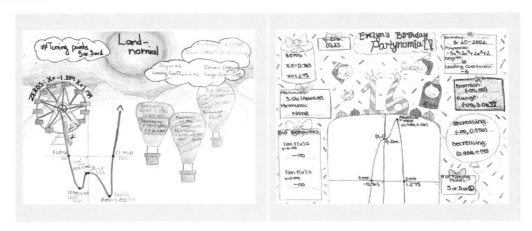

From a High School Visual Arts Teacher: Sharing Clarity

Name: Richard Graham, J. Sterling Morton High School, Cicero, IL

Topic: Self-Portraits and Video (two separate units of study)

Self-Portraits

After making a baseline drawing (without instruction), the students receive instruction in and demonstration of proportions, typical shapes, and variations in portraiture. They then practice using themselves as models and work from proportion, straight on, to developing emotion or alternate points of view of the head.

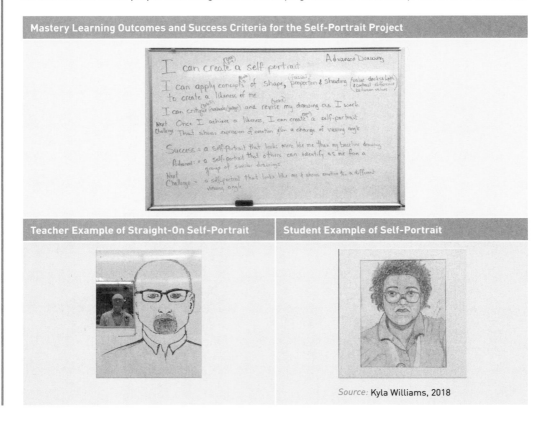

Source: **Kyla Williams, 2018**

In advanced drawing, we are taking concepts from the drawing unit of the visual art class and expanding the student's range or vision. We draw portraits from life, as opposed to using photographs as source material. The change from using a two-dimensional source to drawing from a three-dimensional model increases complexity. In addition, some students in advanced drawing did not have the visual art class experience.

Students gain confidence in their abilities to draw from life. They learn how to render what they see in 3D onto a 2D surface. They also learn that the process is not just copying, but constantly shifting from seeing to drawing, to comparing the image to the model and evaluating the image (both as a likeness and as a work on its own) and back to seeing and drawing again.

Student Work Samples

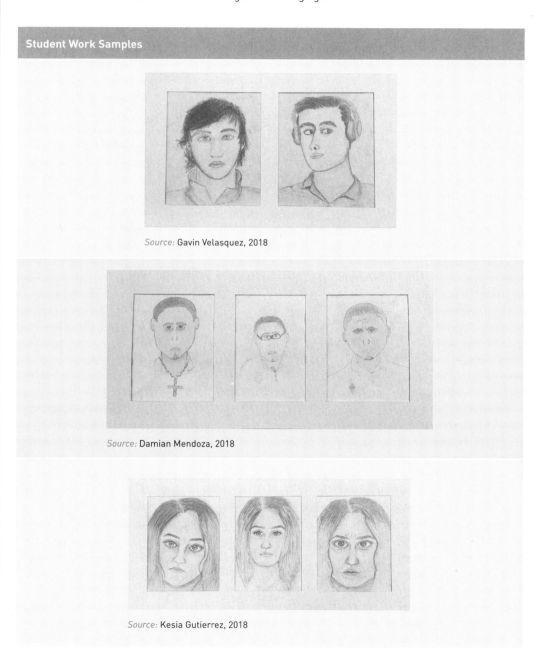

Source: Gavin Velasquez, 2018

Source: Damian Mendoza, 2018

Source: Kesia Gutierrez, 2018

(Continued)

(Continued)

Video

In this unit, students are using detailed analysis of exemplars to learn to create suspense in their own work. They study a film (Alfred Hitchcock's *Strangers on a Train*) to identify, compare, and evaluate different techniques used to build suspense in film. Then they brainstorm story ideas, evaluate the ideas, and create storyboards for the chosen story. They then use the storyboards, and various techniques selected, to create a suspenseful short video.

Success Criteria

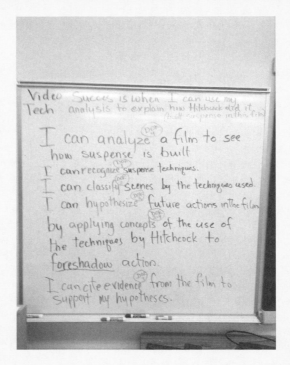

Suspense Video Mastery Learning Outcomes	Anchor Chart of Video Techniques

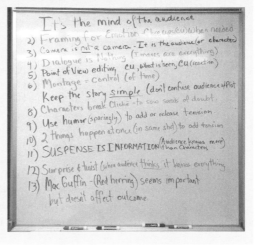

Students are using technical skills they have learned and developing ways to not just show emotion, but to create an experience of emotions for their audiences. Along the way, they discover how films can and do manipulate viewers.

Students often report back on other films they see on their own and marvel at de-constructing the filmmaker's art. Some continue to make videos in college or on their own, but many others take away an understanding and appreciation of the craft.

From a Principal and Instructional Coach: Sharing Clarity

Names: Shay Swan, Principal; Tate B. Castleton, Instructional Coach, Syringa Middle School, Caldwell, ID

Our Goal: Fostering Clarity

At Syringa Middle School, we have worked hard as a staff to transition to and implement the use of learning intentions and success criteria buildingwide. It was our goal to be a school where Visible Learning was happening in every classroom every single day.

We decided that we needed to find a way to both gauge how we were doing as a team, and to help our teachers hear firsthand from the mouths of their students how they were doing in the classroom. After some trial and error, we decided upon a method we feel works best for our teachers and their students.

We set out to pull two students from every teacher's classroom on four different days over the course of a few weeks. Two of those days would be unannounced, and two would be known to the teachers. Each student was brought into Mr. Castleton's office one at a time and asked three questions on camera:

1. What are you learning today, or what is the learning target?

2. Why are you learning that today?

3. How will you know when you've successfully learned this, or what are the success criteria you've been given?

The video of each student was uploaded and sent to each teacher, along with a Google Form that asked the teacher to be reflective and determine how well the student communicated the learning intention and success criteria.

By creating the Google Form, we put the evaluation back in the teachers' hands, and let them decide how well their students understood that day's learning intention and success criteria. After teachers answered each question, the data was sent back to us to compile and share. It came back looking something like this:

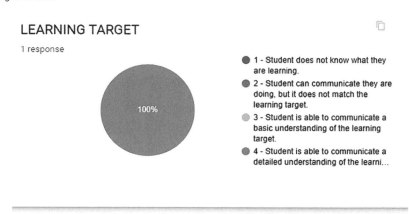

LEARNING TARGET

1 response

100%

● 1 - Student does not know what they are learning.

● 2 - Student can communicate they are doing, but it does not match the learning target.

● 3 - Student is able to communicate a basic understanding of the learning target.

● 4 - Student is able to communicate a detailed understanding of the learni...

(Continued)

(Continued)

SUCCESS CRITERIA

1 response

- 1 - Student does not have an anwer
- 2 - Student can communicate some expectations, but it does not match the success criteria.
- 3 - Student is able to communicate a basic understanding of the success criteia.
- 4 - Student is able to communicate a detailed understanding the success criteria.

We then compiled the data each time and shared it with our staff in intentional ways.

Why We Went About It This Way

As stated earlier, this process was not brought about to cast judgments on teachers. We did not want them to feel like they were under a microscope; instead, we wanted them to be an integral part of this critical benchmark process. By videoing their students and then sending the teachers the videos with some simple reflection questions, we put the evaluation in their hands—and rightly so, since they're the ones who taught the material. This method allowed us to have open, honest conversations about where we were and where we needed to go next.

How We Are Accomplishing It

We decided to create four benchmark videos over the course of several weeks. We let the teachers know in advance when two of the videos would be made, and the other two we kept a surprise. Our hope was that what students knew and could articulate about what was being taught in their classes would improve with each video. We also used the data that we gathered from these benchmark videos to help us construct more useful professional development activities that were delivered to the staff as a whole and by the instructional coach in one-on-one situations.

What Our Impact Has Been So Far

Thus far we feel that this undertaking has been valuable for our staff. We have seen steady improvement with each benchmark video, and students come more prepared to articulate what they are learning and how they will know when they've learned it. Students have become more aware of learning targets and success criteria. Teachers have also been more intentional in their teaching and have placed a much greater emphasis on learning intentions and success criteria.

Here is some of the data. You can see the improvement from the first benchmark to the fourth and final benchmark:

Learning Targets

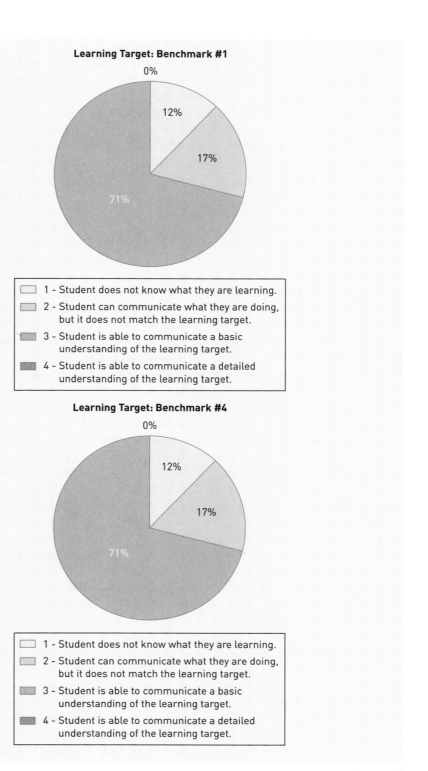

Learning Target: Benchmark #1

0%

12%

17%

71%

1 - Student does not know what they are learning.

2 - Student can communicate what they are doing, but it does not match the learning target.

3 - Student is able to communicate a basic understanding of the learning target.

4 - Student is able to communicate a detailed understanding of the learning target.

Learning Target: Benchmark #4

0%

12%

17%

71%

1 - Student does not know what they are learning.

2 - Student can communicate what they are doing, but it does not match the learning target.

3 - Student is able to communicate a basic understanding of the learning target.

4 - Student is able to communicate a detailed understanding of the learning target.

(Continued)

(Continued)

Success Criteria

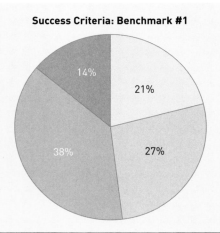

Success Criteria: Benchmark #1

- 1 - Student does not have an answer.
- 2 - Student can communicate some expectations, but it does not match the success criteria.
- 3 - Student is able to communicate a basic understanding of the success criteria.
- 4 - Student is able to communicate a detailed understanding of the success criteria.

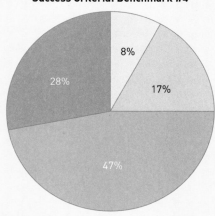

Success Criteria: Benchmark #4

- 1 - Student does not have an answer.
- 2 - Student can communicate some expectations, but it does not match the success criteria.
- 3 - Student is able to communicate a basic understanding of the success criteria.
- 4 - Student is able to communicate a detailed understanding of the success criteria.

While this undertaking is a work in progress, we feel its impact is being felt and is making a differ-ence in every classroom at Syringa Middle School. We continue to use this platform with our teachers in the hopes that we continue to see consistent growth and improvement.

REFLECTION

How will you think differently about clarity, based on what you have read?

What ideas have you generated that you will try in your own classroom or school?

ASSESSING WITH CLARITY: OPPORTUNITIES TO RESPOND

LEARNING INTENTION

I understand the impact and strategies around providing opportunities to respond in the clarity journey.

SUCCESS CRITERIA

I will be successful if

- I can analyze and explain the relationship between learning intentions, success criteria, and opportunities for students to respond.

- I can create opportunities to respond that align with specific success criteria.

Notice the different wording with the learning intention and success criteria for this chapter. How is the wording different from that of the previous chapters? Do the learning intention and associated success criteria have the characteristics presented in Chapter 2? What approach to learning intentions and success criteria fits you best?

Let us recap our clarity journey up to this point. The first two steps in teaching and learning with clarity are

1. Gaining clarity by developing learning intentions and success criteria

2. Sharing clarity by co-constructing learning intentions and success criteria with the learners in our classrooms

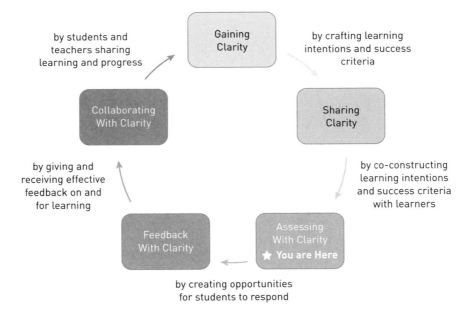

Our journey thus far brings us to the next component of using success criteria to make learning visible. In addition to articulating the evidence that learners must demonstrate, success criteria provide a clear framework for planning, developing, and implementing opportunities for learners to demonstrate their learning and provide information to us about their progress. Assessing with clarity involves the creation of opportunities for students to respond.

WHAT ARE OPPORTUNITIES TO RESPOND?

Do you recall the set of directions to the local frozen yogurt bar in Chapter 1? We asked you to find the unnamed, unidentified, and unspecified destination. After using that rather frustrating task to demonstrate the concept of a clarity problem, we can now revisit that scenario from a very different angle. When there are clear learning intentions and success criteria, teachers and learners have programmed the destination into the GPS: in this case, GPS stands for Gauging the Progress of Students. With your vehicle's GPS, there are many routes to your destination, and with some GPS systems, you are offered a choice of routes at the start of your journey. What happens if you take a turn that is not along the selected route? That electronic voice quickly chimes in, "recalculating." Assessing with clarity works the same way.

Once the destination is set (learning intentions and success criteria), opportunities to respond offer learners multiple pathways for actively progressing toward that destination. Only when learners are actively progressing toward the destination do we, as teachers, have the necessary information about their progress to provide effective feedback. We will engage in a thorough discussion about feedback in Chapters 8 and 9. Our focus now is on planning, developing, and implementing these multiple pathways for actively progressing toward the destination.

Opportunities to respond include any strategies, activities, or tasks that make student thinking visible and allow both the teacher and learner to observe learning progress. When planning, developing, and implementing opportunities to respond, two essential questions should guide our thinking:

GUIDING QUESTIONS FOR OPPORTUNITIES TO RESPOND

1. What opportunities to respond will tell me how learners are progressing in their learning related to the learning intention(s) and success criteria?

2. What am I going to do with their response that will support their next steps in learning?

Providing students with opportunities to respond gives us feedback about the impact of our teaching. Each opportunity to respond is driven by the learning intention and success criteria for that particular lesson or learning experience. For example, if the success criteria say *describe*, the opportunity to respond should focus on or provide deliberate practice in *describing*. Thus, they should make thinking visible so that teachers and learners can see where they are with regard to each learning intention and success criterion.

MORE THAN ASSESSMENT AND EVALUATION

Opportunities to respond are more than assessments. Consider the following questions:

1. If you were to provide your learners with a formative assessment, say, an exit ticket, what would you do if all or almost all of your learners demonstrated proficiency or mastery? How would that influence instruction?

2. If you were to provide your learners with a summative assessment, say, an end-of-unit test, what would you do if a majority of your learners did not demonstrate proficiency?

The previous two questions point out the challenge of a limited view that formative and summative assessments are the only means for monitoring learning progress. This dichotomy places too much emphasis on the performance, or grades, rather than the learning. Not to mention that dichotomizing assessments as either formative or assessment limits how we use the information about learner progress and then provide effective feedback. Opportunities to respond are more than formative versus summative assessments. Yes, entrance tickets, exit slips, quizzes, and unit assessments are examples of opportunities to respond. However, think-pair-shares, classroom discussions, questioning, laptop dry erase boards, student-generated videos where students explain their thinking, and level of mastery and journal prompts are also examples of opportunities to respond. Whether they are done individually, in small groups, or as a whole group; formally or informally; silent or out loud; opportunities to respond are purposeful and intentional moments that make student thinking visible and allow both the teacher and learner to observe learning progress.

Notice that certain opportunities to respond fit into multiple categories. For example, an exit ticket is a formal opportunity to respond that is silent and individual. Furthermore, these opportunities do not require a number recorded in the grade book. Informal opportunities to respond are often impromptu checks for understanding that inform the next steps in teaching and learning. While informal, to get the most out of providing students an opportunity to respond, they should

Type of Opportunity to Respond	Description	Examples
Individual	Each individual student has an opportunity to respond.	An individual student answering a question; completing an exit ticket; one-on-one conversation, listening to a student explain his or her thinking
Small group	A small group of students generates a response; three, four, or five students contribute to a single response.	A group of students complete mathematics problems, answer questions in social studies, meld individual summaries into one that represents the thinking of the group, or complete a science laboratory.
Whole group	All students in the class respond to the same question or prompt.	Choral response; using clickers or plickers, where responses are representative of the class as a whole; Kahoot or Poll Everywhere questions; responses on dry erase boards
Silent	The response does not involve social interaction.	Exit ticket, short constructed response, writing a summary, journal reflection
Out loud	The response involves social interaction or dialogue between learners and teacher.	Think-pair-share, turn and talk, read aloud, cooperative learning task, discussion circles
Formal	The response is formally recorded.	Summaries in an interactive notebook, exit slip, data from plickers, solving a mathematics problem on paper or the computer, running record, students rate their progress against the success criteria paired with evidence of their work
Informal	The response is not formally recorded.	Conversations with/between peers or the teacher, response to impromptu questions, quick verbal checks

be planned for and thoughtfully aligned to instruction. Opportunities to respond come in many varieties, opening the door for us to use them on a regular basis to monitor learners' progression toward the learning intentions and success criteria. Providing opportunities to respond should be a routine, not an occasional, occurrence. The role of opportunities to respond in student learning is well documented in the literature (Black & Wiliam, 1998; Hattie, 2009, 2012). The more time that is devoted to providing learners with opportunities to respond, the higher student achievement climbs (Black & Wiliam, 1998; Hattie, 2009, 2012; Marzano, 2007).

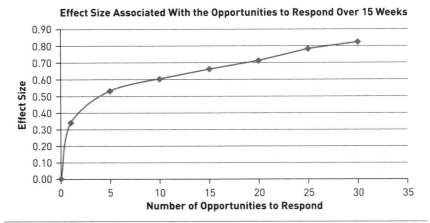

Effect Size Associated With the Opportunities to Respond Over 15 Weeks

Source: Bangert-Drowns, R. L., Kulik, J. A., & Kulik, C. C. (1991). Effects of classroom testing. *Journal of Educational Research, 85*(2), 89–99.

As teachers, we continually emphasize the importance of developing a conceptual understanding about the ideas taught in our classrooms. As our content becomes more rigorous, opportunities to respond become increasingly more important so that teachers have a firm awareness of whether or not students are progressing in the learning *of terms, concepts, ideas, procedures,* or *processes.* This can only happen if both the teacher and the learner spend the necessary time to make thinking visible through engaging and rigorous tasks.

The planning, developing, and implementing of opportunities to respond are about teachers seeing learning through the eyes of the students and helping students take an active role in their learning by developing an enhanced awareness of their learning progress—again, making thinking visible to both the teacher and the student.

TIMING THE OPPORTUNITIES TO RESPOND

The timing of opportunities to respond is just as important as the specific strategy used to offer students a chance to respond. Offering an opportunity to respond to students at the wrong time, either too soon or too late, will diminish the impact on learning. The information generated by student responses will not provide clear evidence about where students are in their learning journey. For example, asking students to participate in discussion circles or a debate—before learners have the necessary skills, knowledge, and understanding to engage effectively in such a task—will reduce the nature of the conversations and thus the evidence about the learning. On the other hand, asking students to summarize a basic concept in a three-minute writing task when they have a deep level of conceptual understanding and are ready to transfer their learning to a new context or tackle a next-level problem can be just as counterproductive. They may demonstrate a high level of mastery of the concept that is not representative of their readiness to engage in deeper and more rigorous content or problems. The alignment between opportunities to respond and the desired level of thinking facilitates the progression of learners toward meeting the learning intention and success criteria.

Consider the use of a Venn diagram. This graphic organizer is familiar to almost every classroom teacher and learner. However, we need to view this from the students' perspective. Your teacher has just asked you to complete a Venn diagram. What are you going to do? Really, what are you going to do? Odds are high that you will simply put facts or excerpts from a reading, video, or web quest into one of two categories. When you notice that you have added a fact to both sides of the Venn diagram, you quickly erase the fact and put it in the middle. Thus, what students are really doing is identifying and sorting, not comparing and contrasting, which is the intent of the Venn diagram. Instead, asking students to analyze or compare and contrast two concepts across three or four big ideas, using the framework shown here, increases the level of thinking and zeros in on the desired level of complexity for this task:

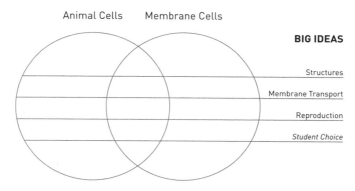

This is an example asking students to compare and contrast animal and plant cells. (Antonetti and Garver, 2015)

It is not always safe to assume that students are ready to identify patterns or similarities and differences. This example points out the importance of intentionally and purposefully selecting and implementing opportunities to respond at the right time and when they align with the level of thinking expected by the learning intention and success criteria.

Simply drawing an opportunity to respond from a bag of tricks, even if the bag is full of evidence-based tricks, will not necessarily lead to the desired clarity about student learning. The right choice of opportunities to respond should take into consideration the following guiding questions:

GUIDING QUESTIONS THAT ADDRESS THE TIMING OF OPPORTUNITIES TO RESPOND

1. What levels of thinking or complexity are (surface, deep, or transfer) called for in the learning intention and success criteria? In other words, with regard to student thinking, where in the SOLO taxonomy (Biggs & Collis, 1982) or in Webb's (2005) Depth of Knowledge guide do these particular learning intentions and success criteria fall?

2. What specific opportunity to respond evokes that level of thinking or complexity?

3. What do I need to do to get learners ready for that level of thinking (Almarode & Miller, 2018)?

Timing matters!

CHARACTERISTICS OF OPPORTUNITIES TO RESPOND

There are essential characteristics of opportunities to respond that both make thinking visible (Ritchhart, Church, & Morrison, 2011) and engage learners in rigorous tasks (Antonetti & Garver, 2015). The difference between (1) you asking your learners if they understand the concept of *author's purpose* and (2) your learners demonstrating that understanding by selecting a text, determining and then stating the author's purpose, and finally justifying their answer provides a window into students' thinking. The latter also establishes the reliability and validity of the evidence about their learning. The evidence generated by asking students to "give me a thumbs-up if you understand how to solve this problem" is significantly different from the evidence generated by having shoulder partners explain to each other how to solve a similar problem, recording each other on video for your review and their own self reflection. So, how do we ensure that we are making thinking visible and providing learners with engaging and rigorous tasks through opportunities to respond?

Consider the following two scenarios:

1. A fourth-grade teacher provides her learners with a two-step word problem that involves multiplication and subtraction:

    Michael buys two bags of dog food that each cost $18.99 with a coupon. He hands the checkout person $50.00. How much change will he get back?

    The teacher also provides four possible answers. Once the students solve the two-step problem, they are to select the answer that they believe is the correct response.

2. Across the hall, her colleague provides the following prompt on slips of paper:

    Create a two-step word problem that involves adding, subtracting, and/or multiplying money, and solve it. Write an explanation of how you solved the problem.

What do these two scenarios have in common, and how are the scenarios different from each other? Both of these scenarios provide an assignment to their learners that focuses on the same skill: solving two-step word problems involving money, addition, subtraction, and multiplication. Where these two scenarios differ is the visibility of student thinking and the specific nature of the assignment. The first scenario does not provide any insight into student thinking, relying solely on the student selecting the correct answer. At the end of this particular scenario, the teacher definitely knows one thing: The learner did or did not select the correct answer. Beliefs or feelings about each learner's understanding of the concept are only assumptions. The evidence provided by selecting the correct choice is neither reliable nor valid evidence of student learning.

In the second scenario, learners are required to make their thinking visible through an engaging and rigorous task. From this task, both the teacher and the learner can identify (1) the learner's level of understanding, (2) what the learner does or does not know, and (3) what the learner can and cannot do, yet, with regard to solving two-step word problems involving money, addition, subtraction, and multiplication.

MAKING THINKING VISIBLE

There are several ways to make learners' thinking visible. Consider some of the characteristics highlighted by Ritchhart et al. (2011):

1. Ask learners to provide descriptions of terms, concepts, ideas, procedures, or processes.

2. Encourage learners to develop explanations and interpretations of concepts, ideas, procedures, or processes.

3. Check that learners' reasons, explanations, and interpretations are accompanied by evidence.

4. Ask learners to take different viewpoints and perspectives on concepts, ideas, procedures, or processes.

5. Ask learners to make connections between what they are learning and what they have already learned.

6. Ask the right question—this will get students to reveal their thinking.

Let us look at each of these six characteristics individually and with examples.
Tasks that make thinking visible should ask learners to *provide descriptions of terms, concepts, ideas, procedures, or processes.* This is different from asking learners to give a definition or simply repeat a specific process or procedure. In the second

of the two math scenarios above, learners described a scenario that would involve a two-step word problem involving money, addition, subtraction, and multiplication.

Other Examples

- In science, learners might describe a particular habitat or ecosystem instead of reciting definitions of what tundra, grasslands, or other biomes are.

- A social studies (world history) teacher could ask his learners to describe how *imperialism* is represented in a specific political cartoon rather than provide a flashcard definition.

- In English language arts, describing the use of symbolism in *The Great Gatsby* makes learners' thinking more visible than simply giving a definition of symbolism.

Tasks that make learning visible should also encourage learners to *develop explanations and interpretations of concepts, ideas, procedures, or processes.* Instead of simply answering a question or responding to a prompt, information about learners' progress is clearer if they have to provide an explanation for a specific answer. As part of learners' explanations, we should encourage them to *incorporate evidence to justify their explanations and interpretations.* Referring back to the two scenarios, which assignment promoted the development of an explanation that also required learners to reason with evidence? The second scenario elicited student thinking that allowed both the teacher and the learner to see the depth of understanding within these mathematics concepts and processes. Because of this evidence, both the teacher and learner can better identify where the learner is in the learning progression.

Other Examples

- In science, learners might have to justify or provide an explanation for their prediction that an object would follow a particular pathway or trajectory.

- A social studies (US history) teacher might ask learners to justify, with evidence, their assertion that the balance of powers actually favors one branch of our federal government over another. Specifically, the teacher would encourage the learners to identify specific examples to support their claim or assertion.

- In a middle school English classroom, the teacher might ask students to interpret a poem by considering the key elements (e.g., literal meaning, theme, tone, structure, sound, rhythm, language, and imagery) and then provide an explanation and justification for the interpretation. This provides a clearer view of student understanding than simply having them describe key elements by which readers analyze a poem.

Explanations, interpretations, and justifications can be incorporated into any opportunity to respond by simply asking students, "What makes you say that?"

If we ask learners to *take different viewpoints and perspectives on concepts, ideas, procedures, or processes,* we are better able to unpack the level of depth in their understanding. For learners to look at an idea from a viewpoint other than their preferred perspective requires that they analyze the idea, extract the essential characteristics, and then compare and contrast those characteristics with the characteristics as they would be seen from the students' preferred perspective. Take for example, the second scenario that asks learners to create their own two-step word problem. Although the current version of the assignment does not require them to take different viewpoints, asking each learner to create a two-step word problem to exchange with a neighbor does. In this version of the assignment, learners will have to engage in solving two-step word problems with money, addition, subtraction, and multiplication from the perspective of their neighbor. This added element of this task will provide reliable and valid evidence for learners' ability to generalize the skills and concepts to different contexts. Which skills did the learners generalize to the different scenario, and which ones were not generalized to this new scenario? What concepts did the learner generalize to the new word problem?

Other Examples

- A high school earth science teacher could offer students a choice of three questions as part of a writing assignment in class:
  - What would happen if the tilt of the Earth's axis, or obliquity, changed to 0 degrees?
  - How might our lives on Earth differ if our planet did not have a liquid mantle?
  - How would an atmosphere composed primarily of carbon dioxide change our planet?

- A social studies (government or civics) teacher could use role-play to support learners in their understanding of the processes of our government and international systems of government. For example, this teacher could have learners role play in mock jury trials, a session of Congress, or a meeting of the United Nations General Assembly. The perspective of the students will change with different roles in the process.

- In a 10th-grade English classroom, learners might predict and infer how a specific story, the characters, the plot, the conflict, and the resolution of the conflict would differ from the viewpoint of different characters or in different settings. For example, students might take the perspective of Walter Cunningham in *To Kill a Mockingbird* when he comes to dinner at the Finches' house. How might that change the story, narration, or dialogue? Or, how about *The Scarlet Letter?* Take the perspective of Roger

Killingsworth and explain the story through his eyes. What is *The Scarlet Letter* of today? Would the perspectives of the people involved change? Why or why not?

Developing a strong understanding of individual concepts, ideas, procedures, or processes is important. However, finding connections across different content areas and generalizing understanding is the goal of teaching and learning. Can I use knowledge and understanding from one area and apply that learning to another area? This requires practice and for students to move from surface to deep learning and then transfer that learning to a new scenario or problem. Refer back to the second scenario near the beginning of this chapter. It requires learners to make connections between writing, mathematics, and authentic experiences outside of the classroom (i.e., the context of the word problem). *The connections that students make between what they are learning and what they have already learned* must be visible so that teachers and learners can see the interconnectedness of concepts, ideas, procedures, or processes.

Other Examples

- An elementary science teacher can help learners make connections by using thinking maps or concept maps that relate two concepts in science. For example, how are climate and weather connected to the characteristics of ecosystems and habitats? More specifically, what role do climate and weather play in food webs, food chains, and resource scarcity?

- A social studies teacher might ask students to identify connections between the first European explorers of the Americas and their motivations and that of their sponsors, as well as how they influenced and were influenced by the Native Americans. What changes did the Native Americans experience to their culture and environment? What changes did the explorers experience?

- In an elementary English language arts classroom, the teacher could ask students to make connections between figurative language in poetry and the use of figurative language in music. For example, how does Katy Perry use figurative language in her song, *Firework?*

If we want to make student thinking visible, we have to ask the right questions. *Asking the right questions gets students to reveal their thinking.* There are two broad categories of questions: open and closed (Allen, 2001; Boaler, 1998; Dohrenwend, 1965). The most salient difference between these two broad categories of questions is the type of thinking involved in responding to an open versus a closed question. Consider the following two questions:

	Question 1	Versus	Question 2
Math Questions	What is the best way to solve a system of inequalities?	Or	Given a system of inequalities, what are your ideas on how to solve the system?
Science Questions	What is the most important difference between a transverse wave and a longitudinal wave?	Or	What are some differences between a transverse wave and a longitudinal wave?

Semantically, the difference in these questions is subtle. In terms of thinking, one provides an opportunity to make thinking visible, while the other leads to simply getting an answer. *Getting students to reveal their thinking requires us to ask the right question.* In both the mathematics and the science example, the first question is a closed question, and the second an open question. The words *best* and *most important* close the responses down to one acceptable answer. The exchange of these words in the second questions for phrases like *your ideas* and *some differences* opens the question up for multiple acceptable answers that open the door to teachers asking, "What makes you say that?" Returning once again to the two scenarios, which question is an open question and which question is a closed question?

Other Examples

- **Science**
  - *Open:* Are certain simple machines more useful or readily used in today's world than other types of simple machines? What makes you say that?
  - *Closed:* Which simple machine is most useful in today's world?
  - *Open:* What are some of the ways the periodic table of elements helps me understand atoms, elements, compounds, and molecules?
  - *Closed:* What are the three most important features of the periodic table of elements?

- **Social Studies**
  - *Open:* What are some of the possible events that lead to the United States entering into a civil war?
  - *Closed:* What is the main reason the United States engaged in a civil war?

- ○ *Open:* What are some of the outcomes of the Industrial Revolution?
- ○ *Closed:* What is the single most influential change to come about from the Industrial Revolution?

- **English Language Arts**
  - ○ *Open:* In your view, which character is primarily responsible for the conflict?
  - ○ *Closed:* Who causes the problem in the book?
  - ○ *Open:* What are some things you notice about this text that are different from last week's reading?
  - ○ *Closed:* What makes this reading an epic?

TASKS VERSUS EXERCISES

In order to continue to develop effective opportunities to respond, we not only want to consider the ways we make thinking visible but also the way we make the "doing" part of learning visible. Up to this point, there has been a lot of discussion about tasks. What separates an engaging and rigorous task from an exercise is the nature of the engagement required to complete the task or exercise. In exercises, learners simply repeat terms, concepts, ideas, procedures, or processes. As a result, learners have fewer, if any, opportunities to make their thinking and doing visible. In tasks, learners are asked to make meaning of their learning by developing multiple representations of the content, identifying patterns, and establishing an emotional connection with the content (Medina, 2014). In other words, learners make meaning of the terms, concepts, ideas, procedures, or processes. In 2015, Antonetti and Garver reported on data from over 17,000 classroom walkthroughs and identified eight features of classroom activities that differentiated those tasks from mere exercises. The following are these eight characteristics of opportunities to respond that are truly engaging and rigorous tasks and not exercises:

1. **Personal Response:** Do learners have the opportunity to bring their own personal experiences to the learning experience? Examples include any strategy or learning experience that invites learners to bring their own background, interests, or expertise to the conversation. This might be an activity that provides learners with the option to create their own analogies or metaphors, allowing learners to select how they will share their responses to a question (e.g., writing, drawing, speaking, etc.), or letting learners select the context in which a concept is explored (e.g., allowing learners to select a specific book or create their own problem). These examples have one thing in common: They allow learners to personalize their responses to meet their background, interests, or expertise.

2. **Clear and Modeled Expectations:** Do learners have a clear understanding of what they are supposed to do? This characteristic refers us back to clear learning intentions, success criteria, learning progressions, exemplars, models, and examples. Do your learners know what success looks like, or are they blindly hoping to hit the end target that you have in mind for them?

3. **Sense of Audience:** Do learners have a sense that this work matters to someone other than the teacher and the grade book? Tasks that give learners a sense of audience are those tasks that mean something to individuals beyond the teacher, and these tasks provide authenticity. Sense of audience can be established by cooperative learning or group work where individual members have specific roles, as in a jigsaw activity. Other examples include community-based projects or service projects that contribute to the local, school, or classroom community (e.g., conservation projects).

4. **Social Interaction:** Do learners have opportunities to socially interact with their peers? Providing learners with opportunities to talk about their learning and interact with their peers supports their meaning-making and development of conceptual understanding. In addition, teachers and learners get to hear other students' ideas.

5. **Emotional Safety:** Do learners feel safe in asking questions or making mistakes? To be blunt, if learners feel threatened in your classroom, they will not engage in any activity, whether it is a task or exercise. Preservation of self takes precedence over the development of a response to "What makes you say that?"

6. **Choice:** Do learners have choices in how they access the learning? As learners engage with concepts, ideas, procedures, or processes, we should offer choices around whom they work with, what materials and manipulatives are available, and what learning strategies they can use. In addition, we should offer them multiple ways to show us what they know about concepts, ideas, procedures, or processes.

7. **Novelty:** Do learners experience the learning from a new or unique perspective? How can we present content in a way that captures their attention? Examples of this characteristic include engaging scenarios, discrepant events, scientific phenomena demonstrations, or games and puzzles.

8. **Authenticity:** Do learners experience an authentic learning experience, or is the experience sterile and unrealistic (e.g., a worksheet versus a problem-solving scenario)? We can offer them a scenario around animals on the verge of extinction and have them address the changes to their own habitat that would possibly prevent plants, animals, and humans from going extinct.

ENGAGING SCENARIOS

Going deeper in the areas of novelty and authentic tasks, is to work to establish an engaging scenario that makes learning relevant by providing a meaning-making experience that allows students to assimilate new learning into an authentic context or framework. As an opportunity to respond, an engaging scenario combines the essential features of making thinking visible with an engaging and rigorous task. Teaching any concept as abstract, independent, or isolated information makes it very difficult for learners to attach it to other concepts, ideas, procedures, or processes. For example, teaching the key elements of poetry (e.g., literal meaning, theme, tone, structure, sound, rhythm, language, and imagery) as a checklist of things to look for in a Robert Frost poem limits the opportunity for students to make meaning of their learning. Similarly, presenting quadratic equations as a series of algorithms about how to solve for the set of solutions (i.e., graphing, completing the square, factoring, or the quadratic formula) offers very little meaning to mathematics students.

An engaging scenario provides an authentic context that then creates an engaging learning experience for students (Ainsworth, 2010) by providing (1) context for learning concepts, ideas, procedures, or processes; (2) an active role for each student in this learning; and (3) multiple opportunities for learners to make their thinking visible to the teacher, classmates, and themselves. Let us look at two examples of an engaging scenario.

ENGAGING SCENARIO #1

Physics or Chemistry: Nuclear Reactions

You are a world-renowned nuclear scientist who works for a university in the same city in which you live. One evening, your local six o'clock news announces that the United States has decided to increase the nuclear infrastructure to reduce the country's level of carbon emissions. As a result, your city has been selected by the Department of Energy as the next location for a nuclear power plant. As you are well aware, there is significant debate about the use of nuclear energy, and it is sure to be a contentious debate amongst your neighbors and fellow citizens.

The mayor of your city calls you in desperate need of some advice and your expertise. You are being asked to serve as a consultant to the city and help guide them in deciding whether to fight this decision to build a nuclear power plant or embrace the selection of your city. You must develop a presentation to inform the public and city officials that will be presented at a public hearing. How can you get ready for this very important presentation and ensure that you provide unbiased, well-supported information to your fellow citizens?

- *Performance Task #1:* Use Cornell notes to gather relevant information on nuclear reactions.

- *Performance Task #2:* Compare and contrast nuclear reactions with other types of reactions in chemistry or physics.

- *Performance Task #3:* Design or create a model or drawing that illustrates the function of a nuclear power plant.

- *Performance Task #4:* Develop a comprehensive list of the pros and cons, risks and rewards of nuclear energy.

- *Performance Task #5:* Compare and contrast nuclear energy with other forms of energy production.

- *Performance Task #6:* Develop a 20-minute presentation making a case for or against the use of nuclear energy.

Notice that the engaging scenario presented above included an authentic story line, an authentic role for the student, an audience for fulfilling this role, and a series of performance tasks. With regard to the performance tasks, teachers can then develop rubrics or guidelines for the successful completion of these tasks based on clear learning intentions and success criteria.

ENGAGING SCENARIO #2

Advanced Algebra: Quadratic Equations

You are an exceptionally talented mathematician who also happens to be a movie buff. You have been contacted by Mythbusters to help them bust a movie myth wide open . . . or validate that the stunt is possible. In the 1994 action-adventure film *Speed*, a bad guy equipped a Los Angeles bus with a bomb that was set to explode if the speed of the bus fell below 50 mph (22 m/s). The police discovered the bomb and routed the bus on to a segment of freeway that was still under construction— their intention being to keep it out of the notoriously heavy Southern California traffic. In a twist of the plot, however, they overlooked a 50-foot (15 m) gap in the construction of the freeway. In other words, there is a 50-foot part of the freeway missing. Since the bomb would explode, killing everyone on board, if the bus slowed down, the police decided to bring another bus up next to the one rigged to explode and jump the gap in the freeway at a speed of 67 mph (30 m/s).

The producers and hosts of Mythbusters need your help! You will provide the mathematical calculations for this episode and present them in a way that the television audience will understand. How will you go about doing this?

- *Performance Task #1:* Compare and contrast quadratic equations with linear equations.

- *Performance Task #2:* Create a visual display of the graph of a quadratic function that illustrates the essential features of the function.

- *Performance Task #3:* Select two examples of a quadratic equation, and find their solutions. Create some record of yourself solving the two quadratic equations. Prepare these records so that they can be used as a study aid for other students.

- *Performance Task #4*: Prepare a video segment of you busting the myth or validating the veracity of the Los Angeles city bus scene from the movie *Speed*.

When engaging scenarios are placed within any content, these authentic contexts allow the student to make meaning from these concrete experiences. Although these scenarios are ideal for the beginning of the unit, they can be easily adapted to jump-start student learning in the middle of a unit or chunk of learning or as a way to bring learning to a close.

CONCLUSION

Teachers and administrators are awash with data about students, so much data that we could get on our blow-up floaties, take our beach towels and sunscreen, and float off into an ocean of meaningless number crunching. It is quite enough. Yet all educators worth their salt want desperately to know how to make a greater impact on students. In this way, we are hungry, thirsty for more feedback. Not just any feedback—feedback that provides us with the clarity to know what's next for our students and how to better support their learning. Better yet, we would like evidence that allows our learners to explain what is next for their learning. If it is gathered thoughtfully, the evidence generated from opportunities to respond will provide a high level of clarity about where to go next in the learning process for teachers and students.

In order to find this elusive feedback, we must first wonder, "Who should we be asking about our impact?" Are we asking the principal who has popped into our room for 10 minutes or the evaluator providing our formal evaluation of effectiveness? Does this give us the feedback we are all craving to tell us about our impact daily, weekly, or with specific students? Typically, the answer is no. Their feedback and evaluation are important, and their coaching can be invaluable. However, our best source of information about how to better meet the learning needs of our students and make a greater impact on them _is_ the students. Yes, just ask the students! Our learners can tell us about those things better than anyone in the school building can. We, as teachers, have to have the disposition to ask (Hattie, 2012). If we train our questioning eyes on our students and pull ourselves from the ocean of charts and graphs that represent them, we will find our thirst quenched, our hunger satisfied, and our next steps clear as day. So free yourself from the floaties, sunscreen, and the data dive! Ask the learners, "How was your learning today?" "What moved your learning forward?" "What didn't work for you?" "Where are you stuck in your learning?" "What are your next steps?" Give your learners multiple opportunities to respond so that both you and your learners can receive feedback that provides everyone with the clarity to know what's next for learning. This leads us to the topic of our next discussion: effective feedback.

LITMUS TEST

Lack of Progress Monitoring of Learning: Do you have a clear picture of where your students are in their learning progression? If we walked into your classroom and randomly selected a student, could you tell me where that specific student is in his or her learning progression?

Never   Sometimes   Always

Unhelpful Assessment Data: Do you engage in data meetings where you have large amounts of data that do not contribute to your knowledge of what the students are learning, how they are learning it, and where they are going next in their learning?

Never   Sometimes   Always

If you selected "sometimes" or "always" for either of the above questions, you may have a clarity issue that relates to developing meaningful opportunities to respond. You will want to focus on planning, developing, and implementing those opportunities in order to improve the evidence about what would move learning forward. Let us look at the reflection and next steps to help address this challenge.

REFLECTION AND NEXT STEPS

1. Gather several examples of opportunities to respond from your school or classroom. What evidence do these opportunities to respond provide about student learning?

2. Are the opportunities to respond aligned with the learning intention and success criteria for a given learning experience?

3. After you collect examples of opportunities to respond, what conclusions can you draw from the examples? Do you want to make changes to instruction?

Conclusions

4. Referring back to Chapter 1, which aspects of the clarity problem need to be addressed in your school or classroom? What evidence supports your claim?

Aspect Needing Attention	Evidence
Fragmented teaching and learning	
Activity-driven instruction	
Misaligned strategies	
Lack of progress monitoring of learning	
Unhelpful assessment data	

ASSESSING WITH CLARITY IN ACTION: VOICES FROM THE FIELD

Assessing with clarity uses learning intentions and success criteria to make student thinking visible. This, in return, allows teachers to monitor student progress toward the specific learning and success criteria and allows students to see their own learning progress. Assessing with clarity generates purposeful tasks that lay the groundwork for feedback on teaching and learning. These tasks generate the evidence we are looking for as learners progress toward meeting the learning intentions and success criteria.

When listening to the voices in the field, we found a multitude of approaches for providing students the opportunity to respond and make their thinking and learning visible. The following examples demonstrate the many ways we can assess with clarity, gathering the necessary evidence of student learning. We continued to encourage this conversation by providing guiding questions about each component of assessing with clarity.

VOICES FROM THE FIELD

From a School: Opportunities to Respond

Names: Mike Cerullo and Claudio Tulipano, Lake Wilcox Public School, Richmond Hill, Ontario, Canada

Examples of Opportunities to Respond

Our learners have opportunities to respond and share their learning in different ways. We honor the learners' choice of presentation (e.g., visual, oral, performance, written, multimedia, digital) in sharing of their learning. Examples include these:

- Literature congress
- Quick write and share
- Museum exhibit

- Inside/outside circle
- Google Classroom Q & A
- Infomercial

- Google Slide Deck learning documentation
- Conversations and dialogue
- Short film

- Collaborative scavenger hunt activity—*The Amazing Race* format
- Mind maps
- Sketchnoting

- Small group presentation
- Modeling of learning—use of manipulatives

(Continued)

(Continued)

- Think, pair, share
- Trial and error

We used the information generated by the opportunities to respond to be responsive to student voice and thinking. These opportunities allowed for students' thinking to become visible. Students were able to come to a conceptual understanding of the curriculum based on co-created criteria and constructive feedback (peer-to-peer, student-educator). The opportunities to respond led to modifications of future lessons based on student need and voice.

Opportunities to respond were based on the development of the learning in the project. For example, discussions were used as opportunities to respond when debating criteria needed for the project. Models were made to assist in making thinking visible and to support students in their confirmation of their thinking.

Our biggest challenges in planning, creating, and implementing opportunities to respond are in aligning these opportunities to effective success criteria based on the learning intention. We noticed when our success criteria were not effective, our student responses were vague and without focus on the learning intention.

Support is needed in the planning process to ensure success criteria and the learning intentions are aligned with curriculum expectations. This will help us in understanding what success (learning) looks and sounds like for each learning intention. With a better understanding of what success looks like, we can plan for opportunities to respond more effectively. We also need support in implementing different ways to respond and in learning how to be more responsive to student thinking.

At Lake Wilcox, the teachers devote a significant amount of time to planning, developing, and implementing of engaging opportunities to respond. As you look back at the examples from this elementary public school, can you identify elements of an engaging opportunity to respond? How could the opportunities to respond be designed to

1. Ask learners to provide descriptions of terms, concepts, ideas, procedures, or processes?
2. Encourage learners to develop explanations and interpretations of concepts, ideas, procedures, or processes?
3. Give reasons, explanations, and interpretations accompanied by evidence?
4. Ask learners to take different viewpoints and perspectives on concepts, ideas, procedures, or processes?
5. Ask learners to make connections between what they are learning and what they have already learned?
6. Get students to reveal their thinking requires us to ask the right question?

These features promote visible learning and thinking. In addition, how could these opportunities to respond allow for personal choice, support emotional safety, incorporate social interaction, provide a sense of audience, offer choice, involve an authentic scenario, or incorporate novelty? Let us consider other examples of opportunities to respond.

Conclusion

To have the greatest impact on student learning, opportunities to respond must make learning and thinking visible. This provides important evidence to both teachers and learners as they strive toward the intended learning outcomes in a lesson or unit. However, gathering evidence of learning is only worthwhile if the evidence is used to make decisions about where to go next in the learning trajectory. The opportunities to respond presented here as examples pave the way for effective feedback and subsequent learning.

From Middle School Math Teachers: Opportunities to Respond

Names: Angelica Blanco and Kevin Sitts, Jefferson Middle School, Caldwell, ID

Self-Assessment Posters

The biggest reason I changed was that I wanted to have clarity on what I was teaching and how to communicate that with my students. I think that as teachers we know what we are teaching but forget to share that with students. One of the first things I did was to complete every assignment, quiz, and test to see exactly what I was going to ask the students to do. After completing this, I created the learning intention for each lesson. This step helped me gain greater clarity.

Not only do students know what the learning intention is for each lesson, I was able to give students immediate feedback on their understanding of that specific learning intention. The feedback at first was either they understood it or they did not. If they got the answer correct, they would sign a poster with the learning intention. This was a way of showing them that they were able to correctly complete this learning intention. We would revisit the learning intention throughout the unit, and each time they demonstrated proficiency they would add a sticker.

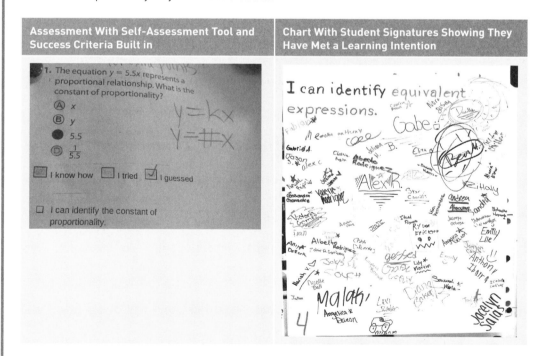

Assessment With Self-Assessment Tool and Success Criteria Built in	Chart With Student Signatures Showing They Have Met a Learning Intention

This was a clear picture to me of what students could do, but I felt that it was missing something, because students had different levels of understanding. So I made some changes to the next unit, based on what Mr. Sitts was doing in this classroom and the results he was having. I added self-assessment along with signing of the posters. I would give students a problem and have them quickly self-assess how well they could complete the problem with no instruction. They had a choice of four colors: green (I can teach/explain this to someone else), blue (I understand for myself), yellow (I am trying but still need help), and red (I need help). After some instruction and practice, students were given another opportunity to reassess. The great thing about student self-assessment is that students can see their own progress as we go through the unit. It also allows me to focus my instruction and work in small groups or one-on-one with students that still self-assess as "reds." I can also pair up blues and greens.

Example of Student-Self Assessment From Mr. Sitts' Classroom	Close-Up of Stickers Showing a Second Day's Self-Assessment

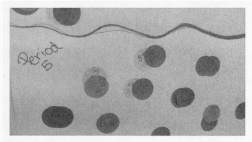

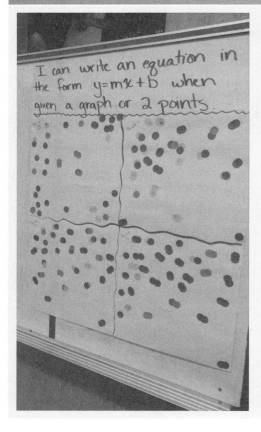

At the end of class, Mr. Sitts asks students to self-assess their progress. In the above photo, students put one day's dot over the previous day's, showing their growth in understanding the concept. For example, some went from a yellow to green or blue.

The biggest impact this change has had are the conversations students have with me and other students. I hear students share what they know and what they do not because they have the posters they can reference. In addition, when we are reviewing, students can tell me what they need help on, rather than simply saying "I don't get it." Students are able to focus on what they still need to study/improve on.

REFLECTION

How will you think differently about clarity, based on what you have read?

What ideas have you generated that you will try in your own classroom or school?

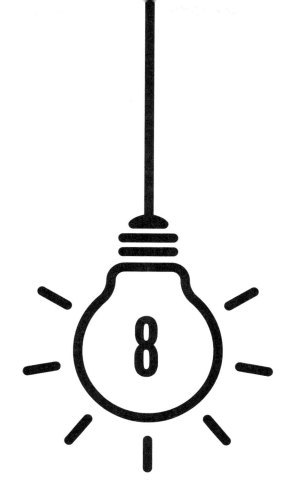

FEEDBACK WITH CLARITY

Giving and Receiving Feedback on and for Learning

READER'S LEARNING INTENTION

In this chapter I am learning about effective feedback—so that I can use opportunities to respond to gain feedback from my students about my teaching.

READER'S SUCCESS CRITERIA

I'll know I have it when I can:

- apply the research on effective feedback to both the learners in my classroom and myself, and
- adjust my feedback based on the specific learning intentions and success criteria.

Notice the wording for the learning intention and success criteria for this chapter. How is the wording different from that of the previous chapters? Do the learning intention and associated success criteria have the characteristics presented in Chapter 2? What approach to learning intentions and success criteria fits you best?

As we have moved through the clarity journey, we have discussed the clarity problem and mapped out a plan for gaining clarity with learning intentions, success criteria, and learning progressions. This plan allows us to include our learners in the clarity journey by co-constructing success criteria with them for their own learning. Then we transitioned to the development of opportunities to respond or ways to make student thinking and learning visible. Only when we make student thinking and learning visible can we and our students have an accurate account of learning progress. Moreover, as we will see in this chapter, opportunities to respond that align with the learning intentions, success criteria, and learning progressions allow us to provide effective feedback on and for learning. According to Hattie (2009, 2012), effective feedback yields an effect size of 0.70. This is approximately equivalent to two years' worth of growth in one academic year. Therefore,

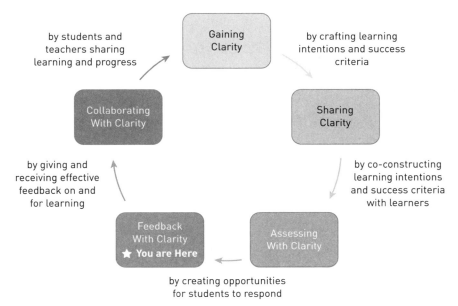

making sure that we are giving the right amount of feedback at the right time in the right way has a significant influence on teaching and learning. Giving and receiving effective feedback on and for learning is the next step in our clarity journey.

WHAT IS EFFECTIVE FEEDBACK?

According to the Merriam-Webster's dictionary (Feedback, 1999), *feedback* is "the transmission of evaluative or corrective information about an action, event, or process to the original or controlling source." Put differently, feedback provides information about a person's performance that is *used as a basis for improvement.* John Hattie (2012) explains the concept of feedback as information that should feed-forward learning, meaning it should equip the receiver to take action. O'Connell and Vandas (2015, p. 98) explain that, "When we break the word feedback down to its parts, we find the word *feed*, meaning to *nourish*, and *back*, meaning *in return* or *in exchange*. Therefore, ***feedback*** *is meant to nourish learning through an exchange.*"

The above definitions of feedback help us formulate the criteria for effective feedback. What is effective feedback, and what is not effective feedback?

Unpacking the definitions, we first see that feedback requires an action, event, or process—a person's performance. In our classroom or schools, these are the opportunities to respond developed so that we can assess with clarity. Without opportunities to respond, feedback is not possible. Take, for example, a classroom where students file through the door and take their seats. The teacher begins to lecture and continues to talk until the end of the class period. Unless learners interrupted the teacher, they were provided no opportunities to respond. There was no student performance for effective feedback. Thus, the teacher and students missed opportunities to provide information about how learning was progressing that day. Effective feedback requires a classroom that makes learning visible.

The second aspect that guides our understanding of effective feedback is the phrase *used as a basis for improvement.* Effective feedback provides information that helps learners close the gap. In other words, effective feedback helps learners identify where they are and where they need to be for success. Through effective feedback, they have the information to make adjustments in their learning to achieve success. If learners are working on argumentative writing, feedback from peers or a teacher that their thesis statement is "not very good" does not provide any information for improvement. What is "not very good" about the thesis statement? What should the learner change about the thesis statement? Effective feedback requires information that helps learners improve.

The definitions say that feedback is the transmission of evaluative or correct information *about an action, event, or process.* Although subtle, the definitions are clear that feedback is about the task and not the individual completing the task. In other words, my thesis statement needs improving, not me as a person. My solution to the mathematics problem is wrong, but I am not a wrong person. My answer on a multiple-choice assessment is a bad one, but I am not a bad person. Effective feedback focuses on the task, not the person.

Simply looking at the definitions of feedback allows us to formulate the criteria for effective feedback. Susan Brookhart (2008) labels these characteristics as *timely, specific,* and *constructive.*

Timely. The opportunity to provide effective feedback to learners requires that learners have opportunities to respond within close proximity to engaging in the content. Let's look at a few examples that highlight the difference between feedback that moves learning forward and feedback that isn't useful to learners.

The key difference between each of the above examples is the availability of a timely opportunity to respond. The examples on the right do not offer opportunities to respond within a timely manner. Thus, the teacher and the learners do not have opportunities to provide feedback in a way that improves performance. In each case on the right, the feedback comes at the conclusion of the performance without time to adjust or modify the process as it is occurring.

This . . .	Not this . . .
As the teacher presents information on cell reproduction (mitosis and meiosis), she stops after each phase and asks learners to turn to a partner and summarize the specific phase. The partners then write summaries in their interactive notebooks. Finally, they pair with another pair to share summaries and check for differences, misconceptions, and questions. Before leaving class, they provide the teacher with a collective summary from their group of four with questions and misconceptions they may still have and would like addressed in the next day's lesson.	The teacher presents all phases of cell reproduction to her students. For homework, learners must answer questions at the end of the chapter.
A math teacher models four ways to solve a quadratic equation: graphing, completing the square, using the quadratic formula, and factoring. After each method or approach is presented, learners use that approach to solve a problem on their miniature whiteboards. They compare their solutions with a neighbor and discuss the problem-solving process.	The teacher works out multiple problems during the class period and asks learners to complete problems 19–39 on page 263 for homework.
Learners view a short video on the balance of powers in the United States. The teacher often stops the video and asks students to discuss what they have learned so far, what they will include on their graphic organizers, and what questions they have about the balance of powers. They are given time to ask questions, and then they return to the video. Once it is complete, students finalize the graphic organizer that requires them to determine the similarities and differences among each of the branches of government.	During a civics class, learners watch a video on the balance of powers in the United States. For homework, they are to write an essay comparing and contrasting the different branches of government.
In an English language arts class, learners investigate three examples of a narratives. As a group, learners compare and contrast the three examples to develop criteria for successful narrative writing. They then develop their own narratives, using a framework provided by the teacher for prewriting and the rough draft. After each phase, they use the criteria the class established to conference with a peer to gain feedback before moving forward.	Using a rubric, students must write a narrative essay on a topic of their choice. The essay is due on Friday.

This leads to a second aspect of timely feedback. Information about learners' performance within a specific timeframe allows learners to use the information for improvement. The effectiveness of feedback can depend on whether the feedback is delayed or immediate. For example, delaying feedback can be helpful by providing students with additional opportunities to respond through error analysis or test corrections (Butler, Karpicke, & Roediger, 2007). However, without error analysis or test corrections, this positive gain disappears. On the other hand, immediate feedback produces significant gains when learners need that information to make corrective modifications during continued practice (Eggen & Kauchak, 2004). In other words, immediate feedback on the current mathematics problem allows me to make adjustments on the approach to solving subsequent problems.

This . . .	Not this . . .
Computer-assisted instruction provides learners with immediate feedback on their solutions to a problem before moving on to the next problem.	A teacher collects a problem-solving set on rational expressions. He marks which answers are not correct and returns the problem-solving set to learners at the end of the week.
A teacher marks incorrect solutions in a problem-solving set on balancing equations and returns the set to learners at the end of the week. She asks them to partner up and identify where they made mistakes in each incorrect solution. They are to describe, in their own words, how they would solve the problem differently in the future.	A teacher returns a problem-solving set on balancing equations to learners at the end of the week. She informs the students that these problems will be on the final test and they should review this set prior to taking the test.
As learners discuss their graphic organizers on the balance of powers, the teacher circulates around the room responding to student comments, questions, and conversations. The teacher then poses several scenarios and asks students to discuss in pairs which branch of government is responsible for addressing each issue.	The teacher returns the comparative essays on the branches of government. The grade for each student is on the top of the essay.
As students complete their rough drafts of their narratives, they schedule time to conference with their teacher. During the conference, the student and teacher collaboratively develop a list of revisions they will make to their story.	Students write narratives and turn them in to the teacher. One week later, the teacher returns the students' narratives. They have the option to revise or not revise and resubmit their stories by next Friday.

Specific. Effective feedback must be specific about the action, event, or process as well as specific about what additional steps will improve a learner's performance on a particular task.

This . . .	Not this . . .
Your supporting details do not align with your thesis statement.	Your paper is confusing. Please revise.
Look at numbers 3, 6, and 10. What do we do when we divide an inequality by a negative number?	You got a 7/10 on this problem set. You need some more practice.
What resources could you use to identify additional factors leading to the fall of the Soviet Union?	This response is not enough. You need to put in more effort.
Confer with a fellow classmate. Make sure you have all of the components of a laboratory report included in your notebook.	This is not a complete laboratory report. You will not get full credit on this experiment.

Comparing and contrasting the above examples, the column on the left provides specific information to the learner that serves as a basis for improvement. In each of the four examples, learners could use the information to identify specifically how they were progressing in their learning and where they needed to go next in the action, event, or process. Students have information that allows them to mind the learning gap.

Constructive. As mentioned before, effective feedback focuses on the action, event, or process and not the person. By being constructive, effective feedback serves a very useful purpose: *learning.* If the goal in each of our schools and classrooms is growth and achievement in learning, constructive feedback supports learners as they progress in their learning. Growth implies that all of our students may not be where they need to be today, but they are farther along today than they were yesterday. Constructive feedback makes the journey about learning, not the individual.

Take a few moments and return to the previous "This" and "Not this" tables. Identify examples of constructive feedback where the feedback zeroed in on the learning. Identify examples of feedback that focused on the student or completing work.

Effective feedback is timely, specific, and constructive. The clarity journey requires that we give and receive feedback on and for learning that is timely, specific, and constructive. Without these characteristics, feedback does not provide clear information, reducing the effectiveness of that feedback for both the teacher and the learner.

TYPES OF FEEDBACK

Because feedback is only effective if it feeds-forward learning or nourishes learning, it is critical that it is structured in a way that moves students from surface learning to deep learning to the transfer of that learning to new problems or situations. Research has identified three types of feedback that are supportive of learning: *task, process,* and *self-regulation.* The timing in the use of each type of feedback is dependent on the learning intentions, success criteria, and current level of performance of the student (i.e., novice to highly proficient).

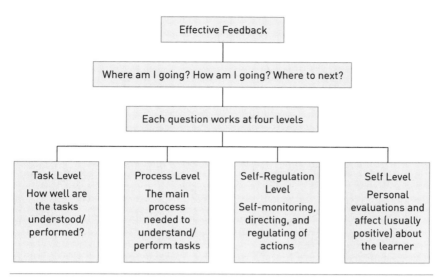

Source: Hattie, J., & Timperley, H. (2007). The power of feedback. *Review of Educational Research, 77*(1), 81–112.

As learners initially engage in learning, *task feedback* develops student understanding of specific content, ideas, and terms. It is corrective, precise, and focused on the accuracy of the new idea, concept, or task. Learners rely on task feedback to add structure to their conceptual understanding, which comes from the teacher providing examples and nonexamples as well as explanations of procedural steps, key features, and context. Task feedback provides clear information to learners that sorts out their understanding. Each learner's successful assimilation of feedback, and use of the feedback to decide where to go next, rests solely on whether each learner understands what the feedback means and how he or she can use it to move forward in the learning. Effective feedback and effective use of that feedback supports this initial learning (see Almarode, Fisher, Frey, & Hattie, 2018).

Process feedback is critical as learners explore the why and the how of specific content knowledge. Learners have likely identified clear boundaries between concepts and have developed awareness of examples and nonexamples associated with specific concept. In their initial learning, students assimilated task feedback into their work to develop an initial understanding of content, terms, and ideas. To move learners beyond what is simply right or wrong, or what is an example or a nonexample, they must receive and incorporate feedback that focuses on the process or strategies associated with accomplishing a specific task.

As learners begin to develop proficiency with specific content, ideas, and terms, the feedback should increasingly shift to process feedback. Whether from the teacher or peers, learners should receive feedback on their thinking, not just the accuracy of their response. For example, teachers might engage students in further dialogue about the use of figurative language to convey an author's purpose: "Remember, the use of a simile or metaphor is an intentional and purposeful decision by the author. What is the author's purpose in this example?" This feedback does not tell students that they are right or wrong. Instead, the feedback, in the form of a question, asks students to think about the process by which they determined the author's purpose in using figurative language.

Process feedback supports making connections, use of multiple strategies, self-explanation, self-monitoring, self-questioning, and critical thinking. For example, a teacher may ask learners what strategies they used in making the calculations for a number of math problems, and ask whether the strategy worked well or whether a different strategy may be more efficient. During a social studies lesson, a teacher may ask a student if primary or secondary sources were used to generate the historical inferences included in the student's essay, and if the difference in the type of source might affect the accuracy of the inference. Rather than focusing on the correct answer regarding the relationship between an independent and dependent variable, a teacher may ask a student, "What is your explanation for your answer?" The focus of process feedback is on relationships between ideas and students' strategies for evaluating the reasonableness of an answer or solution. Process feedback enables students to explicitly learn from mistakes and helps learners identify different strategies for addressing a task.

Like task feedback, process feedback should be specific and constructive and should support learners' pathways toward self-regulation feedback. That is, it should deepen thinking, reasoning, explanations, and connections. Does the teacher prompt learners through strategic questioning related to the learning process? What appears to be wrong, and why? What approach or strategies did the learner use or apply to the task? What is an explanation for the answer, response, or solution? What are the relationships with other parts of the task?

Self-regulation feedback refers to learners' ability to know what to do when they approach a new and different problem, are stuck, or have to apply their understanding in a new way. Students who have reached a deep level of conceptual understanding and are armed with multiple strategies are equipped to self-regulate, as they transfer their learning to more rigorous tasks. Highly proficient learners benefit from self-regulation feedback, although self-regulation feedback is not the only type of feedback that is important to these learners. For example, when teachers detect a misconception, or when a gap arises in foundational or background learning, learners benefit from both task and process feedback. However, a majority of the feedback at this part of the learning process should be self-regulation through metacognition. The teacher's role in the feedback at this level is to ask questions to prompt further metacognition.

Eventually, learners practice metacognition independently through self-verbalization, self-questioning, and self-reflection. They take personal ownership of their learning, which provides increased motivation and understanding. This is a well-documented finding in education research (e.g., National Research Council, 2007). The ability to think about their own thinking promotes learners' self-awareness, and it enables them to problem-solve around the learning task and to understand what they need to do to complete the task. To reiterate, learners know what to do when they get stuck, when a new challenge arises, or when their teacher may not be available. This is self-regulation feedback. Metacognitive processes boost student achievement.

Learners, at this point, are what John Hattie refers to as Visible Learners, as they see themselves as their own teachers. They have clear knowledge about where they are in their own learning process and about how they are progressing to or beyond the learning intention and success criteria, and they can monitor their own progress. Yet students need scaffolding as they progress toward this metacognitive awareness. To develop their metacognitive skills, students need to learn the art of self-questioning. Teachers must model this through the questions they pose to students as students move from processing to and through self-regulation.

The next step in our discussion on effective feedback is the delivery. Beyond the characteristics of effective feedback, does the delivery of the feedback matter? The answer is, yes.

THE DELIVERY OF THE FEEDBACK

Think back to your days as a student in school. How was feedback about a specific action, task, or assignment delivered to you? Was it simply a numerical value, a 5/10 or 75%, at the top of a piece of paper? Was it a letter, an A, C, or F, indicating how well you did on a particular activity? The delivery of this numerical value or letter followed the completion of the action, task, or assignment. This grade provided general information about how you did on the assignment as a whole but nothing specific about how you achieved it or how you could improve. This grade was about your performance, but your neighbor could have received the same grade for a very different set of reasons, good and/or bad. The delivery of this feedback limited the ability of the feedback to be specific and constructive. Depending on when you received the feedback, the information may or may not have been timely.

Consider a different scenario. Rather than a general numerical value or letter, you receive a high volume of comments and corrections that fill the pages of your work. A common expression is that "the red pen bled all over your paper." The information is in detail and addresses every element of the work from aesthetics to grammar, from aligning decimal points to the problem-solving approach. Although specific and constructive, the sheer volume of the information was overwhelming, and you may have wondered where to start or maybe if it would be best just to start over or give up all together. How do you sift through this feedback? By sheer volume, this feedback paralyzes a learner as to what to do in response.

Thus, the delivery of the feedback matters and is an essential part of how effective timely, specific, and constructive feedback it is for a learner. Using these two examples as a reference, noting that they are on the ends of a continuum, notice that the feedback is also limited to written, teacher-to-student feedback. Just as we had to expand our understanding of checks for understanding or opportunities to respond in Chapter 6, the use of effective feedback requires us to expand our understanding of both feedback in general and effective delivery of that feedback.

EFFECTIVE FEEDBACK WITH EFFECTIVE DELIVERY

If effective feedback is timely, specific, and constructive—but also dependent on the delivery of the feedback, how can we provide effective feedback with effective delivery? When delivered, effective feedback must answer three questions for the learner (Hattie & Timperley, 2007):

1. Where am I going?

2. How am I going (or doing)?

3. Where do I go next?

These three questions are very similar to the three questions introduced at the beginning of this book. Recall from the introduction of this book that clarity in learning requires that both teacher and learners are able to answer three questions: (1) What am I learning? (2) Why am I learning it? and (3) How will I know when I have learned it? Although these questions look very similar, not to mention that we do not need one more list of things to remember, these two sets of questions bring together our clarity journey over the past seven chapters.

Three Questions for Clarity	Three Questions for Effective Feedback
1. What am I learning?	1. Where am I going?
2. Why am I learning it?	2. How am I going?
3. How will I know I have learned it?	3. Where do I go next?

As teachers embark on the clarity journey, they must have answers to the three questions on clarity so that they can make purposeful, intentional, and deliberate decisions about the learning journey in their classrooms. This, of course, includes sharing clarity, creating and implementing opportunities to respond, and now, creating an environment for effective feedback. The scope of the three questions for clarity is reflective of the scale of the journey of learning that is being planned for students.

As learners embark on the learning journey, they must be provided enough clarity to engage with us as teachers. Therefore, they require answers to the three clarity questions so that they can take part in the journey and ownership of their own learning. The research is clear that students who know what they are learning, why they are learning it, and how they can be successful are more likely to take risks, enjoy the thrill of learning, and engage in goal-directed behavior (Hattie & Donoghue, 2016).

Together, both teachers and students require guideposts that provide information about a student's progression through the journey that is the *basis for improvement or persistence.* Put differently, the three questions for effective feedback provide timely, specific, and constructive information about progress on the learning journey so that learners can adjust their heading or maintain their current heading.

Once the teacher and the learners have identified the destination through the learning intention and success criteria, feedback is that small voice captured inside of the GPS or Google Maps that provides gentle reminders about whether to proceed, turn, or pause for "recalculating."

Where am I going? In the delivery of effective feedback, *Where I am going?* refers to the initial *learning intention and success criteria.* This information provides a reminder or reframe of the target at which the action, event, or process is directed. Let us return to our earlier examples to see how we might answer the first question, *Where am I going?*

Scenario	Answering the Question: Where am I going?
The supporting details in a learner's essay do not align with the thesis statement.	Remember, we are learning to formulate a thesis statement that will guide us in identifying and developing supporting details.
A learner gets several problems incorrect on a problem set involving the solving of inequalities.	We are learning that the solving of inequalities requires a few different decisions than solving equations.
A student provides one factor that the student believes led to the fall of the Soviet Union.	The fall of a country is the result of many different and related events or influences. Our learning focus is to look at them all through different lenses.
A student submits a science laboratory report with several sections missing.	We are learning that scientific investigation requires full transparency on the part of the scientist. Thus, we are learning about the essential components in communicating a scientific investigation.

Notice that in each scenario, the delivery of the feedback focused on the what and why of the learning journey. Teachers and learners should continue to keep the learning intention and success criteria in mind. This is the first component in delivery effective feedback: a timely, specific, and constructive reminder of where we are going.

How am I going? Aligned with the learning intention and success criteria, the second component of effective feedback provides a clear assessment of how learners are progressing toward the target. Are learners making progress? If not, where and what is the gap in their learning? Returning to the previous examples, effective feedback must deliver clear and concise information about learners' progress.

Scenario	Answering the Question: Where am I going?	Answering the Question: How am I going?
The supporting details in a learner's essay do not align with the thesis statement.	Remember, we are learning to formulate a thesis statement that will guide us in identifying and developing supporting details.	Your thesis statement does not align with your supporting details. How might you better align them?
A learner gets several problems incorrect on a problem set involving the solving of inequalities.	We are learning that the solving of inequalities requires a few different decisions than solving equations.	What do we do when we divide by a negative number when solving inequalities?
A student provides one factor that the student believes led to the fall of the Soviet Union.	The fall of a country is the result of many different and related events or influences. Our learning focus is to look at them all through different lenses.	Because there are multiple factors leading to the fall of the Soviet Union, which might you add that shows a different lens?
A student submits a science laboratory report with several sections missing.	We are learning that scientific investigation requires full transparency on the part of the scientist. Thus, we are learning about the essential components in communicating our scientific investigation.	Confer with a classmate, and review the success criteria. Make sure you have all of the components a laboratory report included in your notebook then let's talk again.

Each of these scenarios provides information about the learning journey so that learners can adjust their heading or maintain their current heading. Although subtle in some of the scenarios, the answer to the question *How am I going?* highlights a difference or gap in where learners are headed in the learning journey and where they are right now. However, we cannot stop there, as learners need support in knowing where to go next in their learning journey.

Where do I go next? The final question in the delivery of effective feedback provides scaffolding or support in how learners can close the gap between where they are in the learning journey and where they are going in the journey. When we think of where to go next for all learners, we have to think of more than just those who struggle. The clarity we have established will ensure that both learners who are struggling and learners who are on track will be able to work toward the learning intentions and success criteria, meeting one success criterion after another. Therefore, the question of where to next is often answered by looking to the next success criterion to be mastered.

However, so often learners who are high achievers finish their work and wait for next steps, and we as teachers struggle to keep up with them. This often results in asking them to do more of the same. The issue is that *Where do I go next?* is a question that focuses on deeper learning, not just on more complete learning. "Oh, you completed the math worksheet; here is another." "Oh, you finished the writing assignment; add another paragraph or start a new one." "Oh, you completed the answers at the end of the chapter; help another student or write a summary." Early finishers learn quickly not to ask where to next when they receive messages that asking just means more work, not more learning. However, when where to next equates to deeper learning, early finishers relish the opportunities and work hard to get there. This inspires others to do the same, and thus encourages deeper, more meaningful learning on the part of all students. That said, it is critical that we think of where to next as deeper learning and are prepared to allow early finishers to dive deeper, explore new problems, apply understanding, and have choice in how they engage in meaningful experiences.

Supporting all learners in closing this gap invokes the principle of gradual release (Fisher & Frey, 2014). Initially, learners will need more support in developing and executing a plan for where to go next. As learners develop more learning strategies and metacognitive strategies, they will need less support. In the end, the part of effective feedback that focuses on next steps will rest predominantly in the hands of learners, as they become self-regulated learners, developing and executing their own plan through the learning progression and beyond.

Scenario	Answering the Question: Where am I going?	Answering the Question: How am I going?	Answering the Question: Where do I go next?
The supporting details in a learner's essay do not align with the thesis statement.	Remember, we are learning to formulate a thesis statement that will guide us in identifying and developing supporting details.	Your thesis statement does not align with your supporting details.	Take a look at the examples and exemplars in the writing center. What do you notice that is different from or similar to your thesis statement and supporting details? How have these writers aligned their thesis statements to supporting details? Use those examples to revise your work.
A learner gets several problems incorrect on a problem set involving the solving of inequalities.	We are learning that the solving of inequalities requires a few different decisions than solving equations.	What do we do when we divide by a negative number when solving inequalities?	What decisions would you make in solving those problems a second time? Write a brief explanation in the margin of how you solve these inequalities.
A student provides one factor that the student believes led to the fall of the Soviet Union.	The fall of a country is the result of many different and related events or influences. Our learning focus is to look at them all through different lenses.	There are several contributing factors leading to the fall of the Soviet Union. You need to include these important factors.	What resources could you use to identify additional factors leading to the fall of the Soviet Union?
For Early Finishers: A student submits a science laboratory report complete with all sections and accurately written.	We are learning that scientific investigation requires full transparency on the part of the scientist. Thus, we are learning about the essential components in communicating our scientific investigation.	You have correctly and accurately reported on the scientific investigation. What have you learned? What does it make you wonder about?	To decide what is next for you, I want you to think about what you have learned so far and what questions you still have. If you were the scientist studying this topic, what would be your plan for how to deepen your learning or investigation?

ADJUST FEEDBACK FOR LEARNERS

Understanding the characteristics of effective feedback (timely, specific, and constructive), the different types of feedback (task, process, and self-regulation), and effective approaches for the delivery of feedback allows teachers and students to adjust the feedback to meet the needs of specific learners.

So that learners and teachers can articulate where we are going, how we are going, and where we will go next, they must receive the right type of feedback at the right time. Every opportunity to respond offered to students should make their thinking visible so that the teacher and the learner can clearly see progress toward the learning intention and success criteria. Therefore, every opportunity to respond is an opportunity for feedback.

Great job! Super work! Now you've got it! Such statements don't work. This type of feedback leaves learners asking, great job at what? Super work doing what? I've got what? Feedback during the learning experience, lesson, or unit should answer three main questions for both the teacher and the student: Where am I going? How am I going/doing? and Where do I go next? (Hattie, 2012) *Where am I going?* refers to the learning intention and success criteria. Therefore, the feedback should be specific to both the learning intention and success criteria. Extraneous feedback that is not related to where the student is going provides cognitive overload and is detrimental to the learning process. *How am I going/ doing?* refers to the current location of the learner in his or her progress toward the learning intention. This feedback should be constructive and concise so that the learner has a realistic view of his or her learning. Finally, feedback focused on where the learner is going next provides timely information about the next area on which the learner should focus.

Feedback on and for learning is crucial in sustaining that learning. This feedback should align all other elements of clarity. At this point, it is up to us to provide feedback during every opportunity to respond that aligns with the learning intention and success criteria, provides information about where learners are in their progress, and helps them decide where to go next. Eventually, teachers can empower students to give each other feedback. Until, then, however, the teacher does not have to be the giver in all feedback scenarios. When students are equipped with the answers to the three clarity questions, they are able to engage in the feedback process as well.

A BALANCED APPROACH

When we consider Graham Nuthall's research (2007) in the *Hidden Lives of Learners*, we find that the majority of the feedback students receive in a day is not actually from us; it is from their peers. The issue is that without clarity, the majority of that feedback is inaccurate. Nuthall states that up to 80 percent of feedback comes from peers, and 80 percent of the time it is wrong or inaccurate. This highlights the need for us to equip our students to provide themselves and others with quality feedback. Otherwise, we are fighting an uphill battle. The first step is clarity, which we have already discussed and have at the ready. The second step is to teach our students how to use the learning intentions, success criteria, exemplars, worked examples, and models to deeply understand what successful learning looks like. It is after we have shared clarity with our students that we have provided the access to such tools and can encourage them to use them wisely. While there are many structures that teachers can model for students and teach students to use for giving and receiving feedback—from feedback frames (O'Connell & Vandas, 2015) to structures like the Ladder of Feedback (O'Connell & Vandas 2015)—we have provided some guiding questions to aid you in finding tools that work well for you and your students.

GUIDING QUESTIONS FOR TEACHING STUDENTS TO PROVIDE QUALITY FEEDBACK

1. Have you modeled the success criteria for students, using worked examples, exemplars, and models?

2. Do all students have easy access to the success criteria, worked examples, exemplars, and models (on the classroom wall, in their notebooks, on laminated sheets for checking off criteria, online, etc.) so that they can begin to use them independently?

3. Have you asked students to use the tools to self-assess? This often is necessary before asking students to engage in peer feedback, so they have an understanding of where they are in relationship to the criteria. How will you ask them to self-assess and be metacognitive using the tools available?

4. Have you provided students with words and modeling to effectively give and receive constructive feedback?

5. Have you provided students with a structure for providing one another feedback (checklist, two wows and a wish, Ladder of Feedback, etc.)?

6. Have you provided students multiple opportunities to practice giving and receiving feedback?

When planning for a balanced approach to feedback, we recommend thinking about the opportunities to respond you have planned thoughtfully and considering how students will interact with them to give and receive feedback. Will the feedback come from (1) teacher, (2) self, or (3) peers? One teacher cannot possibly provide all the feedback for all learners all of the time, nor are students waiting for us to do so. Rather, if we thoughtfully pair opportunities to respond with opportunities for different feedback partners, we can share the work load but also share the learning that takes place in meaningful conversations about learning. How do you begin? Review the opportunities to respond that you have created and planned that align to the learning intentions and success criteria. Decide which you will personally provide feedback on and which will be used for self and peer feedback.

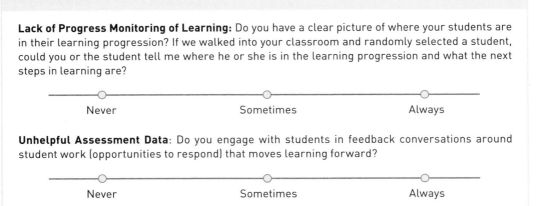

LITMUS TEST

Lack of Progress Monitoring of Learning: Do you have a clear picture of where your students are in their learning progression? If we walked into your classroom and randomly selected a student, could you or the student tell me where he or she is in the learning progression and what the next steps in learning are?

Never   Sometimes   Always

Unhelpful Assessment Data: Do you engage with students in feedback conversations around student work (opportunities to respond) that moves learning forward?

Never   Sometimes   Always

What information do teachers and students receive from the progress monitoring and assessment data? Does the feedback to the teacher and students answer the questions:

1. Where am I going?

2. How am I going?

3. Where do I go next?

REFLECTION AND NEXT STEPS

As you reflect on the feedback in your school or classroom, use the following matrix to guide progress. The reflection questions can support you in considering whether feedback with clarity is happening in your school or classroom. The next steps provide guidance on how to implement specific tasks in your discussions around this part of the clarity journey. Finally, the last column, or evidence, highlights what evidence will give you the best picture about supporting effective feedback in your school or classroom.

Reflection Questions	Next Steps	Evidence
What type of feedback do learners receive in your school or classroom?	Using common planning time, grade-level planning, and/or content area meetings to focus on providing a variety of feedback: • Task, process, and self-regulation • Oral, written, and student-to-student	Students provide the best indicators as to whether or not the feedback is clear. Ask them by: • Polling the class • Hosting a focus group to ask if it is clear where they are going, how they are going, and where they are going next • Using individual student data charts that allow them to map their learning progress

Reflection Questions	Next Steps	Evidence
Is the feedback to learners timely, specific, and constructive?	Align the delivery of the feedback with the learning intentions, success criteria, and learning progression. Make a deliberate decision about the focus of feedback during each part of the learning progression.	Ask students to explain what they need to do next to meet the learning intention and success criteria. Ask students to progress-monitor their own learning using the success criteria.
Does the feedback provide a probable pathway from the learners' current level to the expected level?	Use a preassessment to determine students' current state of understanding.	Ask students if they can explain the steps to meeting a single success criterion.
Are you using a balanced approach to feedback?	Plan for feedback to be given and received by teacher, self, and peers that align with the opportunities to respond you have already developed.	Ask students to engage in feedback conversations, and monitor the quality of discussion. Ask them what is working to move their learning forward and what else would help them.

FEEDBACK WITH CLARITY IN ACTION: VOICES FROM THE FIELD

Feedback with clarity brings together the concepts, skills, and understanding from our clarity journey. Effective feedback is only made possible when clarity exists, has been shared, and learning assessed. Effective feedback between teachers and students guides learners to the learning targets. Feedback provides insight into the new evidence we may be looking for as learners progress toward the learning intentions and success criteria. As you might have guessed, the delivery of feedback differs from classroom to classroom, teacher to teacher, and with each individual student. However, one common feature of this feedback is that it answers the questions:

1. Where am I going?

2. How am I going?

3. Where am I going next? (Hattie, 2012; Hattie & Timperley, 2007)

What follows are multiple examples from schools and classrooms throughout North America. As you explore these examples, consider the quantity, delivery, and audience associated with each instance of feedback.

	What it means	What it looks like
Quantity	The Goldilocks principle	Too much feedback overwhelms the learner and can distract from the learning intention and success criteria associated with the opportunity to respond. Too little feedback leaves the three questions associated with feedback unanswered—neither the learner nor the teacher knows where to go next. Feedback should use the Goldilocks principle—not too much, not too little, but just the right amount.
Delivery	Oral Written Modeling Peer-to-Peer Teacher-to-Peer Peer-to-Teacher	Feedback can and should take many forms. Feedback can be delivered verbally or written on the artifacts of a specific task. We can model what we want learners to say or do, allowing them to adjust their own work. Furthermore, feedback does not always come from teachers, but from the learners.
Audience	Individual Small Group Whole Group	Finally, feedback can be directed toward an individual student—If the student needs very individualized and targeted feedback. Feedback can also be directed to small groups or the entire class.

VOICES FROM THE FIELD

From a Team of Kindergarten Teachers: Feedback With Clarity

Names: Rozanne Gans, Gwen Hogg, & Candace Bilbery, Van Buren Elementary School, Caldwell, ID

Student-to-Self Feedback   Subjects: Reading, Math, Writing

What does success look like and feel like to a five-year-old kindergartener? During collaboration we asked ourselves this question. We talked with Kara, our consultant, and she shared some success criteria with us. We used one of her great ideas. The results are that this year kindergarteners at Van Buren Elementary are able to tell you and show you what they are learning, how they are learning it, and how they will know they have learned it.

Learning Intention: We will become readers by practicing skills on Lexia, doing letter centers, and reading with our teacher.

Content Objective: We are learning to read. **Language Objective (example)**: We will read, write, and discuss the letter A. **Assessment Objective/Success Criteria (example)**: I will know I have it when I can read, write, and tell the sound of A.

Each kindergarten classroom put up alphabet posters for each letter; each poster was about eight by six inches. We then put the names of every child on every letter poster. As each student learned a letter—capital, lowercase, and sound for each letter—we took the student's name off that letter poster and gave the student that alphabet letter to take home to make an alphabet at home. We also gave each student a certificate when the student had learned all the letters and sounds. Students not only took ownership of their learning, they also helped others practice and learn letters and sounds. Just before our winter break, when most students had mastered all their sounds and letters, we had a donut party as a celebration of learning for all students. This year, with our students truly aware of expectations and success criteria, we have seen a measurable difference from previous years.

Alphabet Chart With Student Progress Shown in Stickers

Certificate of Completion of Letter Recognition and Sounds

(Continued)

(Continued)

We also put up number lines for each class with stars marking each child's progress toward counting to 100.

Students' Progress Toward Counting to 100

Students' Progress on Sight Words

Our newest success criterion is for our sight words. (The number of kindergarten sight words has risen over the last few years from 34 to 88.) One classroom has the solar system with rockets traveling to the sun. Another has a tree with woodland animals showing their progress as students increase the number of sight words they know. Our third classroom is in the process of posting a Disney path to the Cinderella Castle marking their success with sight words.

Overall, sharing success criteria with our students has been a good use of time. We have seen our students take charge and be more responsible for their own learning. Learning has become more student driven and less teacher centered. Students have goals, and they own their learning.

From a Second Grade Teacher: Feedback With Clarity

Name: Christina Ramie, Iroquois Point Elementary School, Ewa Beach, HI

Student-to-Self Feedback   Subject: Writing Opinions

I conducted a series of opinion-writing lessons to ensure my students were clear on what was expected. To start, I showed students some sample opinion paragraphs. Together, we used sticky notes to identify pros and cons of each paragraph. Afterward, I created success criteria based on common pros identified. I then modeled writing a paragraph to include all parts of the success criteria. I separated criterion onto a different sheet of chart paper to ensure students could differentiate each step. I also color coded each criterion. When it was time for the students to write, they could refer to the sample I modeled. Once students were finished with their paragraphs, they paired up to confirm that they had all of the parts of an opinion paragraph. To do this, I had students color code all of the parts of their paragraphs, just as I did on the chart paper. Students quickly realized if they were missing a component if they did not see all of the required colors. Students then made necessary changes to ensure they had met all the success criteria.

Example of Success Criteria for Writing an Opinion

Notice: Topic of this writing assignment was, Should Teachers Give Homework? The success criteria are posted one criterion per chart and color coded. The example paragraphs are below the chart papers that students analyzed to determine pros and cons in opinion paragraphs on a different topic.

Why I Did It

As I became more informed and knowledgeable of the philosophy of Visible Learning, I realized that my expectations of my students were not always clear. I had mediocre rubrics that said things like "some reasons included" and "many reasons included." If even I wasn't completely sure about this ambiguous language, then how could I expect my seven-year-old students to understand it? Through my new understanding, I was able to help my students find clarity. They were no longer unable to figure out if they were meeting the standard(s). They knew exactly what proficiency looked like.

(Continued)

(Continued)

The Impact

I saw an immediate positive response to the success criteria. It was great to overhear the students referring back to the success criteria during peer conferencing. I overheard sentences like, "Did you include a topic sentence? I don't see any red on your paper." or "You might get a DP (developing toward proficiency) if you don't include three reasons." It was evident that my young writers knew exactly what was expected of them throughout this writing process. They exuded confidence and sureness as a result of having clarity.

Grade 2 Opinion Paragraph Sample

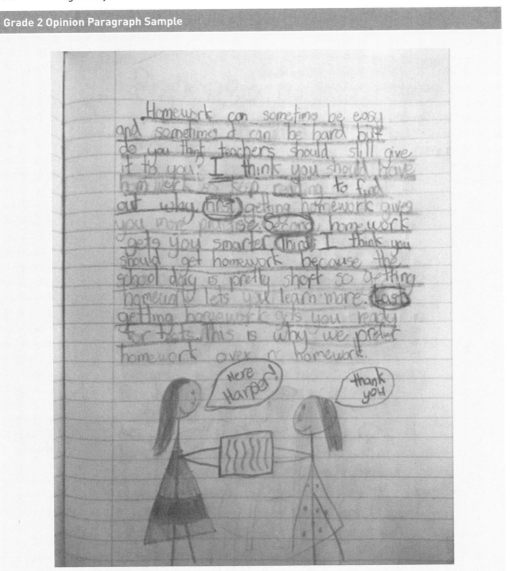

Notice the way the student annotated the writing to show that she met the criteria by underlining or circling the words that met each criterion in a different color.

When outside observers asked a student in Christina's classroom what she would work on next since she had accomplished all of the success criteria, she replied, "I need to get to where I know the success criteria by heart, without the checklist, so I am ready to go to third grade."

From a Fourth Grade Teacher: Feedback With Clarity

Name: Kristian Odegaard, Lone Tree Elementary School, Lone Tree, CO

Student-to-Student and Teacher-to-Student Feedback   Subject: Writing

Co-Creating Success Criteria

I have used success criteria for a couple of years now. I began using success criteria with students in writing. I have always seen the importance and benefit of students having ownership in their learning. I used to co-create rubrics with students; however, I still felt like the rubrics were in "teacher language." I would have students grade themselves based on the rubric but still felt that their writing did not improve. I also found that rubrics were very subjective and full of gray areas, so while the students helped to create it, they still did not have ownership or improve.

When I create success criteria with students, I begin with brainstorming what students know about the topic or what they think should be a part of it. For example, if we are creating success criteria for narrative writing, students already have background and knowledge about what a narrative should include. We then look at the standards to determine what the state says we need to include in our narratives. Finally, we look at exemplars to determine other components that should be a part of a narrative.

The first time I tried success criteria, I was nervous to see what my students would generate as success criteria. As a teacher, it can be hard to give up control. We all know the standards we are responsible for teaching students and the many skills and strategies we need students to learn. However, once my students looked at their own knowledge, the standards, and exemplars, their created success criteria included every component that I would have placed on a rubric.

Allowing students to co-create the success criteria gave them a voice in the process, but more important, it quickly began to improve their writing. The gray areas of rubrics were now gone. Students could look at their own writing with the success criteria to determine what they had done well as well as the areas they needed to improve. Students could also have quality conversations about their writing based on the success criteria.

Assessing With the Success Criteria

Co-creating the success criteria is only a small part of how my teaching and my students' learning has changed since I started using success criteria. The learning really takes place when students assess using the success criteria.

Descriptive Writing Success Criteria

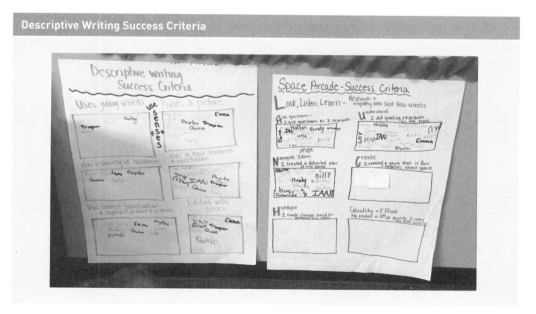

(Continued)

(Continued)

Addi's Writing Conference

Quinn's Writing Conference

To assess with the success criteria, I always start with a conference and a conversation with a student. It is not simply about giving a grade or checking the student off my list; it provides valuable information for me as the teacher. It also allows students to take ownership of what they are doing well and where they need to focus moving forward.

On the poster with the success criteria, I create a box for each criterion. Once students master that criterion, they sign their name in the box. During our one-on-one conference, each student and I spend time going through the success criteria discussing how the student demonstrated or mastered each criterion. I allow students to sign in each box when they have mastered that criterion based on our conversation. The conversation provides crucial feedback for the students while they prove how they met each criterion. As we discuss their work together, students often find areas they need to focus on next. Not only are they able to justify that they have met some of the criteria, it becomes a natural conversation to set goals. Students know what they need to work on next to improve. Use the QR codes in the margin to view my conferences with Quinn and Addi as we discuss how their work meets our descriptive writing success criteria.

The impact on students' learning from using success criteria has been huge. Kids have ownership and improve their work based on the success criteria. They are able to have quality conversations with peers and identify how their work meets the success criteria. Even parents have commented on how impressed they are with students' work. Success criteria have drastically changed my instruction as well as my students' learning. I look forward to all the ways I will continue to use success criteria moving forward.

From a Fifth Grade Teacher: Feedback With Clarity

Name: Jenny Hartvigsen, Van Buren Elementary School, Caldwell, ID

Student-to-Self and Student-to-Teacher Feedback   Subject: Math

Knowing the importance of the students being able to assess themselves and see their learning as the year progresses, I have created a system that accomplishes both and works for my class and me. At the beginning of each unit, my students and I construct our learning intentions and success criteria. Afterward, we look through our reflection sheet. This sheet has three major components: a list of all standards that will be covered in the unit, a small area for the students to score how well they are progressing, and a written reflection on their learning. After the students have completed their assignments and the assignments have been graded/scored, I file them in the student portfolios.

Reflection Sheet

Novice (1) I'm just starting to learn this and I don't understand it yet!	Apprentice (2) I can do this if I look at an example or get help!	Practitioner (3) I can do this on my own without any help.	Expert (4) I can do this on my own and explain how to do it.

Reflect on your work in math. How are you doing? Are you an expert, practitioner, apprentice or novice? Attach a piece of evidence.

Standard that I am working towards:	Reflection	Written reflection
I can easily multiply four-digit by two-digit whole numbers using the standard algorithm.	4	
I can divide four-digit numbers (dividends) by two-digit numbers (divisors).	3	
I can illustrate and explain a multiplication and division problem using equations, arrays and/or models.	4	
I can add, subtract, multiply, and divide decimals to hundredths using what I have learned about place value.	4	
I can relate the strategies I use to add, subtract, multiply, and divide decimals to hundredths to contextual problems and explain why I chose the strategies to help me solve the problem.	X	
I can explain my thinking process clearly using high-level vocabulary.	2	I dont use high level vocabulary because we don't use worksheets to explain our reason.

Once a week the students take all the work from their student portfolios. They review each piece, matching the work that they did with the standards listed on their reflection sheet. Students select exemplar work that best demonstrates their individual growth and mastery of the standard, attaching it to their reflection sheet. The students then place the completed reflection sheet with attached evidence into their data folder. As the unit progresses, the students are collecting evidence using the reflection sheets to prove that they are growing and learning. The data folders are then used to help the students guide the discussions with their parents/guardians during student-led conferences. Not only do the reflection sheets help the students see their learning, but they help me as a teacher guide the everyday lessons.

Work Students Select to Add to Their Portfolios to Prove Their Learning

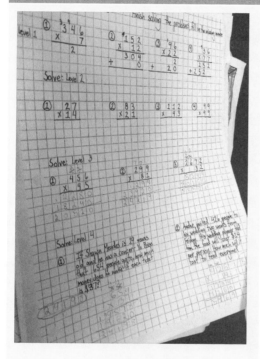

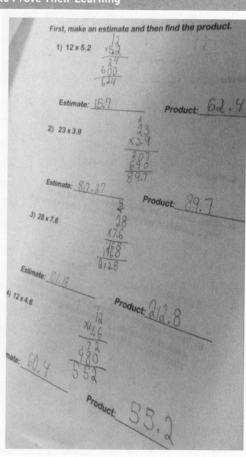

REFLECTION

How will you think differently about clarity, based on what you have read?

What ideas have you generated that you will try in your own classroom or school?

COLLABORATING FOR CLARITY IN LEARNING

LEARNING INTENTION

We are learning to (WALT): understand roles in building clarity in our district, school, and/or classroom.

SUCCESS CRITERIA

What I am looking for (WILF):

Collaboration	• I can explain the power of collective clarity.
	• I collaborate with students, teachers, and leaders to develop clarity at all levels.

Why?
This is because (TIB): Collective clarity matters for student and teacher learning.

Our journey has taken us from the definition of clarity to the recognition of a clarity problem and through the process for building clarity in your own school or classroom. From the very beginning, we aimed to operationalize clarity in learning into five essential components for both teachers and students:

1. Crafting learning intentions and success criteria

2. Co-constructing learning intentions and success criteria with learners

3. Creating opportunities for students to respond (i.e., formative assessment)

4. Providing effective feedback on and for learning

5. Sharing learning and progress among students, teachers, and leaders

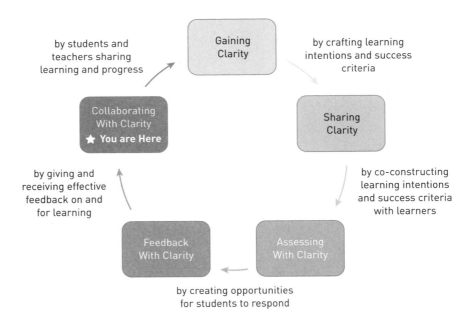

Each chapter worked through an instructional framework that provided a systematic means to ensure that both our students and we had clarity in our learning that also served as a catalyst for accelerating learning. So, what next? How do we change our practice and adjust our instructional decisions to maximize clarity in learning for our learners and for ourselves?

We can accomplish this in two ways: (1) by continually engaging in dialogue with students to gain feedback about progress in learning and next steps and (2) by collaborating with other teachers and leaders to ensure clarity of learning expectations and to use evidence from students to determine next steps. We will highlight each as we chart the journey forward.

CHARTING YOUR CLARITY JOURNEY

Changing our own practice is successful only when we reflect on our own clarity journey and, along with our students, see ourselves as learners. In order to change our practice, we first need to gain insights into where we want to start, why we want to start there, and how we will know when we are ready to move onto the next step in our own learning journey. John Hattie emphasizes that the most successful teachers are those that have the disposition to ask, to examine negative evidence about their own performance, and to make changes based on student feedback. They are the teachers that have the greatest impact (2009).

Take time and reflect on your own strengths and areas of opportunities for growth. At the conclusion of each of the previous nine chapters, you were encouraged to reflect on your own environment. For administrators, this reflection could focus on your school, specific grade levels, or content areas. For teachers, this reflection should focus on your own learners. Let us revisit the litmus tests for each component of clarity.

LITMUS TEST

Bottom line: Do we have clarity? Is it working for kids?

Below we have included several prompting questions that provide an opportunity for reflection as to some of the common issues we see in the area of clarity for learning. If you have struggled, as we have, with one or more of the common pitfalls, we recommend using the question that aligns with your specific need to self-reflect. Later in this chapter, you will be given the opportunity to set a goal and pair it with success criteria to address your personal areas of greatest need, set a course for change, and know when you have achieved your goal, whether it is for your classroom, school, or district.

However, the bottom line in how you or anyone is sharing clarity with students in the classroom comes down to whether it is working, no matter how it is posted, shared, co-constructed, assessed, et cetera. Are students more assessment-capable because of our practices? Are they able to answer the questions: Where am I going? Why am I learning this? How am I progressing? and Where to next? If not, we have missed the mark or aren't there *yet*, and if so, we must continue the practices that are helping us to develop more assessment-capable students.

(Continued)

(Continued)

Fragmented Teaching and Learning: Does learning in your school or classroom feel like a series of discrete topics?

Never   Sometimes   Always

Activity-Driven Instruction: Do you and your colleagues pick an activity first, fitting it into the content? Or do you first determine what learners must know, understand, and be able to do?

Never   Sometimes   Always

Misaligned Strategies: Do the strategies, activities, and tasks in your school or classroom ask students to engage at the same cognitive level as the particular standard?

Never   Sometimes   Always

Lack of Progress Monitoring of Learning: Do you have a clear picture of where your students are in their learning progression? If we walked into your classroom and randomly selected a student, could you tell me where that specific student is in his or her learning progression?

Never   Sometimes   Always

Unhelpful Assessment Data: Do you engage in data meetings where you have large amounts of data that do not contribute to what the students are learning, how they are learning it, and where they are going next in their learning?

Never   Sometimes   Always

After reading through the questions posed above, you may be thinking that you just aren't sure if it the clarity you are providing to students is working or is creating more assessment-capable learners. In that case, we encourage you to ask. Ask students to reflect on the learning intentions, success criteria, feedback, and assessment tools you have employed to provide feedback as to whether it is or is not working for them.

CHARTING NEXT STEPS

Throughout the previous chapters, you may have incorporated some of the ideas presented in each chapter into your school or classroom. You may also have engaged in the **Reflection and Next Steps** activities to understand better the level of clarity in your own school or classroom. Therefore, your responses to the litmus tests now may be different from your earlier responses. Use the following table to summarize your present thoughts. In the column on the right, share several areas of strength and also areas where you see growth opportunities.

	Strength or Opportunity
Crafting learning intentions and success criteria	
Co-constructing learning intentions and success criteria with learners	
Creating opportunities for students to respond	

	Strength or Opportunity
Providing effective feedback on and for learning	
Sharing learning and progress between students and teachers	

For the items that you indicated were strengths in the previous chart, now provide a specific example from your school or classroom that would support your assertion that the item is indeed a strength. What evidence would you point to in your classroom to support such assertions? If you cannot identify a specific example, then change your response from a strength to an opportunity.

	Strength or Opportunity	Evidence or Specific Examples
Crafting learning intentions and success criteria		
Co-constructing learning intentions and success criteria with learners		
Creating opportunities for students to respond		
Providing effective feedback on and for learning		
Sharing learning and progress between students and teachers		

When we include a chart like the previous one as part of our reflective practice, it requires that we have a consistent system of self-reflection on what is happening in our classrooms. Oftentimes we believe we are doing one thing, when we are actually doing another thing or students have yet to notice the change. Valuing evidence, even with self-reflection, prevents our own confirmation biases or misconceptions from barricading our own learning journey. This simple data chart can (1) guide conversations with our students, instructional leaders, mentors, or colleagues; (2) guide our decisions about what professional learning to seek out; and (3) provide clarity in our own learning by answering the three questions for ourselves: What am I learning? why am I learning it? and how will I know I have learned it? "Knowing thy impact" is an essential component of *Visible Learning* and requires self-reflection (Hattie, 2012). The strengths are to provide the foundation for changing practice by identifying successes, things we are already good at doing in our schools and classrooms. The opportunities become the focus for changing our practice.

Now, convert each opportunity into a goal with success criteria for yourself. For example, if you identify that you use too much "sit and get" lecture or packets, then *your* learning intention might be *to increase the number of opportunities for classroom discussion and dialogue in student learning.* If you identify that your students cannot tell you why they are learning something, then *your* learning intention might be *to increase the authenticity of learning tasks to provide more relevancy with content.* As we do with our students, we must set up criteria for success. How will we know that our students have more opportunities for classroom discussion and dialogue? How will we know that learners are finding learning tasks to be more authentic? We must have a clear understanding of what success looks like to better identify resources and supports for implementing our goals and monitoring our own progress. In other words, what are the success criteria for your professional learning intentions? Here is an example.

Goal	I will increase the number of opportunities for classroom discussion and dialogue in student learning.
Success Criteria	1. I will incorporate two or more opportunities for classroom discussion into the learning period.
	2. I will monitor student discussion to better assess student understanding.
	3. I will ask for feedback from students and use evidence from classroom discussions to plan the next step in the learning episode.
	4. I will collaborate with my planning team to develop opportunities for classroom discussion.

Select one of your opportunities and develop a goal and success criteria for that opportunity. Use the ideas from the previous chapters, your responses from the **Reflection and Next Steps** sections, and what you have learned from discussions with your instructional leaders, mentors, or colleagues to select your specific professional learning intentions.

Goal	I will
Success Criteria	1.
	2.
	3.
	4.

This exercise will support your effectiveness in making conscious decisions about what professional learning is necessary to enhance the probability that you will achieve your learning intention and success criteria. As highlighted by Timperley, Wilson, Barrar, and Fung (2007), this professional learning should do the following:

1. Occur over an extended period, as learning takes time: This goal will not be mastered by Friday. It often takes multiple years to deeply change practices.

2. Challenge your existing beliefs: Rather than looking for evidence that you are right, look for evidence that your strategy did not work.

3. Be structured so that you regularly engage in dialogue with colleagues about learning.

4. Garner support from and involve school leadership as fellow learners with you.

It is extremely important that we dialogue among colleagues, gather support from school leadership, take every opportunity to observe effective classroom instruction, and participate in communities of practice or learning groups with teachers who are either seeking to increase their clarity in the classroom or demonstrate mastery of clarity in learning. This gives you an opportunity to gather specific feedback on your progress toward your own learning intentions and the success criteria you have established. Every hallway conversation, teachers' lounge discussion, and classroom observation about learning is an opportunity for feedback.

How we engage in collaborative learning and conversations with other teachers and leaders matters just as much as how we engage with students. There must be time, protocols, evidence to review, success criteria, student and teacher voices, and a commitment to making an impact––just to name a few of the critical elements. In the following paragraphs we will highlight some of the essential components, and in addition, in the following chapter, we have provided several examples from school leaders that show how they have created opportunities for long-term, deep work to take place in the area of clarity. They have created a variety of approaches to coaching, professional development, and networking that are truly innovative and have proven to make an impact. We encourage you to use these examples as a springboard to planning your own journey.

THE JOURNEY TOWARD CLARITY IN BARREN COUNTY PUBLIC SCHOOLS

The Barren County School System in Glasgow, Kentucky, is currently engaged in a systemwide initiative focusing on clarity. Starting with the elementary schools and then expanding to the middle and high schools in the upcoming years, each school has created or will create a school innovation plan at the start of the school year, and one of the components of focus within the plans is clarity. As part of this focus, teachers and administrators prioritize standards and then create learning intentions and success criteria wrapped around each priority standard. The next step is to align rigorous tasks to the learning intentions and success criteria along with meaningful assessments. The goal is for learners in each school to articulate what they are learning, to identify how they will know when they have learned it, and to determine their next steps in learning. However, to model clarity in their own professional learning as well as to practice what they preached, the district created the following learning intentions and success criteria for this work, which they refer to as their *shared vision for clarity:*

> ## Visible Learning
> ## Shared Vision
> ## Teacher Clarity (.70)
>
> **Learning Intention-**
> *We are learning...*
> *How to utilize Learning Intentions and Success Criteria in order to make learning visible to our administrators, teachers/staff, and learners.*
>
> **Success Criteria-**
> *We know we will be successful when...*
> - ✓ *LI/SC are written in kid-friendly language, tied to standards/concepts/skills, and focused on learning.*
> - ✓ *LI/SC are displayed where learners can read (large enough print), access, and refer to them throughout the lesson.*
> - ✓ *LI/SC are consistently referred to by teachers/staff and learners during lesson.*
> - ✓ *Learners can, based on LI/SC, answer the following: What am I learning? How will I know when I have learned it? What are my next steps in learning?*
> - ✓ *Teachers/Staff formatively assess daily based on LI/SC.*
> - ✓ *Teachers/Staff as well as peers reference LI/SC to provide feedback to learners.*
> - ✓ *Learners are able to self-regulate feedback to themselves by referencing LI/SC.*

LI/SC refers to Learning Intentions & Success Criteria

The teachers and instructional leaders from Barren County had this to say about their vision:

> As you can see, our ultimate goal is for learners to tie LI/SC to feedback they give and receive. The goal is for learners to self-regulate feedback to themselves by referencing the LI/SC. As a district, we make this clear through the learning intention and success criteria for our building-level administrators and teachers. However, schools had the opportunity to further focus on an area within clarity around which they felt they needed additional professional learning and support. Data [was] generated from school-based instructional rounds. Many schools chose their area for continuous improvement [from a problem of practice that was revealed through the data.] So, once the teachers realized that the importance of clarity and how it [is] an essential part of the learning process, the other components of clarity fit together, and the work became more meaningful in their classrooms.

As professional learning networks of teachers continue to grow within schools and districtwide professional learning communities, teachers now see the connection between clarity, feedback, and collective teacher efficacy in the teaching and learning in Barren County Public Schools.

The following are three perspectives from classroom teachers and the clarity work in which they have been engaged in the Barren County School System.

Perspective One: From a Primary Grades Teacher

Here is what Lacey Mahaney, a primary teacher in the Barren County School System, has to say about how the work positively impacted her learners:

Increased teacher clarity has not only improved my instruction, but it has also improved my students' experience in the classroom. Teacher clarity greatly relies on knowing what success looks like. As a teacher, I dig into each standard by looking at the verbs that standard contains, as well as the concepts that the standard contains. I develop my picture of what success looks like. One way I have been able to convey to my students what success looks like is through the use of common formative assessments and rubrics. When the common formative assessment has clear expectations of proficiency, the students begin the unit with an idea of what is going to be expected of them. They no longer have to guess what success looks like.

Co-creating success criteria is another way I get my students to look beyond the day's lesson and, instead, to deeply understand what they are learning. The students are able to use their knowledge of expectations from the pre-common formative assessment to help design the success criteria for the unit. This has helped our classroom community develop a common language that we are able to share when discussing our learning and our subsequent success.

In doing all of this, I truly feel that my instruction is more focused than it has ever been because I know what to teach and how to teach it. My students have taken ownership of their learning and are cognizant of what they know, what they need to know, and are actively seeking ways to fill in the gaps.

Examples of Learning Intentions and Success Criteria in Ms. Mahaney's Classes

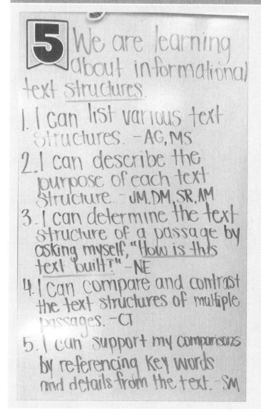

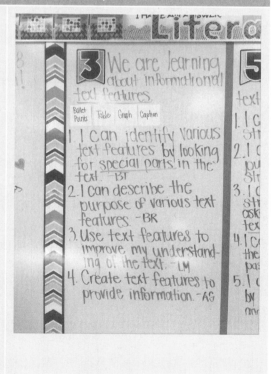

Perspective Two: From a Math and Science Teacher

Broderick Davis teaches math and science in the Barren County School System. He, too, has seen a positive impact on his learners:

Teacher clarity is having a great impact on student learning in the classrooms at Austin Tracy Elementary School. Teachers are utilizing learning intentions and success criteria in ways that make student learning more relevant and meaningful for everyone. Our learning intentions and success criteria are posted in clear view, so learners have access at any point in time during instruction. Also, students have the opportunity to self-regulate at any time by using our "Success Pit" when they move themselves to different points across the pit as learning occurs. Each success criteria in the pit is directly tied to the state standard and learning intention and is scaffolded to promote more rigor as the learner acquires new knowledge. Furthermore, students self-regulate by using our "bucket system." After completing an exit ticket at the end of class, learners will decide where to place their work by choosing the bucket that matches what they perceive to be their current level of proficiency at that time. All of these measures are being taken to ensure that our learners know where they are in their learning journey at any point in time and where they need to work more in attempts to improve understanding of specific standards-aligned skills. Teacher clarity is helping teachers and students be much more intentional about the learning that takes place in the classroom. We are excited to continue making teacher clarity a priority as we seek to best meet the needs of each individual learner.

Examples of Learning Intentions and Success Criteria in Mr. Davis's Math Classes

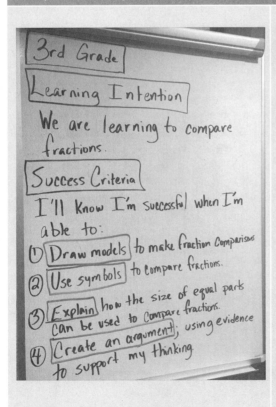 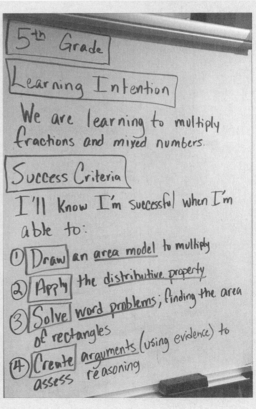

Mr. Davis places his success criteria along the learning pit. Learners have a magnetic number which they move along the pit as they master various levels of the scaffolded criteria. In doing this, they are able to self-regulate their feedback around the mathematical processes in the success criteria.

Examples of Learning Intentions and Success Criteria in Mr. Davis's Math Classes

At the end of each class, Mr. Davis has his learners place their formative assessment in a bin (above), indicating their level of mastery. He then can see if their perception matches their reality in regard to where they are in their learning.

Perspective Three: From a District Lead Teacher

Josh Maples shares his experience:

As Visible Learning District Lead Teacher, I have the privilege of working alongside principals and teachers in developing learning intentions and success criteria. Through our analysis and deconstruction of standards, we create scaffolded LI/SC that are scaffolded and provide a clear pathway to success for all learners. In this role, I have to see where we are going and how we will get there. Through the vision of our superintendent and directors of instruction, I help principals and teachers see appropriate next steps of implementation within our seven elementary schools. Each school is different and the teachers within each school have different needs. I have to meet them where they are in their understanding of teacher clarity. Many teachers look at teacher clarity as a ten-foot long sandwich; one that they can't digest all at one time. So, we chunk it into sections of implementation. Often, I consult with the principal in regard to the feedback I want to give and ask them if they feel that particular teachers are "ready" for all of the feedback. In most cases, we scaffold the feedback; giving them piece at a time. It is important to give them the positive feedback that they need to stay motivated and couple it with appropriate suggestions for improvement.

(Continued)

(Continued)

When a teacher posts LI/SC, the principal and I give feedback by taking what they have and making suggestions on what it could look like and the positive impact that it will have on clarity and learning. The teachers appreciate the feedback. The feedback provides a deeper understanding of the purpose and the relevancy of LI/SC. We scaffold our success criteria so that learners can see what they will do when they master new learning. Teachers are beginning to see the benefit in scaffolding the level of complexity by sometimes using verbs such as define, identify and apply for ELA or build, draw and solve for math. Providing learners with this type of progression helps them see where they are going and what it will take to be successful. We have seen teachers begin a lesson and, based on observation or assessment data, revise their success criteria to meet the current understanding of their learners.

Teacher clarity often comes from the instructional decisions that are made based on formative assessments. We are working toward being more effective in using "real-time" data to make instructional changes to meet the needs of learners. Formative assessments in conjunction with small group instruction have made us more aware of where each learner is and what they need to reach mastery of standards. In Barren County, we have worked on creating formative assessments that are created based on the rigor asked by the standard. We give the assessment at least three times throughout instruction of the standard and chart student progress. When we analyze the results, we document misconceptions demonstrated for those learners well-below the goal, close to the goal or at the goal. We then document research-based strategies to implement within these three groups of students and monitor the success of those strategies based on the next assessment. This process provides teachers the opportunity to be more clear and intentional in their planning; while providing differentiated success criteria to learners based on their current understanding and performance.

An example that I always use with teachers is one that I personally experienced when I was in the classroom. I was teaching an RtI group and assessed them twice per month using a computer-based assessment. The assessment would give me a report on performance, outlining what standards needed reteaching and more support. I would then teach those standards for 4 sessions before a learner would retest. However, one student, on her second testing session, asked for Post-it note. She already had her scrap paper and pencil, but asked for something more. As this student took her assessment, she wrote down each math problem that she struggled with. Out of 35 questions, she wrote down 7 that really confused her. When she brought the Post-it to me, it was like Christmas came early! She took ownership of her learning and told me exactly what she needed. I was able to provide a clear pathway to success based on what the learner told me they needed. I also had assessment data to further inform those instructional decisions. This example provides me the clear picture of what happens when a learner knows where they are in their learning and can compare that to where they know they need to be. It certainly made me more effective at designing instruction.

When a student can take ownership of their learning, the teacher can have conversations reflect on instructional practice and provide students with what they need with greater accuracy.

WHAT IT TAKES TO MAKE CLARITY HAPPEN

Achieving clarity in learning works best, and doing what works best matters. The question is how to scale the work in the classroom as well as for an entire school system. Chapter 11 provides additional examples from schools and districts that have deeply engaged in this work and have taken different approaches to addressing clarity, answering the question, "How do we learn and change together?"

In addition to the work in Barren County, Kentucky, the subsequent chapter looks at the collaborative process undertaken by each of the following schools and classrooms:

- Lone Tree Elementary School, Lone Tree, CO

- Bauder Elementary School, Fort Collins, CO

- Caldwell School District, Caldwell, ID

- J. Sterling Morton High School District 201, Cicero, IL

IN THE CLASSROOM

Success in our classrooms and schools comes down to the decisions we as teachers make each and every day. For each of these decisions to have the greatest impact on student learning, the decisions have to strike the ideal balance between deliberate and instinctive thinking. To be deliberate, we recommend checking in regularly on the success criteria you set for yourself earlier in this chapter. Are you making progress? How do you know? What are your next steps in learning?

In addition, to being deliberate, we recommend considering the other influences from Professor John Hattie's *Visible Learning* books (2009, 2012). When planning for deliberate learning that comes from a place of clarity, teachers can ensure that high-yield strategies—those that show greater gains in student achievement than are expected in a typical school year—are at play regularly in their classrooms. Not only are these strategies used, but teachers with clarity know how best to employ them to achieve the desired learning. For example, with clarity, teachers may have students engage in classroom discussion (effect size = 0.82) and know exactly what they want learners to accomplish during the discussion. Without clarity, classroom discussion may be less focused and less productive, and may result in a lot of class-room chatter. Without clarity, teachers and learners are less likely to engage in productive questioning (effect size = 0.48) and self-questioning (effect size = 0.55), respectively. Not to mention, without clarity, success criteria (effect size = 1.13), opportunities to respond (effect size = 0.90), and feedback (effect size = 0.70), the focus of this book, are not possible. All of these influences are tasks or strategies in our schools and classrooms that require clarity in learning if they are to be effective. Are these deliberate and effective strategies making an impact in your classroom? How do you know? What are your next steps in intentionally incorporating them to deepen learning?

The instinctual part then comes after all the planning and hard work of preparation. It encompasses the small and unique changes teachers make daily in the class-room as learning develops. When clarity truly exists for teachers, these intuitive moments become highly effective, as they are focused on the critical learning that must take place and yet deepen, challenge, and question current understandings and next steps. These are brought on by questions students pose, moments when everyone is stuck in the learning, lightbulbs exploding when someone "gets it" and shares with others, and times when the learning takes an unexpected turn. The beauty of the moments is in their authenticity, but that beauty is brought on by the clarity teachers use to make these instances possible and then the way they capitalize on the moments when they happen. For a teacher that has clarity, these instinctual moments become deep learning experiences, but for the unclear teacher, they are simply a bird walk, a moment of interest that dissipates, or a missed opportunity. Are you ready to better capitalize on such moments? What are your next steps in being ready?

The term *efficacy,* by itself, refers to the ability to produce a desired or intended outcome. Self-efficacy, then, is the belief that *I* have the ability to produce a desired or intended outcome. Using clarity both deliberately and instinctually in your classroom will build self-efficacy. Why does that matter? Teachers that have the greatest impact have high self-efficacy. They know what they are doing and why they are doing it, they still have the disposition to ask if it is working, and they get results. Clarity is the pathway to efficacy and higher achievement. How efficacious do you feel? What evidence builds your self-efficacy? How will you collect and share that evidence?

IN THE SCHOOL OR DISTRICT: COLLECTIVE TEACHER EFFICACY AND INTENTIONALITY IN PROFESSIONAL LEARNING

When considering collective teacher efficacy, we are talking about the collective belief that teachers have the ability to produce the desired or intended outcomes in their specific educational setting (i.e., the school and classrooms), despite what other factors may affect those outcomes (Forsyth, Adams, & Hoy, 2011; Goddard, Hoy, & Woolfolk Hoy, 2004). Put differently, collective teacher efficacy represents the overall belief of a school and its teachers that they can make a difference in the learning of their students regardless of where the students came from and what they bring with them to the school doorway (Woolfolk Hoy, Hoy, & Davis, 2009).

To make work on clarity scalable, impactful, and lasting, collective teacher efficacy (see Goddard et al., 2004) is a critical piece and must be part of the journey. Collective teacher efficacy has a high impact on student achievement, with an effect size of 1.57. An effect size of 1.57 is almost *four times* the average effect size associated with one year of formal school (0.40). This is not to say that a school must begin with collective teacher efficacy already in place, but rather that the professional learning teachers engage in must continue to build it. Let's take a look at how the two relate and how they can build on one another.

CLARITY

First, let us review clarity. As you recall from the introduction to this book, Fendick (1990) defined *clarity* as the compilation of organizing instruction, explaining content, providing examples, guiding practice, and assessing of learning. Hattie (2009) describes clarity as communicating the learning intentions and success criteria for the learning intentions. Teachers and students have clarity if they are able to answer three questions:

1. What am I learning?

2. Why am I learning it?

3. How will I know when I have learned it? (see Almarode, Fisher, Frey, & Hattie, 2018)

With an average effect size of 0.75, clarity provides almost twice the average effect of one year of formal schooling. When teachers are clear on what students are learning, they can better select learning experiences that specifically target that learning. Similarly, when teachers know why students are learning what they are learning, they can better design learning experiences that are authentic and relevant to learners. Finally, when teachers know what success looks like, they can show learners what success looks like, design opportunities for students to make their own thinking and learning visible, and gather evidence about where to go next in the teaching and learning. All this, because of clarity.

PUT THEM TOGETHER

The last sentence in the previous paragraph hints at the answer to my original question: How is collective teacher efficacy related to clarity? Just as planetary orbits are not possible without gravity or the gravitational force, and thus baking is not possible without specific ratios, collective teacher efficacy is not possible without clarity. Just as sulfur vapor is yellow and iodine vapor is purple, collective teacher efficacy is fostered by clarity.

There are four sources of efficacy and self-efficacy (Bandura, 1995): mastery experiences, vicarious experiences, feedback, and emotions. When we do something and do it well, we develop self-efficacy. When we interpret how well we do something, we develop self-efficacy. These are *mastery experiences*. As teachers, we evaluate how well a particular strategy or lesson worked in our classrooms. Our interpretation of that contributes to our belief in our ability to be effective teachers.

When we observe or watch colleagues do things in their classrooms, and their approaches work, we increase our beliefs about our ability to do those same things in our classroom. These are *vicarious experiences*. This same thinking applies to the third source, *feedback*. Feedback from our peers or students shapes our beliefs as well.

Finally, our *emotions* are a source of efficacy. Our beliefs in our ability are associated with how confident we feel prior to engaging in a task. Feeling confident before teaching a lesson increases our belief in our ability to do so effectively.

Funneling mastery experiences, vicarious experiences, feedback, and emotion into collective teacher efficacy hinges on clarity. Walking into your classroom knowing what students must learn, understanding why they are learning this content, and grasping what successful learning looks like provide an unmatched feeling of confidence and positive emotion about your ability to get your students to that successful learning outcome (Source #4: emotions). Having clarity on the what, why, and how questions allows you to purposefully and intentionally select the right approach to teaching and the right strategy, at the right time, for the right content and the right student. This purposeful and intentional decision making will lead to greater gains in learning (Source #1: mastery experiences). Furthermore, you can interpret those learning gains as the result of *your* preparation, planning, and decision making (Source #1: mastery experiences).

By sharing clarity with your students—making them aware of what they are learning, why they are learning it, and what success looks like—you will make them better able to communicate when they have gaps in the learning progress. This feedback will allow you to make adjustments—adjustments that are just as purposeful and intentional as the approach and strategies selected at the onset of the lesson. You will know what is necessary to close the gap, because you have clarity on the learning target (Source #3: feedback).

When clarity is present throughout a grade level, content area, and school, teachers have a greater opportunity to collaborate with peers and address problems of practice. "My learners are not progressing in their understanding of author's purpose. What do you do in your classroom that works?" "My learners are having difficulty selecting the best approach for solving quadratic equations. What works for your learners?" Asking and addressing these specific questions requires both clarity on our part and clarity amongst our colleagues. Colleagues are our best source of ideas as long as we are clear on what we are asking (Source #2: vicarious experiences).

OUR CLARITY PURPOSE

Teaching and learning are complex. Teachers and learners are complex. When all four of these items are blended together in our schools and classrooms, there are many factors that can and do contribute to the most important and intended outcome: student learning.

Therefore, at the end of the day our purpose, above all else, is to equip students with the skills and confidence to take on any goals or challenges and to come out on the other side victorious (O'Connell & Vandas, 2015). It is to build the self-efficacy of students. Why? Because we have no idea of the challenges, types of careers, or goals our students will be required to tackle. Thus, in doing this work, we are not only building our own efficacy and that of our colleagues, but most important, we are building the efficacy of our students. They will come out on the other end better equipped to learn and more prepared for future endeavors. This is our ultimate purpose and the great payoff of the work on clarity . . . our students . . . better equipped . . . more successful.

Enjoy the journey; relish the learning; celebrate your impact!

COLLABORATING FOR CLARITY IN LEARNING: VOICES IN ACTION

It is true that we are often better when we collaborate and do work collectively, and the same holds true for the work around clarity for learning (Protheroe, 2008). When groups of teachers and leaders dive into the standards, the best practices around creating clarity, and their curricular resources, students can only benefit from that work. It stands to reason that as teachers and leaders become clearer about what the learning expectations are, that clarity will be passed along to students. In fact, this collective work has the potential to greatly accelerate learning for students (Hattie, 2012), and so we have highlighted several school systems that have championed this work to the benefit of all learners. Each has taken a different approach, and each has shared his or her journey. Use this chapter to dream about what this work could look like in your system as a collectively powerful learning journey.

VOICES FROM THE FIELD

From an Elementary School: Collaborating for Clarity

Name: Kay Tucker, Innovation Specialist, Lone Tree Elementary School, Lone Tree, CO

Building Clarity and Implementing Success Criteria Schoolwide: Coaching Teachers

Lone Tree Elementary implements an innovative model for learning that weaves together three elements: personalization and student autonomy, real-world inquiry promoting entrepreneurial thinking, and participating in a global setting. As we grow this model, we continually look for specific systems and practices to implement that will empower both teachers and students to be successful.

During the 2016–17 school year, we felt we needed to build strategies specific to personalization and student autonomy. In our self-directed, flexible learning environments, students collaboratively create personalized learning plans with teachers as they align their interests, strengths, and learning styles. Students have a voice in what and how they learn as well as choice in how to demonstrate mastery of concepts and skills. A piece that was missing for us as a school was the common language and research-based methods that would allow us to implement strategies across all grade levels and drive the change in instructional practices to help us reach our goals in this area.

Connecting our staff to author experts is part of our vision for a strong professional development plan, and so we reached out to Kara Vandas and Mary Jane O'Connell, coauthors of *Partnering With Students: Building Ownership of Learning* (Corwin, 2015). In September, Kara presented to our staff an overview of the book and the big picture of the "why" behind the philosophy of building ownership of learning. She focused on Chapter 3, "Defining Criteria for Success," and talked about using data from preassessments to co-construct learning goals with students, and the power of gaining clarity to promote the "hand-off" of learning.

Kara's examples and the reasons behind the "why" of doing this were very powerful, and yet made so much sense and seemed easy enough to implement. Our staff left her session inspired and ready to try some of these new strategies. Literally, the week following our professional development day, teachers were engaging students in the process of building clarity—they were co-constructing success criteria with their students, and exemplars were created and being used to empower students. We immediately saw the application of professional development to practice, and better yet, we saw the impact on learning.

One of the biggest changes was in goal setting. We moved from setting vague, long-term goals (DRA level 28 by the end of the year) to setting clearly defined short-term goals on a regular basis. Students now analyze data with their teacher and understand where they are, where they want to go, and what they need to do in order to reach their goals. They determine how they want to demonstrate their understanding and set a timeframe to do so. Even in kindergarten, our students align what they need to know and learn with their passions and interests and use the timeframe of "soon" in setting

Co-Constructed Success Criteria for Ownership of Learning in Math—4th Grade

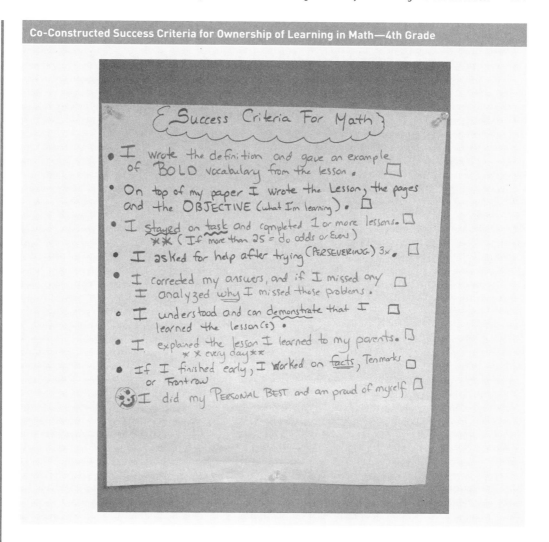

goals. This new approach replaced a system where teachers analyzed the data and then created and assigned pathways for learning.

As all of this was taking place in our classrooms, we simultaneously implemented the same strategies for our teachers. All teachers have personalized professional growth plans where they document their current state of practice and their desired state of practice aligned with the clarity of our model. Within a matrix, they create steps that will show progress to their desired state and reflect on these steps across the year. We saw tremendous growth in our staff using this process, but after our training with Kara we saw how we could more effectively impact professional growth by modeling with our teachers what we want them to do with students. We now co-construct success criteria with our teachers as we meet with them regularly in one-to-one conferences. Understanding where they currently are as teachers (using student achievement data) and engaging in dialogue to determine specific next steps (success criteria) has helped our teachers grow as professionals at an

(Continued)

(Continued)

Example of a Teacher Matrix—Current State to Desired State				

2017–2018

Area of Focus	Current State	Success Criteria		Desired State
Real World Math Connections	Students complete math topics at a personalized pace, using tools of their choice (usually the text book).	Begin to build understanding about why/ how we use math in the real world. Use CNN to make math connections.		Collaborate with students to identify opportunities for real world application of math skills.
Parent Communication	Collaborate with students to regularly progress monitor, track data, and set goals using online data form.	Familiarize students with their personalized data tracking forms with each student, email links to parents, and explain during conferences.		Empower students to regularly utilize their data tracking forms to independently track and analyze data for goal setting purposes.

even faster pace. They take risks aligned with proven strategies, are given feedback on a timely basis, and then reflect and set new short-term goals.

Implementing this one simple practice of defining criteria for success on a schoolwide basis has had a very positive impact at Lone Tree Elementary. Students are owning their learning across all curricular areas, and they can speak to what they are doing and why. They actively use success criteria as a means to independently check and improve not only their work, but their habits and the processes used in learning. The possibilities for learning are not capped by specific grade-level lessons, and pacing is dependent on the individual, not the teacher or the class as an average. Our schoolwide data in math and literacy, along with parent feedback, proves that this approach to learning is working and that we truly are maximizing learning opportunities for our students. As one parent stated, "I don't know what you have changed in your math program, but it is certainly working!" We were able to respond that we have not changed our resource, but our approach to learning. After implementing for only a year and a half, we feel that we truly are maximizing student learning opportunities.

This collective impact on student learning that is happening in our school is directly related to the speed at which our teachers are effectively implementing new strategies—strategies that are set up as success criteria for them as their next steps in their professional growth. Bottom line, we now know that if we maximize professional growth using success criteria, we will ultimately maximize student growth across all grade levels in our building. So exciting!

From an Elementary School: Collaborating for Clarity

Names: Brian Carpenter (principal), Jami Montoya-Ulibarri, Kelsi Idler, Kelli Hoyberg-Nielsen, Kelly Hogeland, Sue Weisman, Emily White, Shawna Reger, Ashley Torres, Jennifer Morrison, Rebecca Schkade; Bauder Elementary School, Fort Collins, CO

Clarity Through Impact Teams

One of the biggest outcomes for me as a building leader regarding the impact team process is what I call the evolvement of clarity. We recognized the effect size that teacher clarity has on student achievement; what we didn't realize is how this clarity evolves and how this clarity affects the individual teacher, the impact team itself, and student clarity. There is reciprocation in this process that cannot be ignored. Here is what we found:

Impact Teams are teams of educators that partner with students.

- They learn together to build professional capital.
- They scale up their expertise so they can make a difference for all students.
- They utilize a number of protocols that include reviewing evidence of student learning, analyzing it to determine what instruction is working for and isn't working for students, and then taking action, using high-impact strategies to respond to student learning needs. (Bloomberg & Pitchford, 2017)

1. In the past, individual teachers would begin with their own clarity regarding the standard they were teaching. This is what I refer to as individual teacher clarity: They see the standard language, interpret it in their own way, create a target statement so that there is student clarity, and then they teach the lesson. Hopefully some measure of formative assessment occurs to discern what effect the lesson had on student learning, and then interventions are put into place to support further learning if necessary. The unit ends and a new one begins. This is what *used* to happen.

2. With impact teams, teachers now come together to unpack a power standard—one that transcends multiple academic areas—and collectively interpret this standard so that all have common agreement on what the standard is asking of students. Once team clarity occurs, progressions are created, rubrics are made, and target statements can then be similarly created so that individual teacher clarity is brought to the classroom. Lessons are taught, formative assessments occur, and the impact team then collectively looks at the results of learning.

3. The results of the formative assessment then drive next steps. This is where clarity evolves. The student work informs the team as to what is clear and not clear for students. The results gave us insight into what we need to adjust regarding the rubric, the progression, and scaffolds for those needing assistance. Our clarity had to evolve for student clarity to evolve. The Evidence, Analysis, Action (EAA) protocol (Bloomberg & Pitchford, 2017) helped us evolve this clarity. After each meeting we adjusted our strategies for different groups of students to understand expectations and move up the progression of learning.

(Continued)

(Continued)

EAA Classroom Implementation Rubric Formative Assessment Process in Action			
EAA Classroom Success Criteria	NY	S	U
1) Evidence			
Learning Intentions (LI) & Success Criteria (SC)			
Students can articulate learning intentions and success criteria.			
Students engage in co-construction of the success criteria with their classmates and teacher.			
Students can identify success criteria (SC) in student work samples & exemplars.			
Students reflect regularly using essential questions connected to big ideas.			
Assessment Tools			
Formative assessments reflect the LI and SC aligned to focus learning progression/standard(s) (rubrics/checklists).			
Exemplars are annotated by the SC and are visible to students (notebooks, LMS, classroom environment).			
Samples of student work are used so students can practice applying SC (varying degrees of proficiency).			
2) Analysis			
Peer & Self-Assessment, Feedback			
Students use rubrics/checklists when engaged in self-assessment and peer assessment.			
Students get regular practice applying the SC.			
Students can identify SC in each other's work.			
Students can give feedback based on the SC in a respectful manner.			
Students engage in reflective dialogue with peers and teacher based on rubrics/checklists.			
Students get regular feedback from teacher to lift the accuracy of their self and peer assessments.			
3) Action			
Goal Setting, Revision, Feedback, Tracking System			
Students reflect on their strengths and next steps based on feedback from peer/self-assessment & teacher.			
Students create SMARTER personal learning goals based on feedback.			
Students revise assessment based on feedback tied to rubric/checklist.			
Students keep track of their progress and mastery of focus standards (they have a way to organize their learning).			
NY = Not Yet S = Sometimes U = Usually			

Source: Bloomberg & Pitchford, 2017.

Impact team work gave us "permission" to reteach an individual standard three times over the course of three months. Each time we met, clarity evolved. For the example shown next, we chose Standard 2: Informative Writing. We have kindergarten examples and third-grade examples. In each, we found that students improved and moved across the progression after each meeting. This recursive approach to understanding is necessary for student improvement. It must be done more than once.

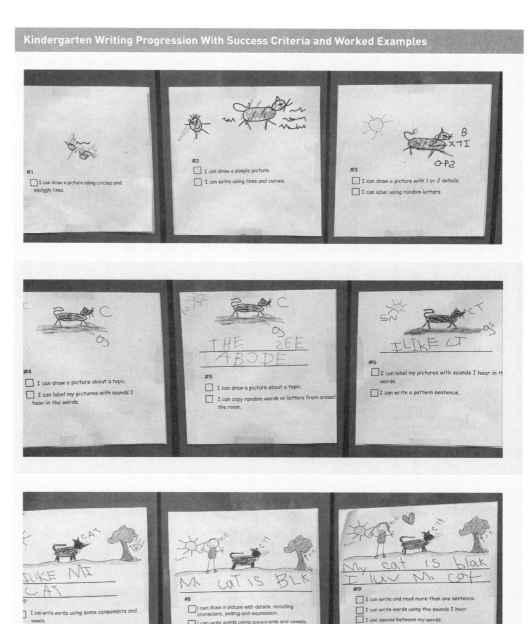

Kindergarten Writing Progression With Success Criteria and Worked Examples

(Continued)

(Continued)

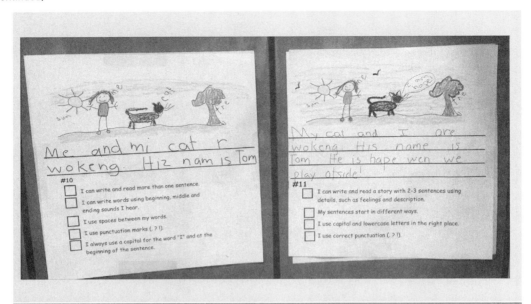

Examples of Kindergarten Writing Aligned to the Criteria

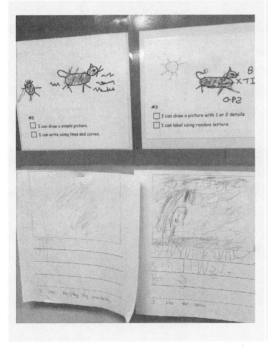

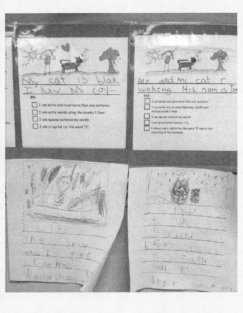

Grade Three Writing Samples and Rubric

ll Seals – Informational Writing (5.1)

Write an informational paragraph that meets or exceeds grade level expectations.

	Grade 1	Grade 2	Grade 3	Grade 4
Introduction	I named my topic	I wrote a beginning sentence that stated my topic.	I introduced the topic and got readers ready to learn a lot of information about the topic.	I introduced the topic and informe readers about the subtopics within my introduction.
Organization/Coherence/Transitions	I may have used a transition word.	I used two or more connecting transitions.	I used linking words and phrases (for example, also, another, more, but...) to connect ideas in a section.	I used complex linking words and phrases (for example, because, als another...) to connect ideas in a section.
	I finished.	I wrote a concluding statement or section.	I wrote a concluding statement or section that refers to the introduction.	I wrote a concluding statement or section that refers to the introductio and gives a final insight.
	I wrote at least two details.	I grouped my supporting details.	I grouped my information into parts. Each section is about one thing that connected to my topic.	I grouped my information into paragraphs and sections including headings.
Illustration	I used facts about my topic.	I used facts and definitions to explain my topic.	I used facts, definitions, and details from my research to explain my topic.	I used facts, definitions, concrete details and quotations from my research to explain my topic.
Craft	I used words about my topic.	I used key words about my topic.	I used expert words that show deep understanding about my topic.	I used precise words and vocabulary that show deep understanding that is specific to my topic.

I am going to teach you about weddell seals. weddell seals have soft fur ther fur is golden too. weddell seals have big flippers so they can swim faster. weddell seals have bright eyes. weddell seals live in cold water in antarctica. weddell seals preaator is a killer whale. weddell seals eat fish, krill, squid, and octopus. weddell seals eyes are big because so they can find food.

Informational Writing

Write an informational paragraph that meets or exceeds grade level expectations.

	Grade 1	Grade 2	Grade 3	Grade 4
	I named my topic	I wrote a beginning sentence that stated my topic.	I introduced the topic and got readers ready to learn a lot of information about the topic.	I introduced the topic and informed readers about the subtopics within my introduction.
	I may have used a transition word.	I used two or more connecting transitions.	I used linking words and phrases (also, another, more, but...) to connect ideas in a section.	I used complex linking words and phrases (for example, because, also, another...) to connect ideas in a section.
	I finished.	I wrote a concluding statement or section.	I wrote a concluding statement or section that refers to the introduction.	I wrote a concluding statement or section that refers to the introduction and gives a final insight.
	I wrote at least two details.	I grouped my supporting details.	I grouped my information into parts. Each section is about one thing that connected to my topic.	I grouped my information into paragraphs and sections including headings.
	I used facts about my topic.	I used facts and definitions to explain my topic.	I used facts, definitions, and details from my research to explain my topic.	I used facts, definitions, concrete details and quotations from my research to explain my topic.
	I used words about my topic.	I used key words about my topic.	I used expert words that show deep understanding about my topic.	I used precise words and vocabulary that show deep understanding that is specific to my topic

imagine it was Hallwen. you carve a pumkin for Hallwen. you selabrat on Hallwen. Hallwen is inport becus you get kanaey. the leves chang culrs wen it is fall. many animal hibrnat. pumkins are cropsd ating auttm. auttm is wun of the for sents. auttm is a wuderfull sesits. in the unitit amaica auttm is imporn we love auttm becus it is impor. finally Desebr is almos Here.

Paydon
Imagine it was Halloween. You carve a pumpkin for Halloween. You celebrate on Halloween. Halloween is important because you get candy. The leaves change colors when it is fall. Many animals hibernate. Pumpkins are crops during autumn. Autumn is one of the four seasons. Autumn is a wonderful season. In the united America autumn is important. We love autumn because it is important. Finally December is almost here.

Clarity evolves through the reciprocation of the process. Staff interpret the standard, and student work shows us how well we did in teaching and clarifying the standard. We must take the information that students provide us to adjust this "clarity," as this drives instruction.

From a School District: Collaborating for Clarity

Name: Jodie Mills, Chief Academic Officer, Caldwell School District, Caldwell, ID

Structuring Ongoing Learning and Support

Link to Corwin White Paper

Educational funding was reduced for the first time in the history of Idaho in 2009. Because of these funding cuts, our district needed to start working smarter and more intentionally with the limited resources. Part of this intentional work was to identify the strategies and resources that yielded the highest impact in addressing the academic needs of our populations of learners. We asked ourselves what would happen if we could actually know the educational impact of what we did before we did it. We needed a framework for empowering teachers and leaders to be critical consumers of professional learning and of the practices they use in the classroom. We went looking for the research, and we found Visible Learning.

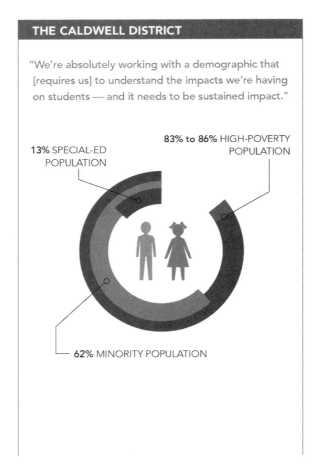

THE CALDWELL DISTRICT

"We're absolutely working with a demographic that [requires us] to understand the impacts we're having on students — and it needs to be sustained impact."

13% SPECIAL-ED POPULATION

83% to 86% HIGH-POVERTY POPULATION

62% MINORITY POPULATION

Through the discovery of John Hattie's *Visible Learning: A Synthesis of Over 800 Meta-Analyses Relating Achievement* (2009) and *Visible Learning for Teachers: Maximizing Impact of Learning* (2012), the first step to our journey was to become students of it by first understanding the research, then making the research visible in the classrooms through implementation. As we continued to explore the power and possibilities of Visible Learning, we took 14 principals, teachers, and district leaders to a conference in Toronto to hear John Hattie speak and deepen our learning. Through the experience, we found that Visible Learning wasn't a checklist of things to do but a culture of how we do the business of learning. Our commitment to implementing the research of Visible Learning was made stronger than ever. We invited John Hattie to Idaho to present to our early adopters and began a district initiative around Visible Learning, utilizing the tools of Evidence Into Action, which helped to identify each school's successes and concerns. These early experiences served as a catalyst, ensuring that the stage was set for successful implementation the culture of Visible Learning in the Caldwell School District.

From these early experiences, our district knew we needed to identify key professional development strategies to empower principals, teachers, and staff members, and set them up for success over the long haul of implementation. The purpose of this professional development process was to guarantee there would be reciprocity between expectations and outcomes. We implemented a series of opportunities for teachers to deepen their knowledge and understanding of their educational practices, and started to lay the foundational work of knowing their impact as educational leaders in their classrooms and buildings. We adopted a two-prong approach to building leadership capacity and adding clarity for principals and teachers. These professional development opportunities included Caldwell School District Summer Institute, onsite consultation and coaching for our building leaders, and ongoing explicit support and coaching for implementation.

The initial step for planning the two-prong approach was to determine our goals and expectations for developing a culture of Visible Learning. We planned a series of trainings that were offered during the summer institute. Leadership teams were provided these trainings prior to the summer institute to assist with implementing the vision and priorities of the institute. During the following school year, onsite consultation and ongoing coaching occurred at all of the buildings to ensure the implementation of the research-based practices presented during summer institute. The focus of the leadership training was to ensure our leaders knew what the research was, were on board for the work, had set clear goals, and were ready to lead the implementation in our district. The purpose of summer institute was to begin to train teachers and leaders in the areas of Visible Learning we felt we needed to start with, and teacher and leader clarity had to come first. We knew our teachers were working as hard as they could and doing the best job they could, but we also knew that Visible Learning occurs when teachers see learning through the eyes of students, and students see themselves as their own teachers. We weren't there yet.

Summer Institute and Ongoing Support and Coaching

The vision of the summer institute was to train as many staff as possible in effective practices, and it has become a consistent delivery model of relevant professional learning,

We aligned to our district goals over several years' time. We began our summer institute in 2013 with 60 teachers attending, and have grown to 250 teachers and leaders attending the 2018 summer institute. With a total district staff of 350, a majority of teachers and leaders are opting to spend some of their summer learning with us, which we consider a huge win. During each institute, we run three concurrent learning sessions so that teachers can engage in all three sessions over the course of the institute. The content of these sessions is targeted toward their grade levels. In order to accomplish this, we have divided the teachers into a secondary group, an upper elementary group, and a primary group that rotate through the sessions. We continue to strive for collective teacher efficacy throughout each grade level and across every school.

After Years 1 and 2 of summer institutes and immersing ourselves even more deeply in the Visible Learning research and the influences that develop Visible Learners, we realized we were missing several components and needed more training on them. As part of our analysis of next steps, we brought in several Visible Learning trainers to support this work and take us to the next level. Every year since, we have focused on developing more Visible Learners and the practices and processes that would get us there; clarity remains a focus of the work year after year. Through cycles of professional

(Continued)

(Continued)

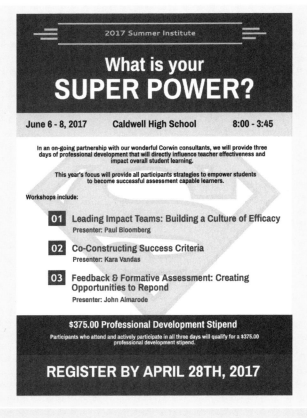

01 Leading Impact Teams: Building a Culture of Efficacy
Paul Bloomberg

Learn how to promote teacher, student, and collective efficacy

Teachers are a school's greatest resource. Excellent teachers make excellent schools. Leading Impact Teams taps into the scheduled team planning time every school already has, and repurposes it in a model that provides the processes needed to build teacher expertise and increase student learning. The model combines two existing practices, formative assessment and collaborative inquiry, and promotes a school culture in which teachers and students are partners in learning. Readers will learn how to:

- Take collective action to build a culture of efficacy
- Embed student-centered assessment in the classroom culture
- Ensure that students are an integral part of the formative assessment process
- Clarify learning intentions and criteria for success
- Leverage progressions of learning for "just right" instruction
- Utilize evidence-based feedback
- Maximize peer and self-assessment in classroom practice
- Implement high-leverage research-based strategies that result in increased learning

02 Co-Constructing Success Criteria
Kara Vandas

Students who know what success looks like and can articulate the progress they have made, are able to not only take greater ownership of their learning but also accelerate their own learning. This highly engaging, hands-on workshop will provide educators with the methodology to co-construct criteria with students, giving them a voice and deep understanding of how to meet the learning intentions. As a result, students will be able to confidently answer: Where am I going?, How am I doing?, and Where to next? (Hattie, 2011). In addition, students will be empowered to develop personalized learning goals and track their own progress toward their learning goals.

Experience the Co-construction Process
- Co-construct and Organize Success Criteria for a Common Learning Intention
- Learn Multiple Approaches to Co-construct Success Criteria with Student

Prepare the Pathway to Success
- Use Learning Progressions to Plan Surface to Deep Learning (Cognitive Rigor Continuum)

Apply the Handoff of Learning
- Increase Student Clarity and Ownership of Learning
- Develop a Comprehensive Plan for Co-constructing Success Criteria

Personalize Learning and Promote Effective Feedback
- Increase Student Ownership of Learning through Goal-Setting
- Use Co-constructed Success Criteria to Provide Feedback and Monitor Progress

03 Feedback & Formative Assessment: Creating Opportunities to Respond
John Almarode

The body of research on how we learn provides well-established principles and practices that enhance the learning outcomes for each of our students. Moving beyond performance on a test and focusing on learning, this workshop links these essential principles to the everyday instructional decisions around formative assessment and feedback you make in your classroom. The application of these key principles will support learners as the ge from surface to deep to transfer even when they may not be ready, yet. "I don't know" and "I don't remember" are phrases that haunt every classroom teacher and learner. How do we create experiences that eliminate these phrases and lead to better learning for all students so that they will "know" and "remember"?

- I can explain the key principles from the science of learning on how my students learn.
- I can recognize formative assessment and feedback practices that apply these principles.
- I can create opportunities to respond (formative assessment) for my students that integrate these principles into my classroom.
- I can analyze how opportunities to respond influence surface to deep to transfer thinking.
- I can apply research on effective feedback in my classroom.
- I can generate additional questions about how my students learn that allow me to assess my impact.

development, we train teachers in the summer, and then support them throughout the school year with coaching. We have quarterly coaching cycles, where each of our schools is provided a half day to work toward accomplishing building-level goals. We also have quarterly leadership meetings and trainings to continue the learning of school leaders and coaches. This work is facilitated with the help of our consultants, Kara Vandas and Ainsley Rose.

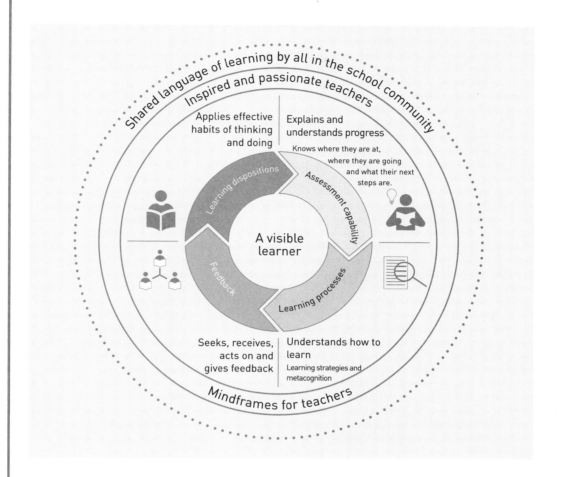

Each school has the professional latitude and responsibility to select a priority within the Visible Learning "donut" that will meet the needs of their students. School SMART goals are developed, based on these priorities and supported through ongoing coaching visits. Therefore, each building is able to select "where to next" for their building and schedule the support visits as they see fit. Some schools engage in small-group coaching sessions with different content area or grade-level teachers, while others host leadership planning sessions and school walkthroughs to determine progress. This structure allows school leaders to have the autonomy to address their specific needs and the professional latitude to determine next steps.

The evidence of the implementation of Visible Learning is being seen through growth from our schools, not only in meeting their goals for teacher practices, but more important, for student learning outcomes. There is strong evidence for a direct connection between the practices we are implementing and the impact on kids. Our district is becoming very rich with educators who are becoming critical practitioners of their profession by understanding and implementing research-based practices that will yield the highest impact for our students. We are not there yet, but we are definitely on the right path by having vision, purpose, and direction for how to get there. We are determined to stay the course.

(Continued)

(Continued)

Caldwell School District: Summer Institute Link to Video From Summer Institute 2017: https://youtu.be/ILNscvx4eJI		
Year	**Learning Topics**	**Focus**
Year 1	• Deconstruction of Common Core Standards in math and ELA • Vertical and horizontal alignment of standards	To have an understanding of what the standards are asking for in terms of student learning, and to ensure alignment of instruction
Year 2	• Review of assessments to align to the Common Core Standards	To align instruction, assessment, and standards
Year 3	• The Visible Learner • Learning intentions and success criteria (included learning progressions) • High-impact instruction	To gain clarity about what is to be learned, and what strategies support learners in owning their learning
Year 4	• Co-constructing success criteria and transferring learner strategies • Feedback and formative assessment: creating opportunities to respond • Impact teams: building a culture of efficacy	To impact student learning through collective efficacy To empower students with clarity and strategies for learning To learn about moving students from surface to deep to transfer of learning, ensuring rigor by providing opportunities to respond
Year 5	• Feedback 101: creating opportunities for teaching and learning • Feedback: aligning feedback to success criteria and learning intentions • Impact teams: lessons learned and building capacity for feedback	To identify what feedback will guarantee that rigorous learning expectations are met by all students To ensure that collective efficacy is impacting student learning

From a High School District: Collaborating for Clarity

Name: Dr. Terrance Mootz, Associate Superintendent, J. Sterling Morton High School District 201, Cicero, IL

Developing Learning Networks That Provide Differentiated but Connected Learning

Background

Teaching is one of the most complex professions imaginable. A good teacher is many things, among them a caring person. But good teachers are also skillful practitioners who are adept at learning and continuing to improve their teaching skills.

Knowing that teaching is a skills-based practice and learning is a social endeavor, J. Sterling Morton High School District 201 is committed to providing choice of professional learning opportunities that are aligned to the district mission—"Every student succeeds," to school improvement processes, and to standards for professional learning. District learning networks are founded on the principles of collaboration, communities, and networking.

Collaboration

Collaborative learning is one of the most powerful ways that educators can understand and address pressing student learning challenges. Collaboration leads to learning when colleagues state an intention to gain new knowledge, skills, attitudes, practices, or beliefs.

Communities

Communities can be among the most powerful forums for learning. Communities of practice that focus on authentic problems and a cycle of inquiry advance their understanding and capacity to serve students. They have protocols and structures that prioritize purposeful learning, and they know whether they are achieving the goals they set.

Networking

As with communities and collaboration, both intentional and incidental learning are valuable outcomes of networking when the conditions are right and participants approach their networking with curiosity and a growth orientation.

Learning Networks

In order to maximize learning and impact on student outcomes provided through professional development days, the district is organizing "learning networks." A learning network is a group of teachers who choose to learn and improve their craft around a specific impactful instructional practice. The purpose is to deepen understanding of content through learning and implementing new teaching practices. In addition, the J. Sterling Morton High School District 201 networks are created to support teachers as they deepen their understanding of the continuum of professional practice.

The seven networks will be offered annually, so that, eventually, all the individuals in the organization will have an opportunity to hone their skills and knowledge in each of seven impactful instructional practices.

During each of the professional development days, which will be designed to support teams in responding to the four critical corollary questions (DuFour, DuFour, Eaker, & Many, 2010) (shown below), teams will meet in their chosen networks to deepen their understanding of best practices, develop lesson plans to be implemented, reflect on implementation, and problem-solve in order to enhance learning and increase student achievement. The four critical corollary questions are addressed through the networks:

Four Critical Corollary Questions

1. What is it we want our students to learn (i.e., know and be able to do)?
   a. Guaranteed and viable curriculum aligned to standards
   b. Learning Networks 2 and 6

2. How will we know if each student has learned it?
   a. Frequent, team-developed common formative assessments
   b. Learning Networks 1, 3, and 4

3. How will we respond when some students don't learn it?
   a. Timely, directive, team intervention
   b. Learning Networks 3, 5, and 7

4. How can we extend and enrich the learning for students who have demonstrated proficiency?
   a. Timely, enriched content and extension activities
   b. Learning Networks 3 and 7

(Continued)

(Continued)

Learning networks strengthen our collective efficacy through (1) providing a structure and process for teams to engage in meaningful collaboration; (2) promoting teacher leadership and extending teams' decision-making power; and (3) deepening our appreciation that it is we, as a collective team, that make the difference in student learning. Network connections to our collaborative work are as follows:

Learning Networks	Presenter	Audience
1. Seven Strategies of Assessment for Learning Over the course of the four training days, network participants will apply the five research-based keys to quality classroom instruction: clear purposes, clear targets, sound design, effective communication, and student involvement. Participants will implement formative assessment practices through application of these strategies in units of study. Time will be provided for participants to design lessons to apply the strategies.	Consultant	Learning Networks
2. Connecting Curriculum and Technology This network will focus on backwards design and inquiry with technology across the curriculum. Participants will revise units and lessons by • Utilizing essential questions and enduring understandings to determine mastery learning objectives • Designing lessons that require students to study and evaluate a variety of resources in order to acquire information, collaborate, and demonstrate their knowledge in a variety of ways • Identifying the technology tools students will need to use in order to successfully participate in the demonstration of the learning • Utilizing OneDrive to guide student learning • Reflecting on the lesson using the substitution, augmentation, modification, redefinition (SAMR) model	District 201 director and instructional coaches	Learning Networks
3. Impactful Common Assessment Design to Guide Instruction Participants in this network will evaluate the quality of existing assessments by • Analyzing the standard/key concept/learning target the question is measuring • Examining the characteristics of effective assessment design Based on research-based design criteria, teams will evaluate and revise current common summative assessments. Teams will also have the opportunity to create additional quality assessments and administrative guidelines, and/or to develop rubrics.	District 201 director	Learning Networks
4. Mastery Learning Outcomes and Criteria for Success/ Partnering With Students Teacher clarity has a significant impact on student learning, and it is built on a foundation of mastery learning outcomes and criteria for success—or the destination and roadmap—of teaching and learning. Network participants will utilize a step-by-step process to ensure clarity about what students need to learn, why they are learning it, and how they will demonstrate their learning.	Consultant	Learning Networks

Learning Networks	Presenter	Audience
Network participants will implement a comprehensive solutions approach to share ownership of learning, and to significantly improve student engagement and learning. Teachers and students will collaboratively develop a plan of action for successful student learning and goal realization.		
5. Differentiation to Engage All Learners Participants will learn how to use differentiated instruction and implement it to help all students succeed, from translating the curriculum into meaningful learning outcomes to using formative assessment to tailor tasks through PLTs. Staff will learn and implement specific strategies to match differentiation needs. In addition to specific strategies, participants will work in teams to analyze and find patterns in formative assessment results and use these patterns to drive instructional adjustments.	Consultant	Learning Networks
6. Curriculum Writing Using Understanding By Design Network participants will support designated content teachers in updating and implementing a curriculum aligned to the Illinois learning standards. We will continue to examine the elements of the Illinois Common Core State Standards, comparing and contrasting them with current teaching and learning practices. Teams will utilize the understanding-by-design process to review and revise curricular units that are have balanced assessment measures. Opportunities will be provided for course teamwork, vertical group discussions across grade levels, and whole-group department work.	District 201 director and instructional coaches	Assigned participation *only*
7. Developmental Counseling and multitiered systems of support (MTSS) Counselors, deans, psychologists, and social workers will spend the training days • Identifying the interventions currently utilized by the student services team and determining objective data sources that can be utilized to assess the impact of those interventions • Exploring the district's Skyward database software system and defining its role in their process of being a data-driven student services team • Considering what critical data elements are pertinent to the district's population and determining whether a comprehensive needs assessment exists that meets the team's goals for choosing appropriate interventions • Developing and implementing a plan that connects interventions that target all phases of student achievement	District 201 administration	Assigned participation *only*

(Continued)

(Continued)

Contribution From Kara Vandas (Coauthor), Leader of a Network

Over the past year, I was invited to lead one of the seven learning networks within the district. We had teachers from math, fine arts, modern language, special education, and physical education, as well as school leaders and instructional coaches in our network. We met regularly throughout the year, sometimes in person and sometimes virtually as a whole group. I also had the pleasure of completing classroom visits and observations. In addition, we communicated on a web-based collaborative platform (SharePoint) set up by the district, which allowed us to share documents, examples, best practices, et cetera.

Example Student Self-Assessment Tool Shared on the Web Platform
Shared by Mary Corbett

Integrated 2 Honors   Name _____ Period _____

What are we learning in Key Concept #7: POLYNOMIALS?

Self Rating:

1: I've never seen this before and I have no idea where to start.

2: I've seen this before, but I don't remember how to do it.

3: I can get started on the problem, but then I get stuck.

4: I can complete the problem, but I am not confident in my answer.

5: I know this well enough that I could teach it to someone else

Target	Examples	Beg.	Mid.	End
7A Identify Key Features of Polynomials	Identify the following key features: 1.) End Behavior: $\lim_{x \to -\infty} f(x)$ and $\lim_{x \to +\infty} f(x)$ 2.) Maximums & Minimums 3.) Domain & Range 4.) Intervals on which Increasing & Decreasing 5.) Zeros 6.) Y-intercept	1.) 2.) 3.) 4.) 5.) 6.)		
7B Apply the Remainder Theorem	7.) Determine if $(3x - 2)$ is a factor of $f(x) = 3x^3 + 13x^2 - x - 6$. 8.) Given $x^3 + ax^2 - 13x - 10$ and that $(x - 5)$ is a factor of the polynomial, what is the value of a?	7.) 8.)		

Target	Examples	Beg.	Mid.	End
7C Solve Polynomial Equations	9.) If $x = 5$ is a zero of $x^3 - 6x^2 - x + 30$, find the remaining zeros using algebra.	9.)		
	10.) The product of 3 consecutive even numbers is 17,472. Create a polynomial function that when supported with technology will help in determining the numbers, then find the numbers.	10.)		
7D Model Polynomials Without the Use of Technology	11.) Graph and describe the transformation between the polynomials $f(x) = x^3$ and $f(x) = -5(x + 1)3 - 2$.	11.)		
	12.) Write a polynomial in Standard Form with zeros of $\{0, -1, 2/3\}$.	12.)		
	13.) Create a rough sketch of a quartic function with the following key features: (maximums and minimums may be approximated) a) zeros: $\{-3, 1, 2, 6\}$ b) end behavior: $\lim_{x \to -\infty} -\infty$ and $\lim_{x \to +\infty} -\infty$	13.)		

The work was powerful because the teachers engaged in deep conversation about their practices and the practices of students, and twice during the sessions, teachers engaged in a sharing experience so others could learn from them. From these, sessions, we all took away new ideas and ways to share clarity with students.

REFLECTION

How will you think differently about clarity, based on what you have read?

What ideas have you generated that you will try in your own classroom or school?

APPENDIX A

Quick Reference

CLARITY

Definitions
• The compilation of organizing instruction, explaining content, providing examples, guided practice, and assessment of learning (Fendick, 1990)
• Communicating the learning intentions and success criteria for the learning intentions (Hattie, 2009)
• When teachers and students are able to answer three questions:
○ What am I learning?
○ Why am I learning it?
○ How will I know when I have learned it?

(Almarode, Fisher, Frey, & Hattie, 2018)

LEARNING INTENTIONS

Definitions
• The intended learning
• "Learning Intentions are what we intend students to learn" (Hattie, 2012, p. 48).

Also Known As . . .
• Learning goals
• Learning outcomes
• Objectives
• Aims
• Learning targets

Quality Criteria for Learning Intentions
• Written
○ As the learning *destination*—"*Where* are we going?"
○ As a summary or general restatement of the standard
○ As a global statement without specifics (e.g., "learn to write an opinion piece" or "learn to use a ratios and proportions to solve a problem")
○ In age-appropriate, kid-friendly language that retains the rigor and intent of the standard

(Continued)

(Continued)

Quality Criteria for Learning Intentions

- Include
  - ○ No specific details from the standard (Specifics will be addressed in the success criteria.)
  - ○ Key terms and vocabulary
  - ○ No references to specific *context* (textual, curricular, situational, procedural, etc.)
  - ○ Explanations of *why* this is important—for students *and* teachers

Guiding Questions for Developing Learning Intentions

1. In reading through the standards, does a "big-picture" learning outcome emerge? If so, what is it?

2. Does the big-picture learning outcome encompass what all of the standards in that section, chunk, or grouping are aiming for in terms of student learning?

3. Would a set of more specific components or success criteria provide the needed clarity as to how to successfully reach the big-picture learning outcome?

SUCCESS CRITERIA

Definitions

- The evidence students must produce to show they have achieved the learning intention

- "Success criteria help students to gain a better understanding of what successful learning might look like in ways that they can recognize from what they know now. . . . They spell out in greater detail the Learning Intention" (Absolum, 2010, p. 83).

Also Known As . . .

- Key competencies
- Evidence of learning
- Components to include on a scoring guide or rubric

Quality Criteria for a Success Criterion

- Specifies what students are to *do* to demonstrate learning
- Provides a "map" to the learning destination—"*How* are we going?"
- Identifies the *details* needed to achieve the learning intention
- Uses specific terms from the standard and maintains the rigor of the standard(s)
- Includes objective wording only; no subjective language (e.g., *some, few, many,* etc.)
- May include *other* details not included in the standard, but necessary to achieve the learning intention(s)

In achieving the standard(s) and meeting the learning intention(s),

1. What evidence would show you that students have achieved conceptual understanding? What language will they need to use to share their evidence of learning?

2. What process might they need to follow to show their understanding?

3. What product would show that they know?

LEARNING PROGRESSIONS

Definitions

- Represent the incremental steps that begin with surface or foundational evidence and build up

- Are our professional estimation of how learning will progress from one idea to another

CO-CONSTRUCTING SUCCESS CRITERIA

Definition

- Simply the practice of working with students to develop a shared understanding about what success looks like

Steps to Co-Constructing Success Criteria

1. Determine *when* to co-construct success criteria with students.

2. Gather the tools students will use: worked examples, exemplars, models.
   - Examples of attainment of the learning intention(s)/standard
   - Examples of exceeding the learning intention (exemplars)
   - Nonexamples or works in progress
   - Processes, steps, or multiple approaches to meet the same criteria

3. Determine the method that will be used to share the criteria with students.
   - Studying and differentiating between exemplars in small groups to generate success criteria
   - Modeling by teachers or students—demonstration with a think-aloud
   - Modeling of worked examples, which are then posted for reference
   - Comparing exemplars to other, less exceptional examples or nonexamples to determine which is better and why

(Continued)

(Continued)

Steps to Co-Constructing Success Criteria

4. Generate initial success criteria with students.
   - Allow students to share criteria after modeling, worked examples, and exemplars have been shared.
   - Add any missing success criteria (teacher noticing if anything is missing and needs to be added, based on the standards and expectations).

5. Categorize and organize criteria to create:
   - T-chart
   - Checklist
   - Rubric (Meets & Exceeds Learning Expectations portions of rubric)
   - Other way of representing the criteria

6. Model/practice using the criteria to provide feedback and set personal goals as to which criteria are to be worked toward next.

7. Revise success criteria and goals over time as learning deepens.

ASSESSMENT-CAPABLE LEARNERS (ACL)

Definition

- Students who are able to articulate what is to be learned, articulate what success looks like, describe and discuss their progress toward meeting the criteria, and determine their next steps in learning. Assessment-capable learners are able to select the right tools, at the right time in their learning journey. In addition, such students are able to set, monitor, and attain personal learning goals, while exploring and selecting learning strategies that work for them. Assessment-capable learners seek feedback, recognize their mistakes as learning opportunities, and support their peers in the learning journey (Frey, Hattie, & Fisher, 2018).

3 Questions of ACLs	Powerful Practices	ACLs can . . .
Where am I going?	Learning intention Success criteria	• articulate what they are learning
How am I going/doing?	Success criteria Examples and exemplars Feedback and formative assessment	• monitor their own progress • articulate which success criteria have been met
Where to next?	Success criteria Examples and exemplars Feedback and formative assessment	• explain what they have not yet mastered • how to transfer their learning to a new challenge or problem

OPPORTUNITIES TO RESPOND

Definition

- Any strategies, activities, or tasks that make student thinking visible and allow both the teacher and learner to observe learning progress.

Characteristics of Opportunities to Respond: Making Thinking Visible

There are several ways to make learners' thinking visible. Consider some of the characteristics highlighted by Ritchhart, Church, and Morrison (2011):

1. Ask learners to provide descriptions of terms, concepts, ideas, procedures, or processes.

2. Encourage learners to develop explanations and interpretations of concepts, ideas, procedures, or processes.

3. Ask learners to provide evidence for their reasons, explanations, and interpretations.

4. Ask learners to take different viewpoints and perspectives on concepts, ideas, procedures, or processes.

5. Ask learners to make connections between what they are learning and what they have already learned.

Note that getting students to reveal their thinking requires us to ask the right question.

Guiding Questions for Opportunities to Respond

1. What opportunities to respond will tell me how learners are progressing in their learning related to the learning intention(s) and success criteria?

2. What am I going to do with their responses that will help with their next steps in learning?

FEEDBACK

Definitions

- Information that should feed-forward learning, meaning it should equip the receiver to take action (Hattie, 2012)

- "Meant to nourish learning through an exchange." (O'Connell & Vandas, 2015)

Characteristics of Effective Feedback

1. Is specific, timely, and constructive.

2. Answers the questions:
   - Where am I going?
   - How am I going/doing?
   - Where to next?

3. Provides different levels of feedback for different learners, including task, process, and self-regulation.

4. Is balanced among teacher, peers and self.

COLLECTIVE TEACHER EFFICACY

Definitions

- The collective belief that teachers have the ability to produce the desired or intended outcomes in their specific educational setting (i.e., the school and classrooms) above and beyond other factors.

- Represents the overall belief of a school and its teachers that they can make a difference in the learning of their students regardless of where they came from and what they bring with them to the school doorway.

Characteristics of Collective Teacher Efficacy

1. Mastery Experiences

2. Vicarious Experiences

3. Feedback

4. Mood or the Upward Spiral

Clarity Self-Assessment

Component of Clarity	Success Criteria	Self-Assessment*		
		NY	S	A
Defining Clarity	• Describe what is meant by clarity.			
	• Explain the relationship between clarity, learning intentions, and success criteria.			
	• Develop a way to determine if I have a clarity problem in my school or classroom.			
	• Apply the language of clarity to my own school or classroom.			
Gaining Clarity	• Describe what learning intentions and success criteria are and are not.			
	• Explain criteria for writing effective learning intentions and success criteria.			
	• Answer common questions and address common misconceptions about learning intentions and success criteria.			
Sharing Clarity	• Define what co-construction is and why it is essential.			
	• Explain what teachers must think through prior to co-constructing criteria with students.			
	• Describe several methods for co-constructing success criteria collaboratively.			
	• Express the rationale for using worked examples and exemplars to further clarify criteria and offer multiple pathways to success for students.			
	• Answer common questions and address common misconceptions about the process of co-constructing success criteria.			
	• Share clarity with students in my own school or classroom.			

Component of Clarity	Success Criteria	Self-Assessment[*]		
		NY	S	A
Assessing With Clarity	• Analyze the relationship between learning intentions, success criteria, and opportunities for students to respond.			
	• Create opportunities to respond that align with specific success criteria.			
Feedback With Clarity	• Use opportunities to respond to gain feedback from my students about my teaching.			
	• Apply the research on effective feedback to both the learners in my classroom and myself.			
	• Adjust my feedback based on the specific learning intentions and success criteria.			
Clarity in Collaboration	• Use feedback from my students to adjust my instruction for better clarity.			
	• Collaborate with students, teachers, and leaders to develop clarity at all levels.			

[*]Self-assessment marks: NY (not yet), S (sometimes), A (always)

AFTERWORD

Whenever educators set out to design meaningful instruction and effective assessment, the need for clarity seems self-evident. After all, how can educators plan instruction and assessment unless they know exactly what they want their students to know and be able to do? Yet understanding the need for clarity is one thing; knowing *how* to actually achieve it is something else entirely.

In 2016 Corwin invited me to create a step-by-step workshop and companion workbook, *Learning Intentions and Success Criteria,* to show how educators and leaders can bring clarity to student learning targets. Since that time, my consulting colleagues at Corwin and I have presented this popular workshop all over the country. But very soon I saw the need for an in-depth book on the subject filled with detailed instructions and accompanying examples across all grades and content areas that would enable K-12 educators to really understand and apply this all-important process in their own instructional programs.

In *Clarity for Learning: Five Essential Practices That Empower Students and Teachers*, authors John Almarode and Kara Vandas have more than fulfilled this need. They have given us an explicit roadmap for the journey to achieving clarity in the classroom. And all we need do is to begin the trip!

As I read this engaging guidebook for creating clarity, especially significant for its detailed instructions and illustrative examples that every K-12 educator in any content area can confidently follow, either individually or as part of a collaborative team, I realized that John's and Kara's doable process is all about making learning and thinking *more visible.*

In addition to providing the necessary what, why, and how of each chapter's particular focus, what distinguishes this book from others on the topic are its "Voices from the Field" sections. These vividly capture real teachers' applications of this process in great detail through a wealth of learning intention and accompanying success criteria samples—created and co-created by teachers with their students. The specific sequence of steps for implementation makes this entire process come to life and is sure to encourage and empower readers to think, "Yes, now I understand! I can do this myself with my own students."

Another powerful feature of this book is the inclusion of very specific suggestions/recommendations readers can use to reflect and evaluate where they currently are with regard to achieving clarity, where they want to go, how they can get there, and what to do when they're just not sure.

But Almarode and Vandas don't stop there. They know the importance of also sharing first-person narratives and implementation plans from school leaders around the country who have already embarked on this journey and want to provide practical guidance and encouragement to their leadership peers about to begin this same quest for greater clarity within their own schools and district.

Clarity for Learning: Five Essential Practices That Empower Students and Teachers may well become the definitive guide for all educators and leaders wanting to achieve crystal clarity of learning intentions and related success criteria—first for themselves and then for their students. The authors' clearly stated three-part goal: to show K-12 educators *how to determine clarity* of learning intentions and success criteria, *how to engage students* in their own learning through this process, and *how to take part in reflective practice* about their impact on student learning, is clearly accomplished in this outstanding book.

Larry Ainsworth
Author, *Common Formative Assessments 2.0:
How Teacher Teams Intentionally Align Standards,
Instruction, and Assessment* and the Corwin
workshop, "Learning Intentions and Success Criteria."

REFERENCES

Absolum, M. (2010). *Clarity in the classroom: Using formative assessment for building learner-focused relationships*. Winnipeg, MB, Canada: Portage & Main Press.

Ainsworth, L. (2010). *Rigorous curriculum design: How to create curricular units of study that align standards, instruction, and assessment*. Englewood, CO: Lead + Learn Press.

Ainsworth, L. (2016). *Learning intentions and success criteria: How to bring clarity to student learning outcomes*. Thousand Oaks, CA: Corwin.

Allen, R. H. (2001). *Impact teaching: Ideas and strategies for teachers to maximize student learning*. Boston: Allyn & Bacon.

Almarode, J. T., Fisher, D., Frey, N., & Hattie, J. (2018). *Visible learning for science. What works best to optimize student learning grades K–12*. Thousand Oaks, CA: Corwin.

Almarode, J. T., & Miller, A. (2018). *From snorkelers to scuba divers: Making the elementary science classroom a place of engagement and deep learning*. Thousand Oaks, CA: Corwin.

Antonetti, J., & Garver, J. (2015). *17,000 classroom visits can't be wrong*. Alexandria, VA: ASCD.

Bandura, A. (1977). *Social learning theory*. Englewood Cliffs, NJ: Prentice Hall.

Bangert-Drowns, R. L., Kulik, J. A., & Kulik, C. C. (1991). Effects of classroom testing. *Journal of Educational Research, 85*(2), 89–99.

Bandura, A. (1995). *Self-efficacy in changing societies*. New York: Cambridge University Press.

Biggs, J., & Collis, K. (1982). *Evaluating the quality of learning: The SOLO taxonomy*. New York: Academic Press.

Black, P., & Wiliam, D. (1998). Assessment and classroom learning. *Assessment in Education: Principles, Policy & Practice, 5*(1), 7–74.

Bloomberg, P., & Pitchford, B. (2017). *Leading impact teams: Building a culture of efficacy*. Thousand Oaks, CA: Corwin.

Boaler, J. (1998). Open and closed mathematics: Student experiences and understandings. *Journal for Research in Mathematics Education, 29*(1), 41–62.

Brookhart, S. M. (2008). *How to give effective feedback to your students*. Alexandria, VA: ASCD.

Butler, A. C., Karpicke, J. D., & Roediger, H. L. (2007). The effect of type and timing of feedback on learning from multiple-choice tests. *Journal of Experimental Psychology: Applied, 13*, 273–281. doi:10.1037/1076-898X.13.4.273

Clarke, R. C., Nguyen, F., & Sweller, J. (2006). *Efficiency in learning: Evidence-based guidelines to manage cognitive loads*. San Francisco: Wiley.

Clarke, S. (2001). *Unlocking formative assessment: Practical strategies for enhancing pupils' learning in the primary classroom*. London, England: Hodder Education.

Clarke, S. (2008). *Active learning through formative assessment*. London, UK: Hodder Education.

Clarke, S. (2014). *Outstanding formative assessment: Culture and practice*. London, UK: Hodder Education.

Claxton, G. (2018). *The learning power approach. Teaching learners to teach themselves*. Thousand Oaks, CA: Corwin.

Dohrenwend, B. S. (1965). Some effects of open and closed questions on respondents' answers. *Human Organization, 24*(2), 175–184.

DuFour, R., DuFour, R., Eaker, R., & Many, T. (2010). *Learning by doing: A handbook for professional learning communities at work*. Bloomington, IN: Solution Tree Press.

Dweck, C. (2006). *Mindset: The new psychology of success*. New York: Ballantine Press.

Eggen, P., & Kauchak, D. (2004). *Educational psychology: Windows on classroom* (6th ed). Columbus, OH: Prentice Hall.

Feedback. (1999). *Merriam-Webster's collegiate dictionary* (10th ed.). Springfield, MA: Merriam-Webster.

Fendick, F. (1990). *The correlation between teacher clarity of communication and student achievement gain: A meta-analysis*. Unpublished doctoral dissertation, University of Florida, Gainesville.

Fisher, D., & Frey, N. (2014). *Better learning through structured teaching: A framework for the gradual release of responsibility* (2nd ed.). Alexandria, VA: ASCD.

Fisher, D., Frey, N., & Hattie, J. (2016). *Visible learning for literacy*. Thousand Oaks, CA: Corwin.

Forsyth, P. B., Adams, C., & Hoy, W. K. (2011). *Collective trust: Why schools can't improve without it*. New York: TC Press.

Frey, N., Hattie, J., & Fisher, D. (2018). *Developing assessment-capable visible learners*. Thousand Oaks, CA: Corwin.

Goddard, R. G., Hoy, W. K., & Woolfolk Hoy, A. (2004). Collective efficacy: Theoretical development, empirical evidence, and future directions. *Educational Researcher, 33*, 3–13.

Hattie, J. A. (2009). *Visible learning: A synthesis of over 800 meta-analyses relating to achievement*. New York: Routledge.

Hattie, J. A. (2012). *Visible learning for teachers: Maximizing impact on teachers*. New York: Routledge.

Hattie, J. A. & Donoghue, G. M. (2016, August 10). Learning strategies: A synthesis and conceptual model. *Nature/NPJ: Science of Learning*. doi:10.1038/npjscilearn.2016.13

Hattie, J., Fisher, D., Frey, N., Gojak, L. M., Moore, S. D., & Mellman, W. (2017). *Visible learning for mathematics: What works best to optimize student learning*. Thousand Oaks, CA: Corwin.

Hattie, J., & Timperley, H. (2007). The power of feedback. *Review of Educational Research, 77*(1), 81–112.

Learning goals and success criteria viewing guide. (2010). Assessment for Learning Video Series. Ontario, CA: Ontario Schools. Retrieved from http://www.edugains.ca/resourcesAER/VideoLibrary/LearningGoalsSuccessCriteria/AssociatedFiles/LearningGoalsSuccessCriteriaViewingGuide2011.pdf

Marzano, R. J. (2007). *The art and science of teaching: A comprehensive framework for effective instruction*. Alexandria, VA: ASCD.

McDowell, M. (2017). *Rigorous PBL design: Three shifts for developing confident and competent learners*. Thousand Oaks, CA: Corwin.

Medina, J. (2014). *Brain rules. 12 principles for surviving and thriving at work, home, and school*. Seattle: Pear Press.

National Research Council. (2007). *Taking science to school: Learning and teaching science in grades K–8*. Washington, DC: The National Academies Press.

Nuthall, G. (2007). *The hidden lives of learners*. Wellington, New Zealand: NZCER Press.

O' Connell, M. J., & Vandas, K. (2015). *Partnering with students: Building ownership of learning*. Thousand Oaks, CA: Corwin.

Popham, W. J. (2008). *Transformative assessment*. Alexandria, VA: ASCD.

Protheroe, N. (2008, May/June). Teacher efficacy: What is it and does it matter? *Principal, 45*. https://www.naesp.org/sites/default/files/resources/1/Pdfs/Teacher_Efficacy_What_is_it_and_Does_it_Matter.pdf

Renkl, A., & Atkinson, R. K. (2010). Learning from worked-out examples and problem solving. In J. L. Plass (Ed.,) *Cognitive Load Theory* (pp. 89–108). New York: Cambridge University Press. doi:10.1017/CBO9780511844744.007

Ritchhart, R. (2015). *Creating cultures of thinking: The 8 forces we must master to truly transform our schools*. San Francisco: Jossey-Bass.

Ritchhart, R., Church, M., & Morrison, K. (2011). *Making thinking visible. How to promote engagement, understanding, and independence for all learners*. San Francisco: Jossey-Bass.

Self-Efficacy: Helping children believe they can succeed. (2010, November). *Communiqué, 39*(3), 1–4. National Association of School Psychologists, http://www.nasponline.org

Stiggins, R. (2015, October). *The role of student growth in teacher evaluation*. Keynote address at the Teaching, Learning, Coaching Conference, Denver, CO.

Stiggins, R. J., Arter, J. A., Chappuis, J., & Chappuis, S. (2006). *Classroom assessment for student learning: Using it right, doing it well*. Upper Saddle River, NJ: Pearson.

Timperley, H., Wilson, A., Barrar, H., & Fung, H. (2007). *Teacher professional learning and development. Best evidence synthesis iteration [BES]*. Wellington, NZ: Ministry of Education.

Webb, N. L. (2005, November 17). *Alignment, depth of knowledge, & change*. Presentation at the 50th Annual Meeting of the Florida Educational Research Association, Miami, FL. Slide deck retrieved from http://facstaff.wcer.wisc.edu/normw/MIAMI%20FLORIDA%20FINAL%20slides%2011-15-05.pdf

Woolfolk Hoy, A., Hoy, W. K., & Davis, H. (2009). Teachers' self-efficacy beliefs. In K. Wentzel & A. Wigfield (Eds.), *Handbook of motivation in school* (pp. 627–655). Mahwah, NJ: Lawrence Erlbaum.

INDEX

A SAGE Publishing Company

Helping educators make the greatest impact

CORWIN HAS ONE MISSION: to enhance education through intentional professional learning.

We build long-term relationships with our authors, educators, clients, and associations who partner with us to develop and continuously improve the best evidence-based practices that establish and support lifelong learning.

Solutions you want. Experts you trust.
Results you need.